ON MY HONOUR

Guides and Scouts in
Interwar Britain

TRANSACTIONS
of the
AMERICAN PHILOSOPHICAL SOCIETY
Held at Philadelphia
For Promoting Useful Knowledge
Volume 92, Part 2

ON MY HONOUR

Guides and Scouts in Interwar Britain

TAMMY M. PROCTOR

AMERICAN PHILOSOPHICAL SOCIETY
Philadelphia ▪ 2002

ISBN: 0-87169-922-2
US ISSN: 0065-9746

Library of Congress Cataloging-in-Publication Data

Proctor, Tammy M., 1968-
    "On my honour" : Guides and Scouts in Interwar Britain / Tammy M. Proctor.
        p. cm. -- (Transactions of the American Philosophical Society ; v. 92, pt. 2)
    Includes bibliographical references and index.
    ISBN 0-87169-922-2 (pbk.)
        1. Scouts and scouting--Great Britain--History--20th century. 2. Boy Scouts
Association (Great Britain)--History--20th century. 3. Girl Guides Association--
History--20th century. 4. Youth--Great Britain--Social conditions--20th century.
5. Youth--Great Britain--Social life and customs--20th century. 6. Social role--
Great Britain--History--20th century. 7. Social change--Great Britain--History--20th century.
8. National characteristics, British--History--20th century. I. Title: "On my honor" :
Guides and Scouts in interwar Britain. II. Title. III. Series.

HS3270. G7 P76 2002
369.4--dc21

                                                                    2002027714

Design and Composition: Book Design Studio II

COVER Male and female Scouts in the Inge family sat for this portrait in July 1910.
Courtesy of The Scout Association.

CONTENTS

ACKNOWLEDGMENTS

This book would never have been completed without the assistance and support of a number of people and institutions. First, I am indebted to my thesis director, John R. Gillis, for his coaching and criticism over the last few years. John has been extremely generous with his time, reading countless chapter drafts. In addition, my thanks go to Michael Adas, Ellen Ross, and Bonnie Smith, who read and commented on the entire work in its dissertation form. Thanks also to those scholars who critiqued parts of the work, including Leonore Davidoff, Gretchen Galbraith, Dee Garrison, Victoria de Grazia, Allen Howard, and Jan Lewis. Special thanks to Ted Koditschek for helping me find my way to graduate school and to Rutgers.

The book has benefited from the comments of several anonymous readers as well as from the editorial work of Anna Davin of *History Workshop Journal* and Mary McDonald at the American Philosophical Society. I would like to acknowledge the Graduate School and the Department of History at Rutgers University for their financial support of my work, Lakeland College's faculty development committee, and Wittenberg University's History Department. My colleagues in the last few years have made my professional life a joy, and they have supported this work in progress in countless ways. Thanks to Margaret DeButy, Dar Brooks Hedstrom, Charles Chatfield, Nate Citino, Bob Cutler, Jim Huffman, Amy Livingstone, Miguel Martinez-Saenz, Nancy McHugh, Shelley Nygaard, Joe O'Connor, Chris Oldstone-Moore, Dick Ortquist, Tony Peffer, Ted Pelton, Julieanne Phillips, Don Reed, Scott Rosenberg, Martha Schott, Bob Smith, Tom Taylor, Claudia Thorndike, Denise Wilson, Richard Wixon, and Molly Wood. In addition, I owe a debt to the archivists and librarians who provided assistance at Alexander Library at Rutgers, Beinecke Rare Books and Manuscripts Collection at Yale, Boy Scouts of America, British Library, British Newspaper Library, Brunell University Library, Firestone Library at Princeton, Girl Scouts of the U.S.A., Imperial War Museum, Kirklees Sound Archive in Huddersfield, New York Public Library, Reed Book Services Library, School of Oriental and African Studies at the University of London, Southwark Local Studies Library, and Uxbridge Local Studies Library. Thanks to Ann Penke and Lori Judy for finding me treasures via interlibrary loan.

I am especially grateful to The Scout Association and The Guide Association for permission to consult their rich materials on interwar youth. Scout archivists Graham Coombe and Paul Moynihan gave

ACKNOWLEDGMENTS

generously of their time and talent during my stays in London, and they provided me with useful leads outside the capital. My thanks goes to them and to Beryl Stacey for allowing me to take up space in their office for several months. Special thanks goes to Guide archivist Margaret Courtney for her enthusiasm, assistance, hospitality, and friendship during my research trips. She and her assistants, Joyce Leas and Pat Styles, always made me feel welcome. In addition, I would like to thank all those who let me interview them and view their Scout and Guide treasures, most particularly Jeanne Holloway, Jane Frenneaux, Sheila Marks, Gwen and Malcolm Pearson, Margaret Pearson, and Roger and Mary Sanderson for opening their homes and archives for me.

My profound thanks goes to the 1991–92 Women's History Seminar at Rutgers, and to all those who read and commented on my work, including Jeanne Bowlan, Michelle Brattain, Malia Formes, Beth Friedley, Beatrix Hoffman, Lisa Kannenberg, Ben Lammers, Pat McDevitt, Colleen O'Neill, Tony Peffer, Scott Sandage, and Martin Summers. Special thanks goes to April Masten and Vince DiGirolamo for their close editing and generous ideas.

Finally, I want to thank my family for their patience and support. My parents, Gene and Eleanor Proctor introduced me to Scouting as a child, and my two brothers, Dennis and Don, never let me forget that I could not go to Boy Scout camp. I especially want to express gratitude to my sisters, Carole McGuire and Gayla Rich, for taking the time to read and comment on parts of this manuscript. To Todd Shirley for his love, encouragement, editorial comments, and the occasional bottle of Scotch, I dedicate this book.

LIST OF ILLUSTRATIONS

INTRODUCTION

On my Honour,
I promise that I will do my best,
To do my duty to God and to the Queen,
To help other people,
And to keep the Scout Law.
—The Scout Promise

Each year in the United Kingdom, well over a million young people promise to do their duty and to live up to the standards of the Scout and the
Guide movements. Although the promises of the Guides and Scouts (and
their younger sections) vary slightly, the meaning of each is clear. As each
child makes a pledge before God, he or she joins the largest youth organization in the world and becomes part of its rich history and tradition. These
new members also become heirs to a program that has been striving to
remain modern and timely since its creation in 1908. In fact, the difficulty
in attracting and keeping members today is not so different from the problems leaders experienced in 1908: how does a youth movement attract the
young and satisfy their parents simultaneously? Should the organization be
co-ed or single-sex? Should it be open to all, regardless of religion, nation-
ality, sexual orientation, political stance, class, and race? What ages should
be included in this organization for youth?

In addressing these questions, I argue that the British Guide and Scout
organizations clearly defined themselves in the period between the two
World Wars, creating institutions that could stand the test of time.
Although founded in 1908 (1910 for the Guides) and developed over the
next decade, Scouting only assumed its modern form when it was redefined
and shaped in relationship to its female counterpart, the Guides, in the
period during and after the First World War. The broadening of the movements to include females and wider age groups transformed the organizations from narrowly defined middle-class reform movements into diverse
and diffuse associations by the 1920s and 1930s. Scouting and Guiding
were able to attract youth from a variety of class, religious, and regional
backgrounds.

The Boy Scout and Girl Guide movements arose in the first decades of
the twentieth century, an era of social and political unrest, and they were
initially the center of intense controversy. By the 1920s, however, they had
become an established part of what came to be seen as the British "way of

life." Guiding and Scouting broke down rigid class, race, and gender divisions with uniforms, mixed companies, and large national and international gatherings. Led at first by the middle classes, by the 1920s the movements were cross-class national movements that helped youth cope with an emerging mass culture. The Guides and Scouts promised social mobility within their ranks and in outside occupations, while emphasizing self-improvement. In addition, these movements became a unique space for youth that allowed boys and girls to stretch gender and generational boundaries.

In many ways the Scouts and Guides defined youth in interwar Britain. As their numbers rose during the 1920s and 1930s, fiction, newspaper columns, shops, and paraphernalia catering to and for Scouts and Guides began to appear. The movements reflected new trends but also retained a bit of the "old world" before the war. For instance, they embraced cinema and saw its potential early, but also participated in music hall entertainment and pantomime. The commodification of service made the organizations a visible presence throughout the country and also created a curious tension in the organization between ideals and possessions as Scouts and Guides became avid consumers of "official" pocket knives, handbooks, cameras, and uniform accessories. The insistence on uniformity and training encouraged members to feel a sense of belonging to a great mass movement. Networks sprang up throughout Britain and the world; a Scout or Guide could go virtually anywhere and be assured of a welcome with just a call to Headquarters.

Scholars of interwar Britain have consistently identified the 1920s and 1930s as a period of redefinition that mixed a reluctant but insistent modernity with an imagined and powerful past. Men and women were redefining homes and sexuality as well as their definitions of nation and empire, often searching for ways to both reimagine the past and reclaim it. The need for a reassertion of sexual difference in family and workplace became the focus of many in the 1920s.[1] As literary scholar Alison Light persuasively argues in a 1991 study of interwar British literature:

> [P]art of the reaction against loss and the ideological rupture which is marked by the Great War, a conservative response might be an increased attachment to the idea of private life, not just as a shell into which the wounded individual might retreat, but as a new locus for the idea of a continuous and stable national history.[2]

The interwar era did indeed witness a longing for home, a nostalgia for some lost ideal, and a general bewilderment at the changes transforming the nation. Other scholars have also examined this reaffirmation of the domestic with its changed meanings in the 1920s, concluding that marital harmony became a kind of indicator of national health and order. In fact, it is quite clear in the histories of this period that the mending and ordering of relationships between the sexes was a vital part of the rebuilding of society after World War I.[3] After all, intimate relationships and family life seem a likely enough retreat for the emotionally scarred men and women of the war generation.[4] Young people in particular were looking for activities that would give meaning to their lives and institutions that would provide stable identities for them in an increasingly impersonal society.[5]

Scouting and Guiding played an important role in the postwar period in developing a mix of modern activities and nineteenth-century values, or to borrow Light's term, a "conservative modernity."[6] In Britain, these youth organizations mixed an older ethos of volunteerism and service, of patriotism and imperialism, of class/race/gender hierarchy, with a newer program of mass leisure, individualism, autonomy and internationalism. Seeking to bill themselves to the young as "modern" and chic, the movements espoused a message of adventure and opportunity, while institutionalizing protections of the older conservative ethos on which the movements had been founded, thereby appealing to parents and civic leaders.

This study begins with the formation of the Scout movement in 1908 and traces the development of a cohesive ideology for Scouting and Guiding in the interwar period. World War II marks the end of an era in the two organizations, and therefore is the terminus for this project. As the Baden-Powells surrendered control to the Scout and Guide councils after 1938 and with Robert Baden-Powell's death in 1941, leaders in both movements felt that substantive changes could then go into effect. Guiding and Scouting began a major transformation in the late 1940s, so that less than a decade after Baden-Powell's death, the movements had different uniforms, badges, tests, rules, and literature. Serious scholarly attention has not yet focused on this period in the history of youth movements in Britain, but the Scouts and Guides could be important starting points for such a study.

Although historians have studied youth organizations in the past, no one has examined these organizations from the bottom up. Because children and adolescents left few formal written documents, scholars have found it easier and more profitable to explore the ideology of youth leaders through their writings and reports. This book takes as its primary subjects the members themselves. The members, mostly children and youth aged eight to eighteen, did have voices. Oral histories, autobiographies, diaries, log books, letters, newspaper articles, handbooks, Scout and Guide publications, census materials, films, and official records are just some of the sources that are used here to get a sense of the participants' experiences, not just the official jargon. Most of the research was conducted at the national Scout Association and Guide Association archives in London. In addition, this book incorporates personal interviews of a number of former members in London, Kent, Hertfordshire, and Yorkshire, and materials gathered at several local studies libraries in those areas. I combined an intimate look at individuals, county organizations, and local troops with information gleaned from the national structure. Collections at the School of Oriental and African Studies at the University of London, at the Beinecke Rare Book and Manuscript Collection at Yale, and at the British Library allowed me to reconstruct the expansion of the movements into the empire.

In short, this study uses diverse source materials to reconstruct the actual experiences of the young people involved in the public spectacle and ritual of the Scouts and Guides, reflecting both the official ideology and the expressed desires of members and leaders at the local level. Within a roughly chronological framework, chapters are structured thematically to include specific questions of race and class, with the unifying theme throughout being gender and generation. On My Honour begins with two chapters that explore the formation of the Scouts and Guides, their transformation during World War I, and their membership and class compositions by the 1920s and 1930s. The interwar period marked a departure for the two organizations as they emerged as large multinational organizations that targeted not only adolescents, but also smaller children and young adults. These first two chapters explore the triumphs and problems of this expansion.

Specifically, Chapter 1 introduces the major arguments and explores the gendering of the Scout movement into the Scout and Guide programs, paying particular attention to the way in which girls shaped both movements. When girls began demanding entrance into the Scouts, leaders made accommodations for a separate girls' movement that would include some of the Scout activities and adventures, but that would be appropriately presented and controlled for females. Issues that arose in shaping both movements between 1908 and 1916 point to a complex negotiation among leaders, youth members, parents, children, and society that contributed to the development of a successful system of education and leisure activities that was flexible enough to withstand the changes of the 1920s.

Chapter 2 traces the development of larger and more diverse movements in the period following the First World War. The 1920s witnessed changing economic and family roles as the government increasingly experimented with defining the family through welfare legislation, public housing, and employment policies.[7] These changes, combined with declining family sizes and increased leisure time, meant that working-class as well as middle-class families were developing new mass leisure activities, fueled by the creation of adolescent consumers with disposable incomes.[8] Historians of British youth have consistently presented Boy Scouting as a pre-World War I, class-based movement, composed of lower middle-class participants. Concerned primarily with social control theories and using Robert Baden-Powell's writing as sources, these scholars assume that the experience of Scouting corresponded with the intentions of its leaders.[9]

New evidence shows that this model does little to explain the vast membership and popularity of the Boy Scout and Girl Guide movements in the 1920s and 1930s, and it simplifies the complex processes involved in the shaping of identity in this period. The addition of females and wider age groups transformed the organizations from narrowly defined and closely controlled middle-class reform movements into diverse and diffuse associations by the interwar period. Scouting and Guiding were able to attract youth from a variety of class, religious, and regional backgrounds. With the inclusion and participation of diverse groups, however, a unified ideology never really coalesced for many members. They embraced the activities and mission of Scouting and Guiding, but had to face the contradictions the organizations created in their lives. For working-class members especially, the movements represented social mobility, education, and travel, but often it also meant a betrayal of community mores, political principles, and family life. Donning a Scout or Guide uniform set a child apart, which could be both liberating and isolating and which created inherent contradictions in the missions of the two organizations.

The next three chapters examine the development of a complex relationship between the two movements that evolved during and after World War I. These chapters constitute the heart of the book's argument, exploring the development of conservative yet modern organizations in the 1920s. In particular, these chapters explain how Scouts and Guides epitomized the postwar citizen that Britons craved, with their selfless pledge to serve the nation, their separate-sex structure, and their prewar moral code. As with the new mass media, cinema, and sport, Scouting and Guiding functioned as national vehicles for expressing the unity and variety of Britain. Eric Hobsbawm described this postwar nationalism as the ability to make "national symbols part of the life of every individual, and thus to break down the divisions between the private and local spheres in which most citizens normally lived, and the public and national one."[10] For a generation of youth, these two organizations helped redefine the meaning of nationalism.

Chapter 3 discusses Guiding's development as an autonomous organization, and Guide leaders' attempts to please both the young women drawn to adventure and parents concerned about respectability and appropriate female behavior. Through the construction of a role I term the "New Mother," the Guides combined adventurous outdoor pursuits and a feeling of purpose and usefulness with a rhetoric of motherhood that emphasized traditional female roles. As Baden-Powell himself described a Guide, she was "to face mountains and difficulties and dangers" so that if "later on she has children of her own . . . she can be a really good Guide to them."[11]

Chapter 4 traces the changing face of the Scout movement as youth participation in both war work and postwar commemoration transformed the mission of Scouting. After 1919, Europe witnessed the growth of a number of youth movements that merged nationalism and masculine pursuits, as a cult of youth emerged that both idealized and shaped the male body.[12] The Soviet Komsomol organization and Germany's Hitler-Jugend are perhaps the most well-known examples, although significant "youth" movements emerged in practically every nation in Europe.[13] While the Scouts shared with these Soviet and German groups an emphasis on outdoor pursuits, marching, uniformity, and loyalty, the Scouts focused their energies on the creation of a service-oriented, international organization, while groups in other countries became highly politicized vehicles of ultranationalism.

Chapter 5 looks at the two movements together, and it focuses on the development of a familial metaphor that boosted the popularity of the movements. The organizations were able to capitalize on the longing for domestic comfort and a harmonious home, using family structures and language to shape the institutional structures. Scouting and Guiding had, and continue to have, the ability to inspire great loyalty in their members because of the creation of an elaborate and highly symbolic language, much of it based on this familial metaphor. The multigenerational nature of the movements and the strong identification of members with Scouting and Guiding ideology in the interwar period shaped a unique and powerful culture for youth.

The final chapter explores the international and imperial aspects of Scouting and Guiding. Within the last two decades, scholarly attention focusing on British imperialism has broadened to encompass the so-called "mythology of empire" including literature, rituals, and language. This new emphasis on cultural manifestations of the British imperial project has brought to the fore groups who had previously only occupied the historical stage in background roles. The British colonial community, long pictured as a unified whole, has become a contested identity as historians examine differences in class, income levels, gender, race, age, and religion in various British communities. Likewise, metropolitan institutions such as public schools, social movements, and organized sports have been scrutinized in an attempt to discover the roots and meaning of the European imperial project.[14]

Eric Hobsbawm and Terence Ranger note in their introduction to *The Invention of Tradition* that a crucial part of British imperialism and patriotism involved the rituals, practices, and "symbolically charged signs" of membership.[15] Perhaps the most frequent targets or recipients of these symbols were the youth of Britain and the Empire; young people were pictured as both the hope and the downfall of British imperial power in the early twentieth century. Young men and women of the middle classes were being trained to be military leaders, administrators, nurses, missionaries and teachers, while the working classes were encouraged to emigrate as soldiers, domestic servants, and farm laborers. Yet even as adults pushed the young toward appropriate roles in the maintenance of the empire, social reformers and politicians worried about the moral and physical decay of the young, which might lead to widespread social upheaval at home and abroad.

Thus, the importance of young people in maintaining and validating the British Empire cannot be underestimated in studies of twentieth-century imperialism. Young people symbolized national revitalization; controlling the youth of Britain in some ways meant controlling the future of the nation and more importantly, ensuring the continued existence of the empire. The rituals, language and symbols that validated the empire at home and abroad particularly targeted the young, who were reading imperial novels and participating in Empire Day celebrations. As the largest and most popular youth organizations in Britain and in the world, the Scouts and Guides are important models for the study of youth and empire. Tapping into the wealth of historical scholarship surrounding World War I and the British Empire, Chapter 6 examines the Guides and Scouts as reflections of anxieties about Britain's moral deterioration, but also as organizations flexible enough to survive the war and the decline of empire. Initially, the movements articulated much of the imperial and militaristic rhetoric of the prewar period and mirrored a growing interest in eugenics and bourgeois fears of the dual threat of decadence and socialism. Focusing on World War I as a turning point, I explore how this meaning of empire, citizenship, and nation changed to fit a growing internationalist ethic and a new definition of patriotism for both boys and girls.

As political scientist Cynthia Enloe has noted, nationalism and colonialism were constructed around real and imagined gender divisions at home and also by memory, nostalgia, and commercial images.[16] Using the insights that such studies of colonial rule, race, and empire can provide, this final chapter uses youth to examine imperial identity at home and abroad. It also helps tie the entire book together. The home imagined and shaped by the domestic movements to help repair the damage of the First World War owed its power and imagery to the empire and in turn gave resonance to the message being transmitted internationally.

Despite the difficulties inherent in any study that tries to incorporate the voices of youth, I still maintain that in the late nineteenth and early twentieth centuries, young people were at the heart of understanding other historical developments. Recent social histories of Britain have been instrumental at bringing youth to the forefront of study and have recognized how important young people can be to the understanding of British history and society.[17] Literary critics have also seen the significance of children and youth to understanding a society. As Jacqueline Rose argued in her study of *Peter Pan*, juvenile fiction can be interpreted as a reflection of adult anxieties and fantasies, and children's books often function as a way to offset challenges to adult identities.[18] Likewise, I contend that yes, the Scouts and Guides are interesting as youth movements, but they are also instructive to those studying British adult society for what they show about gender and class anxieties as well as national and imperial ambitions. The special importance of Scouting and Guiding is that these movements were not just limited to the Edwardian period, but they are still vital identity-forming institutions today in Britain and around the world.

ENDNOTES

[1] For excellent studies of the gendered anxieties emerging in this period of transformation, see Susan Kingsley Kent, *Making Peace: The Reconstruction of Gender in Interwar Britain* (Princeton: Princeton University Press, 1993), and Mary Louise Roberts, *Civilization without Sexes: Reconstructing Gender in Postwar France, 1917–1927* (Chicago and London: The University of Chicago Press, 1994). A challenge to these studies can be found in Susan Grayzel, *Women's Identities at War: Gender, Motherhood, and Politics in Britain and France during the First World War* (Chapel Hill and London: The University of North Carolina Press, 1999), 226–246.

[2] Alison Light, *Forever England: Femininity, Literature and Conservatism between the Wars* (London: Routledge, 1991), 211.

[3] See, for example, Deirdre Beddoe, *Back to Home and Duty: Women between the Wars, 1918–1939* (London: Pandora, 1989), Kent, *Making Peace*, and Eric Leed, *No Man's Land: Combat and Identity in World War I* (Cambridge: Cambridge University Press, 1979).

[4] Recent studies have focused on the impact of wounded male bodies and memory on those living in Britain in 1920s. In particular, see: Joanna Bourke, *Dismembering the Male: Men's Bodies, Britain and the Great War* (London: Reaktion Books, 1996) and Nicoletta Gullace, "White Feathers and Wounded Men: Female Patriotism and the Memory of the Great War," *Journal of British Studies* 36:2 (1997): 178–206. A review of some of this recent literature is Susan Kingsley Kent, "Remembering the Great War," *Journal of British Studies* 37:1 (January 1998): 105–110.

[5] A recent work has looked at youth movements of this period as ways of institutionalizing postmodern elements of informality and spontaneity. See Reuven Kahane, *The Origins of Postmodern Youth: Informal Youth Movements in a Comparative Perspective* (Berlin/New York: Walter de Gruyter, 1997).

[6] Light, *Forever England*, 10.

[7] Many governmental attempts to regulate family life and provide public assistance floundered, yet they were important harbingers of programs implemented in the 1940s. Good discussions of some of these issues can be found in Susan Pedersen, *Family, Dependence, and the Origins of the Welfare State: Britain and France, 1914–1945* (Cambridge/New York: Cambridge University Press, 1993).

[8] David Fowler, *The First Teenagers: The Lifestyle of Young Wage-Earners in Interwar Britain* (London: Woburn Press, 1995), 93–115.

[9] On the scouts, see for example, Michael Rosenthal, *The Character Factory: Baden-Powell and the Origins of the Boy Scout Movement* (New York: Pantheon Press, 1986); John Springhall,

Youth, Empire and Society: British Youth Movements, 1883–1940 (London: Croom Helm, 1977), and Paul Wilkinson, "English Youth Movements, 1908–1930," *Journal of Contemporary History* 4:2 (April 1969). There have been a number of biographies of Robert Baden-Powell, but the best is the most recent one by Tim Jeal, *The Boy-Man: The Life of Lord Baden-Powell* (New York: William Morrow, 1990). On social control as a concept used by historians, see Gareth Stedman Jones, "Class Expression versus Social Control? A Critique of Recent Trends in the Social History of Leisure," in *Languages of Class: Studies in Working Class History, 1832–1982* (Cambridge: Cambridge University Press, 1983), 76–89; and Eileen Yeo and Stephen Yeo, "Ways of Seeing: Control and Leisure versus Class and Struggle," in *Popular Culture and Class Conflict 1590–1914: Explorations in the History of Labor and Leisure*, eds. Yeo and Yeo (New Jersey: Humanities Press, 1981), 128–154.

[10] Eric Hobsbawm, *Nations and Nationalism since 1780: Programme, Myth, Reality* (Cambridge: Cambridge University Press, 1990), 42.

[11] Robert Baden-Powell, *Girl Guiding* (London: C. Arthur Pearson, 1921), 62–63.

[12] Much has been written both about the celebration of youth and the importance of youth to the development of ideologies such as fascism. See, for example Modris Eksteins, *Rites of Spring: The Great War and the Birth of the Modern Age* (New York: Doubleday, 1989), J.A. Mangan, ed. *Shaping the Superman: Fascist Body as Political Icon* (London/Portland: Frank Cass, 1999), and George Mosse, *Nationalism and Sexuality: Middle-Class Morality and Sexual Norms in Modern Europe* (Madison: University of Wisconsin Press, 1985).

[13] For a classic study of the German Youth Movement from 1901 to 1933 that examines the developments of the interwar period in detail, see: Walter Laqueur, *Young Germany: A History of the German Youth Movement* (New York: Basic Books, 1962). Other studies of the development of the Hitler Youth and Komsomol include Kahane, *The Origins of Postmodern Youth*; Gerhard Rempel, *Hitler's Children: The Hitler Youth and the SS* (Chapel Hill: University of North Carolina Press, 1989); Dagmar Reese, "Emancipation or Social Incorporation: Girls in the Bund Deutscher Mädel," in Heinz Sünker and Hans-Uwe Otto, eds., *Education and Fascism: Political Identity and Social Education in Nazi Germany* (London: The Falmer Press, 1997), 102–120; Peter Stachura, *Nazi Youth in the Weimar Republic* (Santa Barbara/Oxford: Clio, 1975); Peter Stachura, *The German Youth Movement, 1900–1945: An Interpretive and Documentary History* (London: Macmillan, 1981); and Kitty Weaver, *Bushels of Rubles: Soviet Youth in Transition* (Westport, CT/London: Praeger, 1992), 32–33. An interesting look at youth (and Scouts, in particular) in Hungary is Eric Hirsch, "Voices from the Black Box: Folk Song, Boy Scouts and the Construction of Folk Nationalist Hegemony in Hungary, 1930–1944," *Antipode* 29:2 (1997): 197–215.

[14] See for example, John Mackenzie, ed., *Imperialism and Popular Culture* (Manchester: Manchester University Press, 1986) and J. A. Mangan, ed., *Making Imperial Mentalities: Socialisation and British Imperialism* (Manchester: Manchester University Press, 1990) on the culture of imperialism; Patrick Brantlinger, *Rule of Darkness: British Literature and Imperialism, 1830–1914* (Ithaca/London: Cornell University Press, 1988), P. J. Rich, *Elixir of Empire: The English Public Schools, Ritualism, Freemasonry, and Imperialism* (London: Regency, 1989), and J. A. Mangan, *Athleticism in the Victorian and Edwardian Public School* (Cambridge: Cambridge University Press, 1981), on specific cultural studies; Ann Stoler, "Rethinking Colonial Categories: European Communities and the Boundaries of Rule," *Comparative Studies in Society and History*, 31:1 (January 1989), 134–161, and "Making Empire Respectable: The Politics of Race and Sexual Morality in 20th Century Colonial Cultures," *American Ethnologist* 16:4 (1989): 634–660, on divisions in the colonial community. Other recent works have contributed to the theme of "appropriate morality" and have questioned

women's impact on the functioning of the empire. Some of these works include Kenneth Ballhatchet, *Race, Sex and Class under the Raj: Imperial Attitudes and Policies and Their Critics, 1793–1905* (New York: St. Martin's Press, 1980); Helen Calloway, *Gender, Culture, and the Empire* (Urbana: University of Illinois Press, 1987); and Margaret Strobel, *European Women and the Second British Empire* (Bloomington: Indiana University Press, 1991). For excellent reviews of work on gender and imperialism and the impact of post-colonial theory, see: Malia Formes, "Beyond Complicity versus Resistance: A Review of Recent Work on Gender and European Imperialism," *Journal of Social History* 28:3 (March 1995), 629–641, and Dane Kennedy, "Imperial History and Post-Colonial Theory," *Journal of Imperial and Commonwealth History* 24:3 (1996): 345–363, and "The Imperial Kaleidoscope," *Journal of British Studies* 37:4 (1998): 460–467.

[15] Eric Hobsbawm and Terence Ranger, eds., *The Invention of Tradition* (Cambridge: Cambridge University Press, 1983), 10–11. Also useful is Benedict Anderson, *Imagined Communities: Reflections on the Origins and Spread of Nationalism*, rev. ed. (London/New York: Verso, 1991), 5–7. Anderson's idea of the "imagined political community" is vital to understanding both colonial communities and the role symbols play in socializing youth to a certain idea of "nation."

[16] Cynthia Enloe, *Bananas, Beaches and Bases* (Berkeley: University of California Press, 1989).

[17] For example, see Michael Childs, *Labour's Apprentices: Working-class Lads in Late Victorian and Edwardian England* (London: Hambledon Press, 1992); Anna Davin, *Growing Up Poor: Home, School and Street in London, 1870–1914* (London: Rivers Oram Press, 1996); Gretchen Galbraith, *Reading Lives: Reconstructing Childhood, Books, and Schools in Britain, 1870–1920* (New York: St. Martin's Press, 1997); Mangan, *Athleticism in the Victorian and Edwardian Public School*; Ellen Ross, *Love and Toil: Motherhood in Outcast London, 1870–1918* (New York: Oxford University Press, 1993), Springhall, *Youth, Empire and Society*, and John Springhall, *Coming of Age: Adolescence in Britain, 1860–1960* (Dublin: Gill and Macmillan, 1986).

[18] Jacqueline Rose, *The Case of Peter Pan, or, The Impossibility of Children's Fiction* (London: MacMillan, 1984), 1–4.

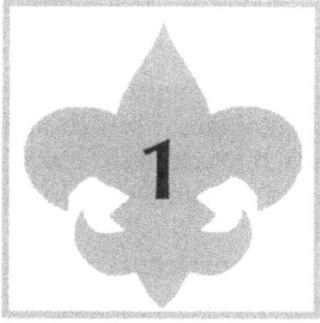

1

DIVIDING THE TROOPS

From Boy Scouting's creation as an experimental camp in 1907 to the present, the movement has had to confront the question of who could, should, and would belong to this uniformed youth organization. Questions of class, religion, race, gender, and sexual orientation have been at the center of the organization's self-definition and, over time, redefinition. In the early years of the movement, founder Robert Baden-Powell and other leaders were preoccupied with such questions, and they spent much of their time shaping and defining Scouting and its membership. The subsequent development of handbooks, media, training programs, and administrative structures as well as ideological constructions of the definition of "youth" and "Scout" helped the organization set boundaries and control entrance.

One of the most important and contentious of these defining issues facing the Boy Scout movement at its inception in 1908 was the question of gender. From the beginning, Baden-Powell wanted a movement that created men of character. As an (at that time) unmarried career soldier in his fifties, Baden-Powell saw the world through a framework of manliness and masculine pursuits, and he was unprepared for the outpouring of interest in Scouting from adolescent girls. Although in later years Baden-Powell maintained that he always had planned for a girls' movement, the Girl Guides were not created until almost two years after the publication of *Scouting for Boys*. It seemed that a girls' movement only became a necessity when girls began a clandestine participation in the boys' movement. By separating the two movements in 1910 and giving girls and boys similar activities but different identities, the Scouts and Guides circumvented public criticism and attracted both sexes with outdoor activities, uniforms, and collectibles, and with appeals to patriotism. The popularity and longevity of the movements were the result of a gendered discourse of service and entertainment that emerged in the first decade of Scouting's history, addressing a more general concern in early twentieth-century Britain with racial purity, degeneration, and appropriate sexuality.[1]

To understand the gendered ideology of these movements, it is crucial to look at the boys and the girls in conjunction, rather than examining each organization separately.[2] Until recent years, the experiences of girls have been marginal to histories of youth and often their lives are portrayed as poor reflections of boys' lives.[3] During the 1970s and 1980s, historians of British youth analyzed male and female youth movements such as the Scouts and Guides as separate entities in order to understand articulations of class and gender. Seminal studies of youth by historians such as Carol Dyhouse, John Gillis, Deborah Gorham, and John Springhall used sex-specific studies to show how youth was constructed and how children fit into the larger sociopolitical history of a period.[4] However, by consciously concentrating on only boys or girls, these studies fail to examine the way sex is understood and defined. The two movements cannot be studied separately because the social categories of "boyhood" and "girlhood" are always constructed in relation to each other. By exploring the interactions between the girls and boys, it is possible to study how these two movements reinforced each other dialectically. By constructing usable categories of "boyhood" and "girlhood," the Scouts and Guides were able to build an active membership of more than a million youth in Britain by the mid-1930s.

SCOUTING FOR BOYS

Scout and Guide history began when Baden-Powell, a soldier nearing the end of his active career, became interested in creating activities to improve the character and training of British boys after inspecting a 1904 Glasgow rally of the Boys Brigade movement, a uniformed Christian youth organization.[5] At first interested in developing a program for use by existing organizations, he began promoting a separate training scheme when he joined forces with newspaper publisher C. Arthur Pearson. With encouragement from Pearson, Baden-Powell tested his ideas on character training by holding a sample Scout camp in 1907 at Brownsea Island, Dorset, consisting of boys from both public school and working-class origins. He invited friends to provide children of the right age from Eton, Harrow, and other elite schools, and he asked the Boys' Brigade organizations in Bournemouth and Poole to provide the working-class boys. Much of the Scout program was tested at Brownsea, including the patrol system, campfire yarns, stalking, camp cooking, competitions, and games.[6] The apparent success of the Brownsea Island experiment meant that Baden-Powell's book, *Scouting for Boys*, and his scheme to regenerate Britain's youth through Scouting might stand a chance.

Baden-Powell, like many of his contemporaries, was concerned with a perceived moral and physical degeneration of Britain. During the last quarter of the nineteenth century, birthrates had dropped and infant mortality rates remained high. Social investigators, such as Charles Booth and B. Seebohm Rowntree, had recorded appalling poverty and disease in urban areas. These vague concerns with the health and vitality of the nation coalesced in a national panic after the Boer War, when military failures and inefficiency exposed what seemed to be physical and moral weaknesses in Britain. Reformers and political leaders called for a reassertion of the virility and power of British men. Unless boys were taught to be "real" men, social critics feared that the family and the nation were institutions doomed to destruction. The literature of the prewar period emphasized the need for boys to learn manliness, as magazines such as *Boys' Own* and adventure books by writers such as G. A. Henty depicted boys engaged in acts of patriotic daring.[7]

The language of national degeneration reflected fears that Britain was becoming effeminate and "soft" in an age of increased nationalist posturing in Europe. Physicians, reformers, socialists, and eugenicists began calling for national efficiency and regeneration as Parliament passed acts providing for health inspections in schools (1907) and for free meals for poor school children (1906), and voluntary associations organized maternal training centers and traveling health visitors for working-class homes. The whole nation seemed to turn its attention to stopping Britain's slide into oblivion.[8] This domestic anxiety mirrored larger imperial and international changes, such as Britain's waning industrial power, Germany's developing navy and industry, and the Empire's nascent nationalist movements. Worries about national degeneration and lack of preparedness led to a series of new pseudo-military organizations for men, women and boys, including Voluntary Aid Detachments (1909), the First Aid Nursing Yeomanry (1907), Officer Training Corps (1908), and the Territorial Force (1908). As Anne Summers has usefully written, the Boer War's aftermath created a nation "organized as a fighting unit."[9]

Combining social and moral reform, imperialism, efficiency, and character training, the Boy Scout scheme was developed as one of many answers to degeneration fears. Scouting sought to improve physical prowess and strength through outdoor activities and games, while teaching morality and nationalism. Baden-Powell borrowed ideas from youth organizations in the United States, from German and Swedish physical training proponents, from the public school sport and games ethos, and from military organizations. In early 1908, his guidelines for scouting appeared serially, and then in book form as *Scouting for Boys*.[10]

Scouting made good use of media resources, propaganda techniques and famous Edwardians to attract boys to its ranks. Baden-Powell had a reputation as a war hero because of his role as "Defender of Mafeking," a town besieged during the Boer War. His name was literally a household word in Britain, thus making his task in publicizing the movement easier. *Scouting for Boys* publisher Arthur Pearson ensured the movement's initial success by cleverly publicizing Baden-Powell along with the scheme. Encouraged by Pearson, Baden-Powell wrote advance articles in magazines, gave a series of lectures, and promoted the idea in newspapers. By the time *Scouting for Boys* appeared, educators, clergy, other youth movements, and boys and girls themselves were eagerly awaiting the appearance of the manual.[11]

Baden-Powell enlisted other people and contemporary ideas to boost his scheme, finding support among men of various political persuasions and of diverse occupations. Commissioners and leaders included Labour MP George Lansbury, Major-General Sir Edmond Elles, and outspoken Liberal reformer Sir Francis Vane.[12] One of his greatest supporters was Rudyard Kipling, who not only composed the official Boy Scouts' Patrol Song in 1909, but whose work, *The Jungle Book*, became the basis for the Wolf Cub Handbook and the whole Cub Scout scheme for younger boys, which was officially created during the war.[13] Kipling attended some Scout events in the early days, served as a commissioner, and publicly supported Baden-Powell's ideas by writing letters of support. In a letter to a headmaster, he wrote: "All I am sure of is that the present trend of legislation is making milksops of the democracy, and for them B.P's plan is about the only way of salvation that I've seen."[14] Kipling's only real disagreements with early Scouting were over discipline and military training. He thought Scouting too lax in its use of punishment and drill.[15]

Ironically, most contemporary observers, many of whom considered Baden-Powell's army background proof enough of his military leanings, voiced concern over too much militarism. In the Scouts, boys were trained in support work for national and imperial defense, and the organization had arisen partly out of concern for the dismal state of army recruits. Parents and politicians might encourage the inculcation of manliness and masculine values, but they did not want a movement that functioned as a feeder for the army. Scouting walked a fine line by denying any military connections, while sanctioning the early Scout patrols, who often drilled, dressed as soldiers, played war games, and learned to shoot with rifles.

Historians have debated the general issue of the militarism of Edwardian society at length.[16] In addition, historians of the Scout movement have focused extensively on the question of whether Scouting was designed as a military organization. In fact, militarism and social control have been the centerpieces of the more critical work on Scouting in Britain. Martin Dedman, for instance, has painstakingly traced the development of

Baden-Powell's ideas to prove that Scouting was not militaristic by design. Instead, Dedman found that Baden-Powell used certain aspects of military organization but focused on training techniques of pioneers in the educational field, such as Maria Montessori and Charles Stelzle. Scouting echoed the general militarism of Britain in the Edwardian period, Dedman argues, but Baden-Powell resisted the identification of Scouting with the War Office, going so far as to deny affiliation during World War I.[17]

Despite Baden-Powell's continual assurances that the movement was not "a form of military instruction, nor is it a Sunday School," critics of the movement were vocal in their belief in Scouting's militarism. The strongest of these critiques in the Edwardian period emerged among trade-union leaders, working-class parents, and Labour Party leaders.[18] These groups distrusted attempts to organize youth into uniformed movements, seeing such organizations as training for the army. They considered Baden-Powell's pronouncements on national defense dangerous and felt that youth were being either directly or indirectly coerced into military service. In the years before the First World War, labor leaders mounted a vigorous campaign against Scouting in its leading newspapers by focusing on the question of militarism.[19]

These outside accusations regarding militarism were fueled by the defection of several top Scout officials who went on to create their own youth movements. The London Scout Commissioner, Sir Francis Vane, left the movement after a well-publicized fight with headquarters in 1909. Vane was dismissed from his post and became the leader of a competing pacifist youth movement, the British Boy Scouts. Another pacifist, John Hargrave, left the position of Commissioner of Camping and Woodcraft in 1920 to take over a youth movement called the Kindred of the Kibbo Kift.[20] Although these and other rival boys' movements never posed a serious challenge to the Scouts, the criticism in the press generated by squabbles over militarism did keep members away. Less strenuous disagreements over militarism took place in the movement as individual Scoutmasters and commissioners tried to define the role of the Scouts. Percy Everett, the publishing representative from Pearson's assigned to the Scouts, became a leading member of both the Guides and Scouts. He pushed for a less militaristic emphasis in the early days, but usually conceded to Baden-Powell over the issue. An example of his gentle persistence on the issue is evident in a letter he wrote to Baden-Powell in 1909:

> I do not know whether you have noticed the correspondence in the daily papers within in the last few days on the military aspect of the Boy Scout Movement, especially in connection with the Manoeuvres which are now taking place. Following on the very Military flavour of the Display at the Crystal Palace, I am sure that a lot of harm is being done to the Movement throughout the country. As an example, I was at Hatfield last night forming a Provisional Committee for that district, and two or three Scoutmasters present mentioned that boys in the country districts were not allowed to join the Scout Movement "because they would have to become soldiers"![21]

Everett's concerns were justified because militarism had become the main focus of criticism of the movement by insiders and the public by 1910. This problem only intensified with the outbreak of World War I and the antimilitary reaction that followed Versailles. In 1915, two prominent Scout leaders expressed concerns in letters over the militarism in the Rover Section, and questioned the goals of the whole organization. By 1922, even Baden-Powell was telling his leaders, "We are anti-war, not anti-defense," in a justification of the Marksman badge.[22] This tension between military discipline and peaceful goals remains in the movement to this day, perhaps providing a more varied membership because of the Scout organization's continued ambiguity regarding its connection with militarism.[23]

Another area of Scout ideology attacked from within and without was the religious philosophy of the movement. Although Scouts pledged their loyalty to God, Christianity was not a focal point of the early movement in the way that it was in other boys' movements, such as the Church Lads Brigade and Boys Brigade. The official stated policy in 1911 was, "It is expected that every Scout should belong to some religious denomination and attend its services…in camp any form of daily prayer and of weekly Divine Service should be of simplest character, attendance being voluntary."[24]

Again, the very openness of Scout policy was suspect to some people, especially as the number of Jewish troops increased. Many Scout troops attached themselves to local churches, YMCA groups, and Sunday Schools, but Scouts were still open to criticism. Sometimes Scoutmasters or Scouts themselves complained about the lack of uniform practice in the movement. The debate over the role of religion in the Scouts intensified as the movement began expanding outside of Britain, bringing in members who were not Christian.[25]

Despite the attacks the Scouts sustained in these early years, the program was undoubtedly a success. *Scouting for Boys* was reprinted, and membership rose steadily in the early years. By the time of the first census of the Scouts in 1910, the movement had more than 100,000 members in Britain alone. That number had doubled less than a decade later. Scout leaders were pioneering new organizations in poor areas such as London's East End and the mining areas of South Wales, while boys at public schools like Eton and Harrow were becoming Scouts. It became a struggle to register and find leaders for all of the prospective Scouts, especially in urban areas.[26]

The decentralized structure of the Scout movement allowed individual troops to develop their own programs and to do their own fundraising, greatly expanding the number of new troops. Despite the existence of a national program, activities often depended on the local leader and his or her interests. One pre-World War I Scout, Edward Ezard, remembered that his Boy Scout troop changed tremendously when his leaders changed. The first leader, a local curate, led the boys in marching, drill, and games. Highlights of Ezard's early Scout experience included mock battles with savage tribes. Afterwards, lemonade was served. When the curate left the area, the new troop leader was a Physical Training (PT) instructor at the local Polytechnic, so drilling, marching, and semaphore were abandoned for gymnastics, boating, and nature study. The boys were even instructed to stop using their staves [long poles].[27] It was not unusual, especially in the first ten years of Scouting's history, to observe such widely varying programs at the local level.

Adventure was central to the Scout ethos, and the movement appeared to be a great game to boys. Scouting made good use of badges, flags, tools, and clothing as encouragement for boys to join. In an essay submitted to Scout Headquarters for a competition in 1909 Robert Clark, a 13-year-old Scout from the north of England, expressed the enthusiasm and excitement some boys felt as Scouts:

> Just imagine for one moment what it means, to get the order from your chief, to carry despatches [sic] through the enemys [sic] lines and country to their destination. You know for sure that it means life or death to you, if you are caught. While I am writing I may say that there are scores of scores of people who have only a very hazy idea of the hardships and hair breadth escapes a scout has to go through.[28]

The movement, its literature, and its heroes seemed to embody adventure. In fact, one recent scholar has described the appeal by saying that Baden-Powell had "a patent on adventure" with the Scout scheme.[29] Adventure was part of the attraction, but the service motive also drew members by making boys feel useful and important to Britain. Scouting was an outlet for their patriotic yearnings, and they considered their service to the nation vital, even though adults often poked fun at their seriousness. In short, the Scout movement allowed them to enjoy themselves as children, while providing them with adult purposes.

Early training was loosely based on Baden-Powell's military experience with the emphasis on campaigning, dispatch running, signaling, and tracking. Scouts used their staves to guard bridges and factories in preparation for national defense. They formed military-style bands and marched through villages and towns. Not one to abide too closely to military regimen, however, Baden-Powell soon expanded the program to include a concern with health, physical fitness, and vocational skills. Some of the early proficiency badges included Airman, Cyclist, Gardener, Interpreter, Photographer, Poultry Farmer, and Starman.[30] In addition to local activities, Scouts held rallies, parades, mock battles, and social gatherings. By 1913, they had a series of annual competitions in place. These competitions included HRH Duke of Connaught's Challenge Shield (running and shooting), Otter Club Challenge Shield (swimming), Darnell Cup (swimming and life-saving), and Imperial Shield (rifle), just to name a few. There were also local and county competitions, and county rallies, which were popular ways to meet other Scout troops.[31]

These large events were important, but the patrol system was the cornerstone of Scout success because it allowed independence and self-government for the boys, while creating a sense of "gang" affiliation and identification within the larger troop. Six to eight boys made up the ideal patrol, and each patrol worked, played, and planned together. They functioned under the leadership of a Patrol Leader and a Patrol Second, usually appointed by the Scoutmaster. Each patrol had an animal name with badges, banners, signs, and corresponding calls. Boys were immediately encouraged to identify with their patrol by signing their names with the patrol sign, learning the call of their patrol, and decorating their corner of the meeting room with identifying symbols. Being a Peewit or a Curlew or a Beaver, complete with appropriate cry, was enough to excite any boy's imagination. Among the most treasured possessions of Scouts were their patrol symbols, second only to their treasured metal Tenderfoot and First Class badges (gained after completing a series of tests).[32]

Reflecting the efforts of other social reformers of the period, Baden-Powell attempted to build a cross-class male community within the Scout organization. He wanted to encourage upper- and middle-class boys to use their leadership skills, and he wanted to inculcate loyalty and selflessness in working-class boys. Scouting shared the aims of settlement movements such as Toynbee Hall, and it built on Christian youth movements like the Boys Brigade and the Church Lads Brigade.[33] However, the Scout program was unique in its methods and in its concentration on a relatively young group of boys. Ages for the first Scouts ranged from about 11 to about 16 years old, but this span was extended up to 18 by 1911. Accommodations for younger and older youth were quickly demanded and delivered. Young boys, aged 8–10, were organized into a new branch, the Wolf Cubs, in 1916. In 1918, Senior Scouts formally became the Rover Branch, which catered to young men aged 18 and older.[34] Despite the development of older sections for the movement, Scouting's strength has always been in its younger branches.

Baden-Powell and other leaders tried some innovative social reform programs for attracting boys and for creating a healthier, more vigorous nation. One such scheme was a farm, which the Scouts set up as a vocational training and Scouting school for poor boys. The idea was that the farm would support itself and that it would be popular enough to attract the requisite number of workers to keep it going. Urban boys could presumably forge a connection with nature, gaining health and strength in the fresh air and building their characters through hard work. Again, this scheme copied other Edwardian reform programs that transported urban children to the countryside such as the Open Air Movement or social experiments in collectivism such as Back to the Land.[35] By December 1911, the Buckhurst Place Farm in Sussex had twenty-five boys in residence, ranging in age from 14 to 18 years. All but two of the boys had been Scouts before they came to the farm, and the boys were from all over the country. The idea was interesting, but the farm had to be abandoned eventually because of lack of funds and problems in administering the scheme.[36] It seemed that the less structured and more creative Scout patrol was a better way of inculcating patriotism and attracting boys

The community Baden-Powell sought to create was one that would bring together men and boys of different backgrounds to build a "British manhood." Historical studies of American masculinity have shown that Scouting and male institutions assuaged adult fears by validating masculine virtues and teaching a masculine ethos. Scouting was a movement that allowed men and boys to be boys without fear of being labeled effeminate. Men and boys could pursue close friendships without censure, and they could test gender boundaries. Scouting became an area outside of work and family where male identity could be created and validated.[37]

This male community was threatened from the beginning by the desires of girls to be Scouts. Youth, regardless of their sex, loved the Scout idea and took up Scouting. It should not be a surprise that the activities that attracted boys to the movement also appealed to girls' sense of adventure. Also, the loose organization of the early years made it easy for boys and girls to start troops with homemade uniforms and a copy of Scouting for Boys, whether they were sanctioned by Headquarters or not [Figure 1]. The following letter to Baden-Powell from 10-year-old "scout" Robert Harrison illustrates this phenomenon:

> My sister, Jenny aged 11 1/2, and I are running a troop of young boys and girls, the members are Magdalen Ogle, age 11, Jack McDougall, age 8, Martin Ogle, age 6, Kathleen Southey, age 11, Nancie McDougall age 6 1/2, Mary Holdgate, age 13, and Evelyn Holdgate, age 11. . . . The girls are not allowed to go out with out a grownup with them, so can you think of any outdoore games we do not have to scatter much. We would love to be reviewed. We usely meet on Saturday afternoons at our house. Also can you somehow design a uniform for boys and girls.[38]

Letters such as this raised the issue of female involvement in Scouting for Baden-Powell and other Scout leaders, but they also created the problem of a coeducational movement. If girls wanted to be Scouts, and unofficial groups including girls were being created, Scout leaders had to make some kind of accommodation for them either within the organization or in a new one. Scouting defined youth and adolescence as a male domain, so girls were problematic in their demands to be part of this masculine terrain. Not only could the inclusion of girls make the program seem less appealing to boys, but it could threaten the respectability of the Scout movement in parents' eyes. After all, coeducational meetings, hikes, and especially camps would undermine the masculine community and the moral purpose of the organization in leaders' opinions.

Girls, however, saw Scouting as an opportunity to experience the adventures and games of male adolescence, something denied them in

FIG. 1 An early group of Scouts, both boys and girls, poses here as a unit. Courtesy of The Scout Association.

Edwardian Britain. More closely guarded than their male counterparts and more confined to private spaces, the thrill of stalking through the forest or learning Morse code communicated both adventure and usefulness to girls. During adolescence, boys were allowed a moment in time when they could do boyish things, but there did not seem to be a corresponding moment in time for girls. As historian Carol Dyhouse has noted, boys reached maturity with their economic independence, but girls seemed condemned to a perpetual state of childhood and dependence in Victorian and Edwardian Britain. Girls, who were controlled and monitored more than boys of the same age, craved the freedom that boys enjoyed.[39] Sally Mitchell has charted girls' demand for a "boyhood" in her work on late nineteenth- and early twentieth-century Britain, writing:

> Dreams of boyhood are hardly unique to the period. Given the cultural valuation of male as better and the visible privileges granted to boys, many girls have envied their brothers. In this period, however, girls' boyishness developed a publicly acceptable face. . . . [T]he boy dream had multiple resonances: girls wanted active games, a serious education, and adult rights and responsibilities.[40]

Despite restrictions on girls, it was becoming acceptable for girls to participate in "tomboyish" activities, if they were controlled. Girls could play sports and bicycle during their teens because it prepared them physically for the rigors of motherhood and mentally for the partnership of marriage.[41] However, what the early girl scouts were demanding of Scouting was the same acceptance as boys into the movement. They sought a coeducational organization, something that would threaten the more important Scout goal of inculcating masculine values. Therefore, the question that arose was "what to do with the girls?" Separation into discrete organizations seemed to be the only answer. As Baden-Powell frequently noted, girls had to know their place in society just as boys had to know theirs: "Teach them from the first that they are like bricks in a wall, or players in a football team: each has to be perfect and efficient, each has to adhere patiently to the rules and to play **in his place** and to play the game" [emphasis mine].[42]

⚜ BEING BRICKS BUT NOT BOYS

The official mythology of Guiding cites the big rally at the Crystal Palace in September 1909 as the point when Baden-Powell realized girls wanted to be Scouts. By this time the Boy Scouts could boast a membership in the London vicinity of 11,000 boys or more. Among the ranks was also a considerable number of girls, some of whom showed up at the 1909 demonstration calling themselves the "Girl Scouts." Adorned in borrowed hats and uniforms copied from the boys, the girls demanded inspection by the Founder as well.[43] This account implies a spontaneous revelation for Baden-Powell about the wisdom of having a girls' movement, when in fact, reports had been flooding into Scout headquarters from schools, churches, and girls themselves citing the popularity of *Scouting for Boys* among female youth. One early female enthusiast recalled how in those early days Baden-Powell's manual had fired the imaginations of girls in her school:

> Six of us decided that we should like to be Scouts, and very soon formed ourselves into a patrol, the Night Hawks. We bought hats, jerseys, haversacks, poles, belts, knives and whistles from Boy Scout Headquarters. We started to build a hut for ourselves, following word for word the instructions given in *Scouting for Boys*. The result was most successful: the hut became our headquarters, and lasted, with repairs, for many years.[44]

This account, along with others, shows that girls themselves negotiated and shaped the movement that became Guiding long before male and female leaders worked out the official outlines.

In examining the girls' role in creating the movement, it is important to look at the initial response to Scouting and to Guiding. Reading *Scouting for Boys* on their own, girls "soon became possessed with a violent desire to be Scouts too," and rushed to get staves and uniforms and merit badges. When denied access to the accoutrements of Scouting, the girls would design and sew their own uniforms, sometimes even using stiff paper to make hats. Other clever girls simply applied for badges and other materials by mail, registering as scouts and signing up using only their initials. Early Guide histories estimate that roughly 2000 girls registered as Scouts using this method. Girls used brothers or friends as fronts for their activities, sending them to get materials or badges. For example, Gladys Commander's brother enrolled her as a Scout in 1909, and she started her own patrol of girls. Elizabeth de Beaumont formed an unofficial group with her brother and her governess. In other cases, schoolmistresses began girl scouting programs as ways of teaching girls character and responsibility, but in a fun way.[45] Simply put, the early Girl Scouts got the same thrill and sense of usefulness that the boys did from Scouting:

> We got our first precious copy of Scouting for Boys by the Chief Scout and read all we could lay hands on, about Scoutcraft. We had Scout hats and poles and scarves and belts. We were the Seal Patrol and were desperately in earnest about it all. It was a wonderful game, so full of something that was utterly lacking in any other![46]

In general, these enthusiastic Girl Scouts reacted unfavorably to the official Girl Guide scheme when it was introduced in late 1909. Suspicious that their programs were about to change, Girl Scouts wanted to keep partici- pating in the excitement of Scouting for Boys: "Armed with staves the Girl Scouts set off to look for adventure. It was found in leaping over dykes, and crawling about in fields on hands and knees, or even on one's tummy."[47] Under the new scheme, girls would be taught "feminine" virtues, as boys were being taught "masculine" ones. The stated aim of the new movement was "to get girls to learn how to be women—self-helpful, happy, prosper- ous, and capable of keeping good homes and of bringing up good chil- dren."[48] One Girl Scout later recounted her reaction to being told of the con- version to Guiding: "One can still remember the feeling of anti-climax, of being let-down, almost insulted. Who wanted to be womanly at our age?"[49] Girls wanted adventure, not "home training."

Although most girls eventually did submit to the change to Guiding, they forced Guide leaders to keep the Scout adventure ethic alive in the new movement. In fact, despite the framework of "womanly" activities that formed the basis of Guiding, girls still pursued Scout badges such as Artist, Cyclist and Signaller to name a few, while engaging in activities like hiking and Morse code. Also, despite new blue uniforms (as opposed to the Scout khaki), some girls refused to give up the hats they had created in the early days, or others modified their uniforms with plumes and tabs and ribbons from their Scout days. Girls were able to do so mostly because of the unor- ganized nature of the Guide movement before World War I. Most local groups had little supervision from the national or regional level, and girls had no special guidebook until The Handbook for Girl Guides appeared in 1912. In fact, Baden-Powell was still receiving letters about unofficial Girl Scout troops as late as 1916.[50]

The Guide movement officially began in 1910, but the conversion and plans began earlier. In early July 1909, Baden-Powell asked editors to insert a note on Girl Scouts in Scout publications.[51] However, it was not until after the September 1909 rally that he articulated a plan for the Guide movement. In the November issue of the *Headquarters Gazette* (one of the early Scout publications), Baden-Powell published his suggestions for Guiding along with a scheme for implementation. Proposing a program similar to that of the boys, but suiting the girls' "sex," Baden-Powell explained his reasons for establishing a separate girls' movement in this short essay and in a pamphlet that was released in early 1910:

> Girls must be partners and comrades rather than dolls. Their influence in after life on the actions and quality of the men is very great—they become their "guides." They therefore need character training quite as much as the boys. As things are, one sees the streets crowded after business hours, and the watering-places crammed with girls overdressed and idling, learning to live aimless, profitless lives; and, in some cases, they run to the opposite extreme and take up manly pursuits, which make them hard and sexless; whereas if an attractive way were shown, their enthusiasm would at once lead them to take up useful woman's work with zeal.[52]

In one short paragraph, Baden-Powell managed to address most of the concerns facing parents in prewar Britain. He talked of making women comrades in a changing society, yet he emphasized their roles as nurturers, wives and mothers. Decadence and moral decay give way to hints of gender deviance in the quotation as Baden-Powell moves from idleness to sexlessness. In the end, he lauds his scheme as "useful woman's work" that would be attractive and appealing to girls and women, not to mention beneficial to their future husbands. Baden-Powell's explanation contains the heart of the Guide paradox: girls must be womanly and motherly (in preparation for marriage), but not sexual; they must be allowed freedom and adventure (in order to attract girls to the movement), but not too masculine.

Just as boys needed manliness training, girls needed to learn femininity and their appropriate role in society. In keeping with this philosophy of teaching girls their place, Baden-Powell wanted "ladies" to organize the girls. While it had been part of the attraction of Scouting that boys took the initiative and formed troops, girls were forbidden the same leniency. In order to ensure that parents had a proper woman on whom to focus, in 1910 Baden-Powell asked his sister, Agnes Baden-Powell, to head the official Guide organization. She was charged with putting together a respectable committee of ladies to administer the Guide movement.

In her 1912 handbook cowritten with her brother, Agnes Baden-Powell used a social reform model to define "useful women's work." Like her brother, Baden-Powell wanted to attract a multi-class group of girls, arguing that training was useful to all, but especially those of the lower classes:

> The girls of the factories and of the alleys of our great cities, who, after they leave school, get no kind of restraining influence, and who, nevertheless, may be the mothers, and should be the character trainers of the future men of our nation . . .[53]

Supplementing this perceived need for Guiding among lower-class girls was a need for upper-class women and girls to do something that counted for their "less well-to-do sisters." This first guidebook asked girls to learn to "Be Womanly/Be Handy/Be Strong/Be Good Mothers" through improved health/hygiene and character training.[54]

This early guidebook adhered to societal norms concerning "proper" womanliness because of widespread attacks on the rise of "tomboys" in the Guides. Tomboyishness was seen as the inevitable result of allowing girls to practice boys' activities. Above all, Guide leaders wanted to distinguish their members from the unsanctioned "Girl Scouting," which was attacked harshly because of the perceived "roughness" of the activities. One of the first attacks came in *The Spectator* in 1909 when anti-suffragist leader, Violet Markham, began a furious letter battle over the existence of Girl Scouts. Concerned that girls and boys were "roam[ing] the countryside together" returning home late and doing who knows what, Markham blasted the Boy Scouts for allowing girls to join in "unwomanly" activities. In one letter, she wrote: "Girls are not boys, and the training which develops manly qualities in the one may lead to the negation of womanliness in the other."[55] Editors of *The Spectator* added a note agreeing with Markham, and eliciting replies on both sides of the issue. One letter from a distraught man in Knutsford called for all the parents who allowed their daughters to join to be pilloried.[56] Many Scout leaders rushed to the defense of the movement, citing the November Guide scheme that called for a separate movement for girls. The Boy Scouts' Managing Secretary made it clear in his letter that "mixed troops of boys and girls are not countenanced" in the movement.[57]

After the heated exchange of letters and an article by Agnes Baden-Powell on the "real" nature of the Guides, *The Spectator* changed its position:

> On a previous occasion we strongly condemned the organization of Girl Scouts, especially under men leaders. Miss Baden-Powell's scheme of Girl Guides is an entirely different proposal, and open to none of the objections to which we drew attention.[58]

As a footnote to this incident, earlier in 1909 Markham had applauded Scout training for **boys** and believed that women could assist boys in their Scouting. She described her own pleasure in hosting a Scout troop on her grounds in 1909, writing: "Personally, I shall never forget the acute delight of crawling along a hedge and capturing an enemy's brigade singlehanded."[59] Unfortunately, Markham did not consider the thrill girls got from experiencing the same kind of games appropriate, or maybe she worried that they had too much fun while scouting.[60] Like Baden-Powell, Markham saw women's role in guiding boys to manhood as a much different endeavor than girls' yearning to be boys.

To stem criticism such as Markham's and to combat perceived threats to womanliness, Guide patrols used feminine symbols such as flowers for patrol names and badges. Many wanted to be Ravens and Wildcats, not

Daisies and Violets.[61] Some of the merit badges were changed to reflect womanly pursuits, so 'missioner" for boys became "sick nurse" for girls and additional laundry badges were added for Guides. Girls wore feminized uniforms based on the Scout model, and girls were told to camp indoors at first. Guide leaders limited parading in public, and marching with the boys was forbidden. As the Founder's wife Olave Baden-Powell wrote in a 1914 article, Guides opened themselves to criticism or harassment when seen in uniform either alone or with Scouts.[62] By limiting public appearances, Guide leaders sought to prove that they controlled the girls in their charge.

Still, in order to attract girls, some adventurous activities had to be justified. Former girl scouts were determined to retain some of their Scout fun, and leaders felt that they should encourage some of these activities. As Agnes Baden-Powell noted in one of her early defenses of the movement, "A girl is no more unwomanly because she can swim in her skirt and boots, or signal in the Morse code, or cook a palatable supper out in the open without civilized appliances."[63] In fact, girls were allowed to enjoy considerable "adventure" in the Guides as long as it fell within the confines of respectable feminine behavior. Baden-Powell herself pursued some unconventional hobbies for a single woman in her fifties, including ballooning, beekeeping, and bicycle polo, and she encouraged girls to be athletic and innovative.[64]

The movement was walking a thin line between conservative forces concerned with women's respectability and feminist forces (in the form of the suffrage movement and the "new women," for example) interested in promoting new opportunities and activities for women.[65] Girls were not yet women, so it was important to teach them respectability in their formative early teen years. Many girls took jobs at age fourteen, so were on the brink of womanhood. Guide leaders and parents thought these girls should be taught appropriate behavior and steered away from all improper pursuits. In a 1911 letter, one headmistress lamented the attack on high school and college education for girls caused by a perceived "unrest among women," saying: "The girls of the present day, we are told, are hard, un-sympathetic (and therefore unmannerly), wanting in the graces hitherto associated with their sex, lamentably indifferent to men and averse to marriage."[66] This headmistress highlighted fears that all organizations for women and girls had to circumvent in order to make their movements work. Girl Guides had to be womanly in order to answer adult anxieties about new freedoms for females. Guides were taught to be sympathetic and trained in home skills, and also they were taught to desire the company of men. Leaders thought girls should become wives, not independent women. Some wanted to train girls to be "companions" for men, but not equals; they wanted to save girls from depravity and moral disintegration, so that as women they, in turn, could save men. As one male lecturer told a prospective Guide group at Notting Hill (London) High School in 1912: "If the hard-up women of

London were able to cook dinners, the drink problem in regard to men would be almost entirely obliterated."[67]

Leaders faced the considerable challenge of presenting appropriate training for mature womanhood so as to be appealing to adolescent girls. Agnes Baden-Powell and her staff accomplished this by offering structured entertainment and merit systems that were exciting, while disassociating themselves from any unauthorized or inappropriate activities, such as raiding boys' camps, wearing short skirts, or creating disturbances. Guide leaders saw nothing funny about such pranks:

> The so-called Girl Guides who made a raid on a Boy Scouts' camp at midnight are not a registered patrol, and the Headquarters of the organization knows nothing whatever about them. The B.P. Girl Guides are not allowed to have anything to do with the Boy Scouts, and are not allowed out after dark. Such behavior can only bring the Movement into disrepute.[68]

CONCLUSION

The continued separation of male and female members was important to the success of the Scout and Guide organizations and to the gendered definition of service that the movements had embraced. Although initially this separation was stark, girls' protests led the Guide movement to adopt and revise many Scout activities for girls. Yet as the movements developed, the emphasis on masculine versus feminine activities increased despite the continued ideological connection between the movements. This emphasis on appropriate sexuality and gender roles allowed the two groups to appeal to youth from a wide range of class and regional backgrounds. Guiding and Scouting reflected societal expectations regarding appropriate activities and interests for boys and girls, while simultaneously participating in the contesting and reshaping of gender roles.

Girls threatened the cross-class male culture that Baden-Powell was trying to create in the Scout movement by demanding acceptance on equal terms. They pushed for a coeducational movement and tried to become boys at least for a short time. In essence, young women and girls created an adolescence for themselves where girls could be boys. This freedom was contained by certain restrictions, such as skirts and more adult supervision for girls, but it was a compromise youth and parents could accept.

In a similar way, the separation of the two movements allowed boys to build the Scout movement into a retreat from the world for men and boys, and leaders could inculcate appropriate notions of manliness. In fact, the Scout cult of masculinity became even stronger when coupled with the creation of its feminine equivalent. Scouts sought to mold ideal citizens, while Guides taught the mothers of the future. Both movements emphasized character building, physical fitness, and nationalism and both organizations promoted adventure for adolescents, but the programs and the meanings of "youth" were gendered and separate.

✿ ENDNOTES

[1] For a classic study of Edwardian Britain, see Samuel Hynes, *The Edwardian Turn of Mind* (Princeton: Princeton University Press, 1968).

[2] Much has been written on the Baden-Powells and the Scout organization, but little has been done on either the Guides or on gender in either movement. The major official histories of the Scouts/Guides include Henry Collis, Fred Hurll, and Rex Hazlewood, *B-P's Scouts: An Official History of the Boy Scouts Association* (London: Collins, 1961); Rose Kerr, *The Story of the Girl Guides* (London: Girl Guides Association, 1954) and Alix Liddell, *The Girl Guides, 1910–1970* (London: Frederick Muller, 1970). Baden-Powell has been the subject of several biographies and the Chief Guide, Olave Baden-Powell, has written an autobiography that is quite useful. The best biography is the recent one by Tim Jeal, *The Boy-Man: The Life of Lord Baden-Powell* (New York: William Morrow, 1990). The analytical books on the movements are limited to work on the Scouts by John Gillis, *Youth and History: Tradition and Change in Early Age Relations, 1770–present* (New York: Academic Press, 1974); Michael Rosenthal, *The Character Factory: Baden-Powell and the Origins of the Boy Scout Movement* (New York: Pantheon Press, 1986); John Springhall, *Youth, Empire and Society: British Youth Movements, 1883–1940* (London: Croom Helm Ltd., 1977); and Paul Wilkinson, "English Youth Movements, 1908–1930," *Journal of Contemporary History* 4:2 (April 1969), 3–23. Allen Warren has written several insightful articles on the Guides and Scouts in various edited collections including, "Mothers for the Empire," in *Making Imperial Mentalities: Socialisation and British Imperialism*, ed. J. A. Mangan (Manchester: Manchester University Press, 1990), 96–109; "Citizens of the Empire: Baden-Powell, Scouts and Guides, and an Imperial Ideal," in *Imperialism and Popular Culture*, ed. John Mackenzie (Manchester: Manchester University Press, 1986), 232–256; and "Popular Manliness: Baden-Powell, Scouting and the Development of Manly Character," in *Manliness and Morality: Middle-class Masculinity in Britain and America, 1800–1940*, eds. J. A. Mangan and James Walvin (New York: St. Martin's Press, 1987), 176–198.

[3] In a thoughtful article from 1984, Mica Nava called for the inclusion of girls in histories of youth. She emphasized the importance of looking at both boys and girls in order to understand the relationship between them. See Mica Nava, "Youth Service Provision, Social Order, and the Question of Girls," 1–30, in *Gender and Generation*, eds. Angela McRobbie and Mica Nava (London: MacMillan, 1984). A recent work that incorporates both boys and girls is Anna Davin, *Growing Up Poor: Home, School and Street in London, 1870–1914* (London: Rivers Oram Press, 1996).

[4] Carol Dyhouse, *Girls Growing Up in Late Victorian and Edwardian England* (London: Routledge, 1981); Gillis, *Youth and History*; Deborah Gorham, *The Victorian Girl and the Feminine Ideal* (Bloomington: Indiana, 1982); Harry Hendrick, *Images of Youth: Age, Class and the Male Youth Problem, 1880–1920* (Oxford: Clarendon Press, 1990); Robert H. MacDonald, *Sons of the Empire: The Frontier and the Boy Scout Movement, 1890–1918* (Toronto: University of Toronto Press, 1993); Springhall, *Youth, Empire and Society*.

[5] Jeal, *The Boy-Man*, 360–362, 371.

[6] For a good account of the Brownsea experiment and the formation of Boy Scouting, see Jeal, *The Boy-Man*, 360–389.

[7] For works on degeneration fears and the fin-de-siecle emphasis on manliness, see: Harry Brod, ed., *The Making of Masculinities: The New Men's Studies* (Boston: Allen & Unwin, 1987); Mangan and Walvin, eds., *Manliness and Morality*; and MacDonald, *Sons of the Empire*. Interesting studies of juvenile literature and nationalism/imperialism include Patrick Brantlinger, *Rule of Darkness: British Literature and Imperialism, 1830–1914* (Ithaca/London: Cornell University Press, 1988), and Jeffrey Richards, ed., *Imperialism and Juvenile Literature* (Manchester: Manchester University Press, 1989).

[8] A well-written account of Edwardian fears of degeneration can be found in Deborah Dwork, *War is Good for Babies and Other Young Children: A History of the Infant and Child Welfare Movement in England, 1898–1918* (London/New York: Tavistock, 1987), 6–22, 123–125, 184. See also Anna Davin, "Imperialism and Motherhood," *History Workshop Journal* 5 (1978): 9–65.

[9] A. J. A. Morris, The Scaremongers: *The Advocacy of War and Rearmament 1896–1914* (London: Routledge and Kegan Paul, 1984), 226, W. J. Reader, *At Duty's Call: A Study in Obsolete Patriotism* (Manchester: Manchester University Press, 1988), 81–89, and Anne Summers, *Angels and Citizens: British Women as Military Nurses, 1854–1914* (London: Routledge and Kegan Paul, 1988), 204, 275.

[10] For a useful discussion of the degeneration worries of Edwardian Britain and the role of youth in combating these fears, see Gillis, *Youth and History*, chapters 3 and 4.

[11] Jeal, *The Boy-Man*, 383–391.

[12] Jeal, *The Boy-Man*, 402–403.

[13] Kipling's work became inspirational in the Scout and Guide movements, especially an excerpt from his poem "The Feet of Young Men," which was inscribed on official log-books and other organizational memorabilia.

[14] Rudyard Kipling to A. Devine, Headmaster of Clayesmore School, 10 November 1911. TC/181, Scout Association–London [hereafter known as SA–London].

[15] Hugh Brogan, *Mowgli's Sons: Kipling and Baden-Powell's Scouts* (London: Jonathan Cape, 1987), 32–43. This book is an intriguing look at the connections between the two men and at their dual roles in creating and maintaining imperial excitement in Britain. Another fascinating investigation of the connections between Baden-Powell, Kipling, and Arthur Conan Doyle can be found in John Neubauer, *The Fin-de-Siecle Culture of Adolescence* (New Haven/London: Yale University Press, 1992), 213–219.

[16] For works dealing with Victorian and Edwardian militarism in general, see Olive Anderson, "The Growth of Christian Militarism in Mid-Victorian Britain," *English Historical Review* 86 (January 1971), 46–72; Alan Penn, *Targeting Schools: Drill, Militarism, and Imperialism* (London/Portland, OR: Woburn Press, 1999); and Anne Summers, "Edwardian Militarism," 236–256, in Raphael Samuel, ed., *Patriotism: The Making and Unmaking of British National Identity* [volume I: History and Politics], (London: Routledge, 1989). Other works on militarism include: Kenneth D. Brown, "Modelling for War? Toy Soldiers in Late Victorian and Edwardian Britain," *Journal of Social History* 24:2 (1990): 237–254; A. J. Coates, *The Ethics of War* (Manchester: Manchester University Press, 1997);

and J. A. Mangan, ed. *Tribal Identities: Nationalism, Europe, Sport* (London/Portland: Frank Cass, 1996).

[17] Martin Dedman, "Baden-Powell, Militarism, and the 'Invisible Contributors' to the Boy Scout Scheme, 1904–1920," *Twentieth Century British History* 4:3 (1993), 201–223. Dedman's article refutes works by Michael Blanch, Stephen Humphries, Michael Rosenthal, and John Springhall, and it echoes earlier articles by Allen Warren, specifically "Sir Robert Baden-Powell, the Scout Movement, and Citizen Training in Britain, 1900–1920," *English Historical Review* 101 (1986): 376–398. An interesting debate on this question can be found in *English Historical Review* 102:405 (1987): 934–950.

[18] Boy Scouts Association, *Boy Scouts and What They Do* (London: Oldfields, 1914), 9. The Baden-Powell quote is taken from an account of the Birmingham Scout Exhibition of 1913. A good study of working-class boys before the war is Michael J. Childs, *Labour's Apprentices: Working-class Lads in Late Victorian and Edwardian England* (London: Hambledon Press, 1992). Childs examines working-class youth and education, family life, and work, and concludes that youth movements had little formative effect on working boys before World War I. For the post-World War I period, see David Fowler, *The First Teenagers: The Lifestyle of Young Wage-Earners in Interwar Britain* (London: Woburn Press, 1995).

[19] For a good discussion of Labour's campaign against the Scouts, see Richard O. Miller, "The New Feudalism: The Origins of the Boy Scouts Movement in Edwardian England" (Ph.D. diss., University of Missouri–Columbia, December 1981), 183–200.

[20] For an interesting look at these rebellions, see Jeal, *The Boy-Man*, 404–409, 501–503.

[21] Percy Everett to Robert Baden-Powell, 16 September 1909; TC/Percy Everett, SA–London.

[22] Roland Philipps to Arthur Gaddum, 17 August 1915, TC/248; Robert Baden-Powell marginal notes in letter from Percy Everett to Robert Baden-Powell 4 September 1922, TC/Percy Everett, SA–London.

[23] For a further discussion of historians' views of the militarism in the Scout movements, see Jeal, *The Boy-Man*, 409–414. Jeal summarizes the positions of historians such as Michael Rosenthal, John Gillis, John Springhall, Anne Summers, and Allen Warren, while making a case for his own interpretation of the militarism of the movements.

[24] *Policy, Organisation, and Rules* (London: Boy Scout Association, 1911), 11–12.

[25] For a discussion of some of the religious controversy surrounding the Scouts, see Warren, "Sir Robert Baden-Powell," 376–398.

[26] Annual Census Figures circular, SA–London.

[27] Edward Ezard, *Battersea Boy* (London: William Kimber, 1979), 81–92.

[28] Robert Black, "An essay on scouting," [handwritten manuscript], 27 August 1909; TC/42, SA-London. Black was a 13-year-old Scout from Hebburn-on-Tyne and a member of the 2nd Jarrow Co. Boy Scouts (Presbyterians).

[29] Richard Phillips, *Mapping Men and Empire: A Geography of Adventure* (London/ New York: Routledge, 1997).

[30] *Policy, Organisation, and Rules*, 17–25.s

[31] Boy Scouts Association, *Annual Competitions: Rules and Conditions* (January 1913), 4–12. TC/225, SA–London.

[32] For a complete list of patrol signs and calls, see Robert Baden-Powell, *Scouting for Boys* (London: C. Arthur Pearson, 1942), 65–69. Please note that this list is available in any edition. The most complete description of the patrol system can be found in Roland Philipps, *The Patrol System and Letters to a Patrol Leader* (London: C. Arthur Pearson, 1917).

[33] On the settlement movements, see Seth Koven, "From Rough Lads to Hooligans: Boy Life, National Culture and Social Reform," in *Nationalisms and Sexualities*, eds. Andrew Parker, Mary Russo, Doris Somer and Patricia Yaeger (New York/London: Routledge, 1992), 365–391; and J. A. R. Pimlott, *Toynbee Hall: Fifty Years of Social Progress 1884–1934* (London: J. M. Dent and Sons, Ltd., 1935). For information on youth movements that preceded Scouting in Britain, see Wilkinson, "English Youth Movements," 3–23.

[34] *Policy, Organisation, and Rules*, 11; Robert Baden-Powell, *The Wolf Cub Handbook* (London: C. Arthur Pearson, 1916); Robert Baden-Powell, *Rovering to Success: A Book of Life-Sport for Young Men* (London: Herbert Jenkins Ltd., 1922).

[35] The Open Air Movement, begun in 1907 in Britain, reflected concern over the large numbers of children with tuberculosis. For information on its history, see Linda Bryder, "'Wonderlands of Buttercups, Clover and Daisies:' Tuberculosis and the Open Air School Movement in Britain, 1907–1939," in *In the Name of the Child: Health and Welfare, 1880–1940*, ed. Roger Cooter (London/New York: Routledge, 1992), 72–95. For information on early British socialist experiments such as Back to the Land, see Peter C. Gould, *Early Green Politics: Back to Nature, Back to the Land, and Socialism in Britain, 1880–1900* (New York: St. Martin's Press, 1988).

[36] Reports on Buckhurst Place Farm, TC/146, SA–London.

[37] On American masculinity in general, see E. Anthony Rotundo, *American Manhood: Transformations in Masculinity from the Revolution to the Modern Era* (New York: HarperCollins, 1993). Especially good are the chapters on Boy Culture (2), Male Youth Culture (3), and Youth and Male Intimacy (4). For works specifically dealing with American Scouting, see Jeffrey P. Hantover, "The Boy Scouts and the Validation of Masculinity," *Journal of Social Issues* 34:1 (1978), and David I. Macleod, *Building Character in the American Boy: The Boy Scouts, YMCA, and Their Forerunners, 1870–1920* (Madison: University of Wisconsin Press, 1983).

[38] Robert C. Harrison to Robert Baden-Powell, 12 July 1916; TC/42, SA–London.

[39] Dyhouse, *Girls Growing Up in Late Victorian and Edwardian England*, 118–119; Leonore Davidoff, "The Family in Britain," in *The Cambridge Social History of Britain, 1750–1950*, ed. F. M. L. Thompson (Cambridge: Cambridge University Press, 1990), 119–120.

[40] Sally Mitchell, *The New Girl: Girls' Culture in England, 1880–1915* (New York: Columbia University Press, 1995), 103–105.

[41] The opening of sports and physical activities to girls occurred along with their admittance into higher education and with the rise of leisure activities for young, single women. See the following works: Sheila Fletcher, *Women First: the Female Tradition in English Physical Education, 1880–1980* (London/Dover, N.H.: Athlone Press, 1984); Jennifer Hargreaves, *Sporting Females: Critical Issues in the History and Sociology of Women's Sports* (London/New York: Routledge, 1994); Felicity Hunt, ed., *Lessons for Life: The Schooling of Girls and Women* (Oxford: Basil Blackwell, 1987); J. A. Mangan and Roberta Park, eds., *From "Fair Sex" to Feminism: Sport and the Socialization of Women in the Industrial and Post-Industrial*

Eras (London/Totowa, NJ: Frank Cass, 1987); and Kathleen McCrone, *Playing the Game: Sport and the Physical Emancipation of English Women, 1870–1914* (Lexington: University of Kentucky Press, 1988). For an interesting article on girls' desires for social and sexual independence in the United States, see Victoria Bissell Brown, "Golden Girls: Female Socialization among the Middle Class of Los Angeles, 1880–1910," in *Small Worlds: Children and Adolescents in America, 1850–1950*, eds. Elliott West and Paula Petrik (Lawrence: University of Kansas Press, 1992), 232–254.

[42] Robert Baden-Powell, *Quick Training for War* (New York: Duffield and Company, 1914), 102. The brick-in-the-wall metaphor was one of Baden-Powell's favorite examples and is located in many of his writings and speeches.

[43] "Girl Scouts: A Popular Contingent," *Illustrated London News*, 11 September 1909, 356. Other accounts also suggest early girl scouts attended Scout rallies. For example, Mary Royden reported her attendance at a Liverpool scout rally prior to May 1909, where Baden-Powell seemed quite displeased at the girls' presence. Mary Royden to Rose Kerr, 20 February 1931, Early Days of Guiding box, Guide Association–London (hereafter known as GA–London).

[44] Kerr, *The Story of the Girl Guides*, 155.

[45] Gladys Commander's 1954 Thinking Day speech, Elizabeth de Beaumont's reminiscences dated 20 October 1931; Early Days of Guiding box, GA–London.

[46] Marguerite de Beaumont, "The Leader's Opinions," IV (April/May 1921), 39. This was a typewritten magazine of the 5th Lene Guide Company put together entirely by Guides and sent to each other in the mail GA–London.

[47] Kerr, *The Story of the Girl Guides*, 39.

[48] Agnes Baden-Powell, *The Handbook for Girl Guides, or How Girls Can Help Build the Empire* (London: Thomas Nelson and Sons, 1912), vii.

[49] Typed reminiscences of Evelyn Goshawk, 1977; Early Days of Guiding box, GA–London.

[50] Lady Betty Balfour to Robert Baden-Powell, 26 March 1916; TC/42, SA–London.

[51] Percy Everett to Robert Baden-Powell, 12 July 1909; GA–London.

[52] Robert Baden-Powell, *Pamphlet A: Girl Guides*, (1910), 3–4. GA–London.

[53] Agnes Baden-Powell, *The Handbook for Girl Guides*, vii.

[54] Agnes Baden-Powell, *The Handbook for Girl Guides*, 22–24.

[55] Violet Markham to the Editor, "Girl Scouts," *The Spectator*, 4 December 1909, 942.

[56] G. A. Seebohm to the Editor, *The Spectator*, 11 December 1909, 994.

[57] J. Archibald Kyle to the Editor, "Girl Scouts," *The Spectator*, 25 December 1909, 1100.

[58] Editor's note, *The Spectator*, 17 June 1911, 923.

[59] Violet Markham to the Editor, *The Spectator*, 25 September 1909, 455.

[60] Markham was known for changing her position on issues, most notably when she abandoned her steadfast anti-suffragism of the Edwardian period after the vote had been won. During the interwar period, she stood for and won a seat in Parliament.

[61] These are examples of common patrol names. The Scouts used animals for names and patrol badges, but the Guides were told to use flowers.

[62] "Lady Baden-Powell's Message to the Girl Guides," *Girl Guides Gazette* 1:7 (July 1914), 3.

[63] Baden-Powell, Agnes, "Our Workgirls," *The Spectator*, 17 June 1911, 923.

[64] Jeal, *The Boy-Man*, 475.

2

C H A P T E R

(UNI)FORMING YOUTH

As war approached once again in the 1930s, it seemed that everyone was in uniform.[1] In England even Princess Elizabeth (future Queen) and Princess Margaret had donned Guide and Brownie uniforms by 1937. This was especially significant in that they were the first members of the Royal Family to join the movement as children not as adult patrons. They hiked and earned badges in the Windsor Great Forest and the gardens of the palace as members of the 1st Buckingham Palace Company, which included girls from other class backgrounds. The princesses functioned as official symbols of uniformed youth by frequently being photographed in their uniforms for newspapers and public occasions.[2]

Significant uniformed youth movements existed in every European country, many organized by political groups such as the fascists, the National Socialists, and the communists. These organizations shared with the international Scout and Guide movements an interest in mass rallies, parades, and spectacles. All of these movements looked to youth as a viable and vital force in the future of Europe.[3] These uniformed movements in size and method were qualitatively different from the British Victorian youth movements such as the Boys Brigade and Church Lads Brigade, many of which sough to create Christian soldiers in the fight against decadence and degeneration. For example, combined membership in the Scouting and Guiding exceeded one million by 1930, and the uniformed Guide and Scout became nationally and internationally recognizable symbols of youth.[4]

Uniforms provide a useful tool for analyzing the Scout and Guide movements at a variety of levels because they meant different things to members and leaders, yet they were important to all concerned with the organizations.

In fact, uniforms were vital to the interwar image of solidarity that the Guides and Scouts sought to create, but for reasons that seemed contradictory. Uniforms apparently erased class boundaries, unifying all youth in a multiclass movement and hiding differences in wealth and position under a wide brimmed hat and a starched tie. On one level, the uniform functioned as the outward sign of the organizations' rejection of class divisions. Within this supposedly "classless" youth society, however, status and rank had not disappeared. Scouts, Guides, and leaders were encouraged to demonstrate their positions in the hierarchy by decorating their uniforms with badges, pins, and identifying symbols. Uniform pieces were available in a variety of fabrics, costing different amounts, and Scouts and Guides could purchase special accessories for their uniforms if they could afford them. These organizations created a seductive consumer paradise for members, with equipment, memorabilia, and literature, as well as uniforms and their accoutrements. The uniforms may have looked uniform to uninitiated outsiders, but Guides and Scouts were only too aware of differences in sex, class, wealth, and talent displayed in the nuances of the uniform.

BUILDING A MULTICLASS MOVEMENT

Before exploring the question of uniforms specifically, the class composition of the movements needs to be outlined. Scholars have long attempted to estimate the membership of these two organizations.[5] How many youth were involved? What were their social positions? Who stayed in the movements and who briefly passed through the ranks? These are thorny questions to answer because of the nature of the organizations and their records. All Scouts and Guides were required to register with headquarters, but those who moved into and out of the organization, who made brief stays, or who aligned themselves with unregistered groups might never have been recorded. Also, records were passed up from the local level through the hierarchy until they reached headquarters, so the accuracy of the numbers may be questionable, especially in the early days of the movement.

Despite the problems with getting accurate figures, it is possible to reconstruct the demographics of the two movements by looking at a combination of national figures and local records. Members were located throughout England, Scotland, Wales, and Ireland (both in Ulster and what became the Irish Republic), and were scattered throughout the British Empire and the world. The Guides and Scouts dwarfed all other British youth movements in numbers.

In the younger age categories (8 to 14) competition came primarily from the uniformed religious youth movements begun in the late nineteenth century, such as the Boys Brigade, the Girls Brigade, the Boys Life Brigade, the

Girls Life Brigade, the Church Lads Brigade, the Girls Guildry, and the Jewish Lads Brigade. Together, all of these organizations had less than half the membership of the Boy Scouts. For instance, the oldest and most popular, the Boys Brigade, reached a membership high in 1939 of only 161,976.[6] Boy Scout membership was then over 400,000. In older age groups competition came mainly from the Young Men's Christian Association, the Young Women's Christian Association, and the club movement. Membership figures for these groups are elusive because of the nature of their programs, with many youth joining temporarily or attending meetings casually. However, evidence does show that the club movement in particular was popular among working-class youth because it was less structured than Scouting or Guiding. Often clubs provided leisure without the moral lessons, and clubs functioned as community meeting houses for youth. Urban clubs did attract more of the youth over sixteen than did the Rangers and Rovers (senior sections of Guiding and Scouting).[7]

In addition to these organized movements, young people joined local clubs and associations, sport teams, and outdoors organizations. Leisure was big business by the interwar period, so the numbers of activities in which youth could participate had grown. As historian Jill Julius Matthews found in her study of the Women's League of Health and Beauty (WLHB), commercialized movements with little interest in service drew large numbers by the 1930s. Multiclass leisure activities like the WLHB, with its program for keeping fit, functioned side-by-side with the older service-motivated clubs, creating a tension.[8]

In spite of competition, the Scouts and Guides sustained growth from their origins in 1908 and 1910 respectively until 1933. After that, membership leveled out and began dropping. See Table 1 for a listing of actual membership figures for the two organizations.

TABLE 1
SCOUT AND GUIDE MEMBERSHIP FIGURES IN THE U.K., 1917–1939

YEAR	GUIDES	SCOUTS	YEAR	GUIDES	SCOUTS
1917	40,350	194,331	1929	518,826	397,648
1919	123,604	218,628	1931	586,616	457,477
1921	236,130	237,633	1933	623,246	480,379
1923	317,862	270,110	1935	581,156	448,396
1925	370,860	305,867	1937	525,276	443,455
1927	433,283	338,053	1939	**	**

** Figures from 1914–1917 and after 1938 are either unavailable or estimated because of World War I and World War II. Early figures (1910–1914) are not available for the Guides.

It is important to note that over a four-year period from 1919 to 1923, the Guides overtook the Scouts in membership, while more than doubling their numbers. They continue to this day to have the larger membership in Britain. Although the Scouts were initially a more popular organization, the Guides surpassed them in the 1920s for a variety of reasons. Demographically, there were more young women and girls many of whom did not work who were available to organize and participate in the movements. Guiding did not face the leadership shortages that Scouting struggled with in the 1920s. In fact, many Guide leaders doubled as Cub or Scout leaders to help ease the personnel shortages in Scouting that followed World War I. Another reason for Guide growth may have been that their organizational structure finally reached the level and sophistication of the Scout structure, making recruitment faster and easier. However, the most important reason seems to be that boys had more freedom and more opportunities to define their roles in post-war society. In addition to a plethora of clubs and organizations, boys could become members of military and paramilitary organizations to prove their commitment to the nation. They joined trade unions and workingmen's clubs, sports teams, and recreational associations. Girls, however, had fewer outlets for their desires to serve Britain and the Empire, and often their activities were more closely monitored by their parents.[10]

Although useful, the Scout and Guide national membership figures mean little without the context of the larger population of Britain in this period. In order to analyze those numbers effectively, it is useful to break down national census figures. As Table 2 demonstrates, Scout and Guide membership varied regionally and by age groups in the interwar period. Generally, the two movements were most popular in cities and towns and less effective in rural areas. In addition, the organizations first gained strength in the south and middle parts of England. Membership in Wales, Scotland, and northern England in the interwar period grew rapidly, but it never reached the levels of the south and midlands. Also, after 1920, the younger branches of Guides and Scouts surpassed the older branches in numbers. Many children joined as Cubs or Brownies, and then they lost

TABLE 2
PERCENTAGE MEMBERSHIP IN THE SCOUTS/GUIDES[11]

	Cubs age 9–11	Brownies age 8–10	Scouts age 12–16	Guides age 11–16
LONDON				
1921*	15%	8%	14%	10%
1931*	25%	24%	16%	13%
YORKSHIRE				
1921*	< 1%	2%	4%	4%
1931*	10%	12%	9%	10%

*Percentage tabulated based on census figures

interest and quit before making the transition to Scouts or Guides. The table only presents figures for two counties in England, but they are representative counties nonetheless.

Examining these two counties in more detail provides an interesting comparison between two different parts of the country, for a clearer picture of the nation as a whole. Yorkshire, England's largest county, is a useful and diverse area to study because of its mix of large and medium-sized industrial towns and its sparsely populated rural areas. Yorkshire, located in the industrial north, was hit hard by the depression of the interwar years. London, of course, presents the picture of a large metropolis with its incredible diversity. These two counties together function as a microcosm of England in the interwar period, so I would like to spend a little time discussing each county and its Scout and Guide movements. When studied closely, each region contributes to the overall picture of class, age, sex, and occupation of the people who composed the Scout and Guide movements in England.

⚜ I. YORKSHIRE

Yorkshire, before its restructuring in 1974, was divided into three areas called "ridings." This study is concerned with largest of these areas, the West Riding, which encompassed the large cities of Sheffield and Leeds, and the smaller industrial towns of Bradford, Doncaster, Halifax, Huddersfield, and Wakefield in the 1920s and 1930s. Major industries included textiles, steel, metal work, transport, agriculture, and coal mining. These industries had prospered in the period up to 1850, spurring growth in the region up through the turn of the 20th century. However, the fall in wool demand, problems in the steel industry, and the increasing competition of other European coal industries meant severe financial distress in Yorkshire in the period around World War I. For instance, by 1921, more than half of the textile workers in Huddersfield were unemployed, and in Sheffield, an estimated one in five workers was on poor relief in 1922.[12] There were major strikes in the coal industry in 1921 and the General Strike of 1926, plus the depression years after 1929 meant long-term unemployment in the region. By 1931, Sheffield's unemployment rate rose to thirty-four percent of insured workers. New industries such as chemicals and engineering were gaining strength, but for many in the West Riding, the interwar period was disastrous.[13]

Huddersfield and Sheffield sustained strong Scout and Guide organizations through the hard times of the 1920s and 1930s. Huddersfield, a center of the worsted wool industry, and Sheffield, world-renowned for its steel, metal work, and cutlery, were circled by green pastureland. The proximity of moors, fields, and parks meant that Scouts and Guides could afford to attend hikes and camps however low their income. The cheap nature of many of the movements' excursions helped create diverse multiclass organizations with membership varying from miners' to mill owners' children in the two cities, although not always within troops.

Huddersfield, city and suburbs, sustained a varied group of Scout troops and Guide companies, which met for county and citywide competitions and camps. There were definite differences in status between companies, as some could ill afford the cost of a uniform, while others took yearly treks to Scotland. It is useful to compare a couple of these groups. The 16th Huddersfield was a Scout troop attached to Huddersfield College (grammar school), and was led primarily by schoolmasters, students, and clerks. This was a particularly active and mostly middle-class group that participated in hikes, and outdoor games and competitions. In 1934, they began taking yearly "tasking treks" to the mountains of Scotland. These were often hundred-mile journeys over rough terrain, necessitating gear and supplies that would have been beyond the means of a working-class group. Working-class groups recognized these differences. As Ralph Whiteley, a Scout in a nearby company remembered: "Only the 16th got King's Scout!" because only they had the time and opportunity to earn the prerequisite badges for this high Scout honor. His working-class group, although keen on the movement, did not have the resources to complete all of the required projects.[14]

In contrast to the more middle-class membership of the 16th, village troops sometimes relied on the generosity of the scoutmaster to buy scarves for the boys' investiture service. Huddersfield Scouts held concerts to raise money for trek carts, tents, and other supplies. If they didn't raise enough, they often could borrow equipment from wealthier groups in the area. Whiteley's troop went camping on nearby Lindley Moor, rather than traveling to Scotland or even to other parts of Yorkshire. Another Scout, whose father was a plasterer, remembered only being in the Scouts a short time. He was allowed to attend camp at nearby Devil's Glen in the daytime but not overnight because, "We'd no blankets that we could spare for me to take to the camp."[15]

Although the activities might have been more modest in working-class troops, advancement was sometimes easier because leadership was more in demand. Whiteley, who joined as an 8-year-old Cub Scout in 1923, became a Cubmaster by age seventeen, and an International Rover Crew Leader in North Africa during World War II. Eventually he was awarded the movement's prestigious Silver Acorn for his forty-five years of service as member, leader and District Commissioner.[16]

The same differences in wealth applied to the Guide troops in the Huddersfield area. In one case, a girl joined the Guides at Roedean, the elite school she attended in the south where Guiding was attached to a larger athletics program. Her father was the rich chairmen of the local Liberal Association and her mother was "always a perfect lady." Her experiences with Guiding in her boarding school contrasted starkly with those of working-class girls in Huddersfield. One girl in a nearby village had to forego the pleasures of the Guides because she could not afford a uniform. Another girl remembered the long process of buying one piece of uniform at a time as she could afford it. A miner's daughter spoke of her pleasures in the movement: making and selling treacle tarts, learning knots, and baking rice puddings.[17]

Likewise, Sheffield encompassed a wide variety of participants in its Scouting and Guiding programs. A majority of groups in Sheffield by 1931 were controlled groups as opposed to open ones, meaning that they were attached to churches, missions or schools. Sheffield warrant records are a useful way to expose a longstanding myth about the Scouts. Many historians have criticized the Scout and Guide movements for admitting working-class children but limiting leadership to the middle classes. Sheffield's records show that by the 1930s, leadership was drawn from a mix of class and occupational backgrounds, as a group of working-class leaders rose through the ranks.

A good example of this phenomenon is the 1st Croft Hall Group, the earliest Scout troop in Sheffield. Formed at the Croft House Settlement in thickly populated central Sheffield, the 1st Croft Hall was run by middle-class reformers. In this slum area, many participants were too poor to participate fully. The settlement had a supply of uniforms, which they loaned to members who proved responsible. However, under the leadership of the warden, Sister Edith Spencer, the troop maintained its numbers throughout the interwar period. By the end of World War II, it was run almost entirely by working-class members who had participated as cubs, brownies, scouts, guides, and assistant leaders throughout the 1920s and 1930s. The Cubmistress was a domestic servant who had held a leadership role in the Cub Pack since 1928. Her assistant, also a domestic servant, had spent eleven years as a Guide and Ranger before becoming a Cub leader. The Scoutmaster in 1944 was a 29-year-old scrapbreaker, who had spent twenty-one years in the movement as a Cub, Scout, and Rover. The warrants show a great diversity in occupations in this one group alone: plumber, housewife, labourer, printer electrician, domestic servant, joiner, metal roller, and store keeper.[18]

Other groups, the 7th Attercliffe Parish Church in the eastern part of Sheffield and the 10th Mount Tabor (Methodist) in Sheffield's center, increasingly looked to working-class men and women for leaders. In the late 1930s, a pattern maker took over the running of the 7th Attercliffe, assisted by a rough turner, a baker, a motor driver, a joiner, and a machinist, all aged between eighteen and twenty-eight. In the 10th Mount Tabor, pearl cutter

George White assumed control in 1935, with help from a brickmaker, a tool and gutter grinder, a driver, and a cinema projectionist.[19]

Although warrant records are not available for Guiding in Sheffield, parallels seem to exist between the two movements and their social compositions. Both Scouting and Guiding appealed to youth and adults in new occupations such as clerks, transport workers, and service workers, and also to skilled and semi-skilled workers increasingly threatened by mechanization and industrial flux. Unemployed people, laborers, miners, and others of the "lower" working class did join the movements, but their staying power was often severely limited by financial constraints and prejudices of other members. Often poor members were "casual" Scouts and Guides, who joined troops for a while but were never enrolled.

What the Sheffield records demonstrate is that middle-class men and women did not have exclusive control of the Scout and Guide leadership by the 1930s. Leaders were drawn from a variety of occupational backgrounds. However, middle-class bias remained in many groups, and often working-class leaders were forced to get employer affidavits to prove their respectability to the Scouts. One such testimonial for a man who had spent more than thirteen years in the movement demonstrates the residue of middle-class mores: "He is honest, sober, and very reliable [and] also has the right temperament for dealing with lads. His parents are very respectable."[20] Scouting was not for the unemployed, the extremely poor, or the dispossessed. In other words, the organizations clearly distinguished between "rough" and "respectable" members, making Scouting and Guiding popular as movements that demonstrated a member's status in a neighborhood.[21]

In all, Yorkshire illustrates several important points about the makeup of Scout and Guide membership. By the 1920s and 1930s, they were multi-class movements, but the very poor were still mostly excluded from their ranks or participating in casual ways. Yorkshire and the north of England, in general, was cut off from Scouting and Guiding as practiced in London and its environs, so often the movements were substantially different in activities and ethos. Finally, although the movements affected fewer people in the north and membership figures were lower, the Scouts and Guides were visible and important presences in the region.

II. LONDON

London, an ever-changing and diverse metropolis, yields perhaps the most substantial information on membership figures because of the variety of studies done on the urban population in the early 20th century.[22] London is home to the very rich and the very poor as well as a large number of people who fall in the middle. However, generalities about the occupational and class structure in London are difficult because it is such a large city. Nonetheless, it is important to delineate certain boundaries and trends. In the interwar period, London grew from 7.25 million to 8.73 million, and about one-third of its population was aged fifteen and under. Also, by the interwar period, more than half of all Londoners lived in the outer suburbs. Since the late nineteenth century an exodus of sorts had been taking place, with railways as the impetus. Those who had the resources were moving out of the central parts of the city and into newly built suburbs.[23] Many of the poor in London were concentrated in relatively small areas of the city located in East, Northeast and Southeast London. These poor areas often featured severe overcrowding and poor housing, in contrast to the richer western and outer suburbs with their neat terraced houses.

Somehow the Scouts and Guides managed to appeal to a variety of groups in London, in the inner and outer suburbs, and in the center. In his *New Survey of London Life and Labour* published in 1935, Hubert Llewellyn Smith devoted two chapters to social organizations for boys and girls in London. Guide and Scout groups were located in most boroughs in the metropolitan area and, as Llewellyn Smith noted, were "found alike in public school and slum." His statistics and analysis are illuminating about age, class, and gender demographics in Scouting and Guiding, and in their comparison to other social organizations.

As on the national level, both the Scouts and Guides were more popular than any other comparable organization for youth in London in the interwar period in most cases. Notable exceptions to the popularity of Baden-Powell's movements existed in East London and the City especially. The stiffest competition came from the Girls Club movement, which drew in older girls and young women of working age [See Table 3].

TABLE 3
COMPARATIVE MEMBERSHIPS OF ADOLESCENTS IN LONDON, 1932[24]

Boys Brigade	7,317
Church Lads Brig.	2,376
Scouts	26,272
Boys Clubs	7,538
Girls Clubs*	33,600
Guides	39,900

*Girls Clubs' numbers include a number of affiliated organizations such as the Girls Friendly Society, the YWCA, and the Girls Guildry. The figures do not include Brownies or Cubs.

Smith also found in his study that in the outer and external suburbs such as Kensington, Hampstead, Hammersmith, Leyton, Barking, West/East

Ham, Acton and Willesden, Scouts and Guides greatly outnumbered other youth movements [See Table 4].[25]

TABLE 4
PROPORTIONAL (PER 1000) MEMBERSHIP OF BOYS AND GIRLS IN
ORGANIZATIONS BY BOROUGH IN LONDON 1932*

	Boys Brig	CL Brig	Scout	Boys Club	Girls Club	Girls Life	Guide
Finsbury	25	0	39	32	52	9	79
Holborn	15	0	102	10	696	8	–
Westminster	4	5	78	70	76	3	162
Stepney	5	5	45	62	61	7	59
Shoreditch	12	4	41	22	103	9	**
Bermondsey	25	13	45	48	83	6	93
Southwark	24	2	42	14	47	14	57
Lambeth	24	6	51	8	37	8	91
Bethnal Green	3	8	47	33	51	–	**
City	26	0	229	0	470	16	**
Battersea	13	0	43	11	7	9	73
Wandsworth	35	0	66	1	20	10	126
Lewisham	26	15	52	6	32	4	120
Camberwell	19	3	63	22	·14	8	80

* This table shows central London and its immediate suburbs.
**These three boroughs are included together under Finsbury.

As in Britain more generally, Guides were more popular in London than Scouts. Smith noted that Guiding was particularly strong in the inner and outer suburbs of London, but rather weaker than the Scouts in the external areas. He concluded that:

> Unlike the Scouts, the proportion of Guides in the external boroughs is actually less than in the Inner Ring. The Guide movement is meant for girls of all classes, but the personnel in London is perhaps drawn from the working classes to a greater degree than is that of the Scouts.[26]

Smith's evidence suggests that Guiding may have had larger numbers than the Scouts in the interwar period because of their ability to attract a wider group of girls. Guides were able to forge ties with Girls Clubs and other girls' organizations, plus they were quite successful at establishing groups in churches and settlements.

One such settlement in Poplar had a thriving Guide company with five full patrols in 1935. Guide records show that leaders targeted girls in the "play-hour" program for inclusion in Brownies and later Guides. Leaders kept detailed records of the girls' lives, including family problems and financial difficulties. One patrol, the Red Roses, provides a useful example. There were six members of the Red Rose patrol. The first, Cissie, aged fourteen, was listed as a "protege of family who is good; poor home, but respectable and clean; poor health." Another, Maud, had just won a scholarship and was listed as a "superior" Guide. Irene and Grace were newcomers and cousins to Cissie, the first Guide listed. The other two members had been watched with some care. Doris possessed a weak and pessimistic family, but "when she had been a Guide a year she had a newish uniform which seemed to develop some self respect." The last girl, Maisie, according to leaders,

> should have her name Drudge, for that she has been ever since I have known her. Her father was in and out of hospital for many many years as the result of the war. He died a year ago. Maisie has been nursemaid to small sister for three years and really a little mother to her two small brothers too.[27]

The personal approach seemed to work. Guide leaders used personnel and structures already in place, such as settlements and church groups, in order to appeal to a larger group of children. The organization funded camps and uniforms for many poorer Guides, and they encouraged well-to-do London troops to hold entertainments for poor Guides. In London especially, the Guide organization made a concerted effort to reach out to respectable working-class areas in the interwar period.

Scouts had less success than Guides in uniting with other groups in London, and from the beginning were plagued with disputes over ideology. After the founding of the movements, London was headquarters and perhaps the most bitterly contested ground. Early Scout leaders had visions (albeit competing ones) of how the organizations could transform the city. In the first years of the Scouts and Guides, letters poured into headquarters asking for policies on forming bands, marching, parading, fundraising, camping, and praying. Leaders asked for confirmation of Baden-Powell's ideas on alcohol, education, religion, and marriage. London especially became an area where ideas were tested and worked out. It became the most visible part of the early movements because much of the membership clustered around the city.

Perhaps the best example of the fight for London is one of the earliest troops in the East End, begun in early 1908 and attached to Toynbee Hall. The troop, led by Scoutmaster Dr. Theodore S. Lukis, had gotten off to an exciting start. However, less than a year later, Lukis was writing that "clouds are gathering over the Scout horizon" as the Scouts were involved in a conflict with other youth organizations over how boys should be trained in the East End. The Boys Brigade and the London diocesan Church Lads Brigade were infringing upon Scout terrain in London by starting groups of their own "scouts," with different methods and badges. Lukis was particularly upset with these occurrences because it seemed that Baden-Powell had sanctioned the Church Lads Brigade scheme. Lukis thought Baden-Powell's actions looked "mighty like a betrayal of our East End council." This conflict over class increasingly divided the Scout movement, as it attempted to stake out turf while remaining on good terms with social reformers, churches, schools, and other organizations. By summer 1909, Lukis was again angry over the Scout leadership's handling of the London situation, writing:

> B.P. [Baden-Powell] is to remain the absolute autocrat of the movement. He is to be the one and only head. Everything is to be decided by him. The movement is absolutely dominated by a middle class type of 'officious' interfering person. . . . One young fellow said that in their district they were discouraging poor boys from joining the movement because they did not look smart and brought the movement into disrepute!!![28]

Lukis' concerns with the running of the Scout movement were only one such example of the upheaval in London in the first few years. In May 1909, the Scouts in Battersea seceded from the movement to begin the British Boy Scouts (BBS). Soon after the Battersea secession, Baden-Powell clashed with his London Commissioner, Sir Francis Vane, over administration. Vane was dismissed, but he called a public meeting of London Scoutmasters in December 1909 to protest his dismissal. The press called Vane's actions a "revolt," publicly embarrassing the Scout movement. After he left the Scouts in late 1909, Vane became head of the BBS, which had about 50,000 members by mid-1910.[29]

These public battles over London Scouting shadowed progress in the interwar period. The BBS was still operating in the 1920s and 1930s, and still constituted a threat to the Scout image. The Scouts and other boys' organizations competed for members rather than uniting and affiliating. Admitting and keeping "rough" lads in the movement, especially beyond the age of twelve, seemed like a losing battle in London. Scout participation in strikebreaking activity in the 1920s and a well-publicized dispute with the Young Communist League from 1927–29 further complicated recruitment among working-class children in the metropolis.

London was the model of Scout and Guide training, and it functioned as a testing ground for the movements' ideas. Disputes arose in the early years that slowed the progress of Scouting in London, but both the Guide and the Scout organizations were the largest youth movements in London by the interwar period. The capital, more than any other area in England, demonstrated the strength of Scouting and Guiding as multiclass movements, while pointing to the clash of middle- and working-class values.

The statistics and records for these counties challenge prevailing opinion about the makeup of the Scout and Guide movements in the interwar period, as local studies of warrant and membership records demonstrate.[30] The Guides and Scouts had many middle-class and upper-class members, but they also attracted large numbers from the working classes in the 1920s and 1930s. The leadership structure was hierarchical and often rigid, with top leadership being drawn from a select few. However, leadership opportunities opened up for a large number of men and women in the interwar period, and with leadership came additional opportunities for travel, employment, and politics. It would be wrong to characterize the Guide and Scout movements using only London or only a small town as a sample because the two movements evoked different responses depending on the environment, the social structure, and the resources of an area.

UNIFORMED YOUTH

Although designed by adults to reinforce social control and conformity, uniforms often allow youth to fashion their own meanings and identities apart from their elders. Scout and Guide uniforms in particular were intended to incorporate youth into society at large, instilling patriotism and self-control. The uniform inspired pride and encouraged responsibility in its members, and the uniforms identified members for both outsiders and insiders. Uniforms and accessories played an invaluable role in the spread of organizations like the Guides and Scouts, symbolizing citizenship, nationalism, and membership.[31] However, youth also used uniforms to construct identities for themselves, for they saw these uniforms as commodities to be exchanged, upgraded, purchased, and sold. Uniforms and their accouterments provided points of negotiation among not only Scouts and Guides, but also between members and outsiders at home or in the community. The value of uniforms often increased for individual Scouts and Guides when they assumed exchange value at international or national gatherings or when they became points of resistance to community or parental pressures.

In the last decade historians, anthropologists, and sociologists have begun to pay more attention to the question of clothing as meaningful communication. Although some have gone so far as to characterize clothing as a language, following modern semiotics, several recent studies have shown that apparel communicates, but not in the same way as a language. Clothing often expresses cultural principles that cannot be verbalized. In 1988 Grant McCracken pointed to dress as "one of the chief opportunities for exercising the metaphoric and performative powers of ritual," arguing that "clothing makes culture material."[32] McCracken and others have stressed the importance of attire as both an instrument of control and a place of resistance, emphasizing that the meanings attached to clothing depend upon the context, the status or social identity of the wearer and viewer, and the period.[33]

During the interwar period, clothing assumed increased importance for youth as points of resistance and identification. One reason for this emphasis was that age and status were marked by outfits that ranged from school jackets to football uniforms. As occupational identifications became less important, some youth may have looked to leisure pursuits to provide identifications. Also, with the standardization of education, age became more compartmentalized. Dress had always marked the boundary between childhood and adulthood, but now differences within the categories childhood and adulthood were being marked and defined through clothing.[34]

Concern with clothing and its meanings reflected a larger focus on the body in the 1920s and 1930s in Europe. Bodies were equated with character by the interwar period, so youth were encouraged to mold and transform their bodies. Sunbathing, tanning, dieting, and slimming entered the vocabularies of British youth as the body became more commercialized. Physical culture and gymnastics had been a part of British society since the late nineteenth century, but physical training became more commercial in the 1920s and 1930s with the advent of "Keep Fit."[35] As Matthews points out in her work on the Women's League of Health and Beauty, pride in the body meant a sound character, and to many interwar reformers, uniforms seemed a good way to ensure uniformity and to mix social classes.[36]

Uniforms had been part of Guiding and Scouting from the beginning of the movements, allowing them to compete with successful youth movements already in place in Britain, such as the Boys Brigade and the Girls Brigade. The Brigades offered free uniforms in a military style, and often recruited working-class youth because of the low cost of membership. Other organizations for children in schools, churches, and missions used uniforms as well. The pre-World War I attempt in Britain to make its citizens healthy and more efficient used uniforms as an important part of that mission.[37]

Beyond the official reasons for instituting uniforms, this clothing constituted a point of pride for individual Scouts and Guides, especially in the early days when members were forced to defend their dress on the streets. In working-class neighborhoods in particular, Guide and Scout uniforms were treated with suspicion and outright violence. Some working-class parents opposed the movements and the uniforms because of the anti-trade union rhetoric expressed in Baden-Powell's writings for popular daily papers such as the *Daily Mail* and the *Telegraph*. Others feared the Scouts were training soldiers, a reasonable fear considering Baden-Powell's military background and the militaristic games and goals of some early troops. Still other parents were suspicious of the ambiguous religious message expressed in the two movements. Socialist and Labour politicians as well as parents castigated uniformed movements for being militaristic and imperialistic, and they saw uniformed youth as even more dangerous because the members were at an impressionable age. As Ramsay MacDonald wrote to Robert Baden-Powell in early 1914:

> I have never been able to take the view that in the long run this Movement was going to be beneficial. I do not believe **in the paraphernalia attached to it**. . . . Moreover,

however much some of its supporters may deny this, I cannot dissociate it from an atmosphere of militarism to which I am opposed. I know how dangerous national habits of slackness have become, but the reason for that, to my mind, is far more deeply seated than the promoters of the Boy Scout Movement seem to recognise.[38] [emphasis mine]

Other politicians and parents took a similar view of Scouting's ultimate aims, especially after the jingoism, militarism, and sacrifice of life that accompanied World War I. They were concerned that Scouting and Guiding might instill principles of conformity and militarism among youth.

In rough neighborhoods hostility to the organizations was often aggressive. There were verbal and physical assaults on uniformed Guides and Scouts throughout Britain before the First World War, especially in working-class areas. They were easily identified by the uniform, especially the distinctive hat. Many early members remembered the insults they were forced to endure in the name of the movements. Edward Ezard, who joined the Scouts just before the war, recalled being taunted while on parade by boys outside of a factory. The boys shouted at the Scouts, calling them "Dustman's Hats and Broomstick Brigade."[39] A Guide from Liverpool had similar prewar experiences: "When on parade, we were generally mistaken for the Salvation Army! Of course we had all sorts of filth thrown at us, and I was generally invited to go to the bathroom immediately I reached home and have a clean up."[40] A London Scout remembered his experience, writing: "Courage was needed to face the ridicule (and the brickbats too at times) to wear Scout kit in the rougher streets. Staves then were a necessary and useful part of the outfit!"[41] In prewar Birkenhead an "officer" and her company were "an excellent target, not only for verbal abuse from the roughs in the neighbourhood, but for the throwing of stones and tomatoes that had seen better days. Opposition, however, only served to strengthen our determination to carry on, as through a glass darkly we caught some faint reflection of our founder's vision."[42] As this Guide hints, however, insults and abuse did not force members to leave the movements. On the contrary, many felt that they had earned the right to wear the uniform by defending their movement against attack. Part of the value of the uniform for Scouts and Guides was derived from its singularity and its easily recognizable hat. Boys and girls suffered the insults and attacks as a sort of rite of initiation. Scout and Guide lore revolved around these stories of bravery and stoicism. Recognition of the uniform, even in the form of abuse, instilled pride in the members who defended themselves.[43]

For Guides and Scouts, uniforms were not only symbols of group membership but also of independence from parental supervision. Many faced opposition from their parents to the uniforms and to their participation in the movements. May Rainer, a working-class girl born in the Fulham Road area of London in 1909, wrote extensively about the Guides and her uniform in her 1977 autobiography. She remembered joining the group, in hopes of escaping the restrictions of home. She found a certain measure of freedom in her weekly Guide meetings, but that freedom was rescinded by Rainer's parents after a domestic dispute involving coins missing from her mother's purse. Rainer's father blamed her for the theft and beat her with a belt until her older brother intervened. The father, not finished with his punishment, burned her beloved Girl Guide uniform on the kitchen stove. Rainer wrote about that incident, "I have never forgotten or forgiven either of them . . ."[44]

As this account demonstrates, clothing, and in this case uniforms, assumed tremendous symbolic importance both for parents and children in the interwar period and could be the focus of tension and resistance in households. It is telling that Rainer's father should seize upon the uniform to punish an infraction that had no relationship to Guiding whatsoever. Her father's burning of the uniform as a punishment shows not only that her parents recognized the uniform's symbolic importance, but also that they understood Rainer's own attachment to the uniform and her recognition of its importance as a sign of independence and identity.

Power negotiations within the household in the interwar period often centered around clothing and possessions that children used to stake out their independence and to defy their parents.[45] William Tucker joined the Scouts in 1910 in London, and got a newspaper job to pay for the uniform. He faced resistance from his policeman father and from his brother, who beat him for joining the organization. He persevered despite his family's disapproval and wore his uniform whenever possible, flaunting his triumph before them. The boy even wore his uniform when the family moved to a farm in Wiltshire in 1912.[46] Another Scout from East London won a raffle and used the money to buy his uniform after his mother told him that he couldn't have a uniform because he already had a Sunday suit. He was proud of his efforts despite his Scoutmaster's attempt to chastise him for the un-Scoutlike behavior of gambling ("Other people bought your uniform").[47]

Stories like these abound in Scout literature, diaries, and memoirs, and combined with the earlier stories of street insults, they constitute an interesting narrative. Uniforms were initially obtained through hard work, they were defended from insult, and they were worn with pride. Unlike members of most other youth movements that provided uniforms, Scouts and Guides usually bought their own uniforms. Ownership, rather than borrowing, inspired in the young owners possessiveness and pride in their raiment. Countless Guides and Scouts recounted the particulars of caring for and wearing their uniforms, such as tying the correct knot in the scarf, sewing the badges in the appropriate spot, and polishing buckles and pins to meet specifications. The ritual of obtaining, wearing, and caring for the

Scout and Guide uniforms symbolized for many children and adults their commitment to the movements and legitimated their roles as citizens in the nation.

The uniform played a significant role for the movements' leadership as well. Guide and Scout leaders consciously spoke of the importance of the uniform in solidifying ideology and creating good feelings among members. In her 1917 guide for leaders, Olave Baden-Powell wrote of the problems of teaching the meaning of citizenship to young girls. She contended that a verbal explanation would leave the Guides confused, but "the day the little Guide joins her company and puts on her uniform for the first time this fact wants no explaining—it becomes a delightful and thrilling reality for her, simply because the uniform is the outward tangible symbol."[48]

Guide and Scout leaders recognized the symbolic power of the uniform, but in some ways underestimated its subversive power. Just because the "little Guide" recognized the uniform as a symbol, did not mean that Guide interpreted its meaning in the same way. Leaders were fond of extolling the uniform's effect as a great leveler, erasing class, regional, sex, and race distinctions. As one middle-class Guide recounted, "It did not matter if you were poor or rich, because you all looked the same."[49] As many poorer Guides and Scouts found out, however, it did matter if you had the money to buy the uniform and its accessories.

G. V. Holmes, an orphan living in a Girls' Village Home, described life as a Girl Guide in the 1920s in her 1948 autobiography. She remembered the great excitement that preceded the formation of the first group of Guides and her anticipation of the day when she would be old enough to join. Holmes spent a good deal of time describing the uniforms that the Guides wore and how they obtained them. They made some, and others were donated, and they made small caps of uniform material because they couldn't afford the official felt hats. Proudly, Holmes and her fellow Guides took up tracking and badge work in their new uniforms, secure in their position in the great sisterhood of Guides. Soon, however, her newfound feeling of importance was shattered by a visitor to the Home, who told the Guides that their hats were not proper Guide hats. As Holmes related: "We had thought that dressed in Guide uniform, we could mix with anyone in the world and become part of it, but no! There were 'Village Guides' and 'Outside Guides' a subtle yet tremendous difference."[50]

As Holmes quickly discerned, uniforms might appear at first glance to be great levelers, but in reality they retained the same class and status distinctions as civilian dress. Likewise, Chaim Bermant, a Jewish refugee from Poland living in Scotland in the late 1930s, joined the Scouts. The only part of the uniform that he could afford to buy was the lanyard and later a kerchief, but he could not afford the hat, shirt, staff and kilt

[Scottish uniform]. He wrote, "I felt apart from the uniformed pack and finally left."[51] He later joined the Jewish Lads Brigade, which provided a free uniform.

Leaders tried to adapt Guiding and Scouting to help poorer members who had little extra money to spend on uniforms. They encouraged fundraising, donations, and trading of used uniforms. Most of the time, however, the youth themselves took the initiative and assumed responsibility for outfitting themselves. Molly Weir, who lived in a Glasgow tenement, bought her uniform from another child who had outgrown it. She raised the money by making and selling toffee apples. She later gathered together money for camp by holding concerts and jumble sales and by cooking and running messages for neighbors.[52]

Alice Linton, who joined the Guides at her church in East London in 1921 when she was thirteen years old, continued in the movement even after she got a full-time job at a laundry. She took her uniform to work with her and changed after she finished work. Their company was "adopted" by a private school company, who provided outings a couple of times per year. Linton's company saved the money for camp, with each person contributing sixpence per week from her wages. They saved enough for camp travel and food, and they borrowed blankets and other supplies.[53] As in Linton's case, if the money for uniforms and equipment could not be raised by the members themselves, often a local association or individual would donate fabric or used uniforms. The Scout and Guide movements' ability to use resources of richer troops to support poorer companies became an important reason for the interwar rise in numbers.

Despite attempts to erase class distinction, money made a difference. In Gamage's 1911 catalog, Guides needed a tunic, a skirt, a belt, a stave, a hat, and a handkerchief to be officially outfitted. They could also buy a variety of accessories such as flags, whistles, lanyards, haversacks, etc. Obviously, the retailers implied that the more "stuff" a Guide possessed, the higher her status in a company. This Gamage catalog is particularly interesting in its selection of hats. Four hats, of varying quality and price, were available for Guides to purchase. Any Guide wearing the cheapest hat that cost a shilling, a felt one with no chin strap, would immediately perceive the difference between herself and the Guide with a hat boasting not only a chin strap but a feather plume that cost two shillings six[54] [Figure 2]. Such options of varying style and material continued into the 1920s and 1930s in both the Scouts and the Guides. For instance, Scout shirts and shorts in 1927 came in six different cloth qualities, ranging in price from 3/6 to 13/-. In 1938, Guides had moved from skirts to overalls, but they had kept the variety of qualities, with four different versions of their standard cotton tunic.[55]

Like G. V. Holmes, less wealthy Guides and Scouts who might feel pride in their uniform when alone often felt ashamed when they compared their

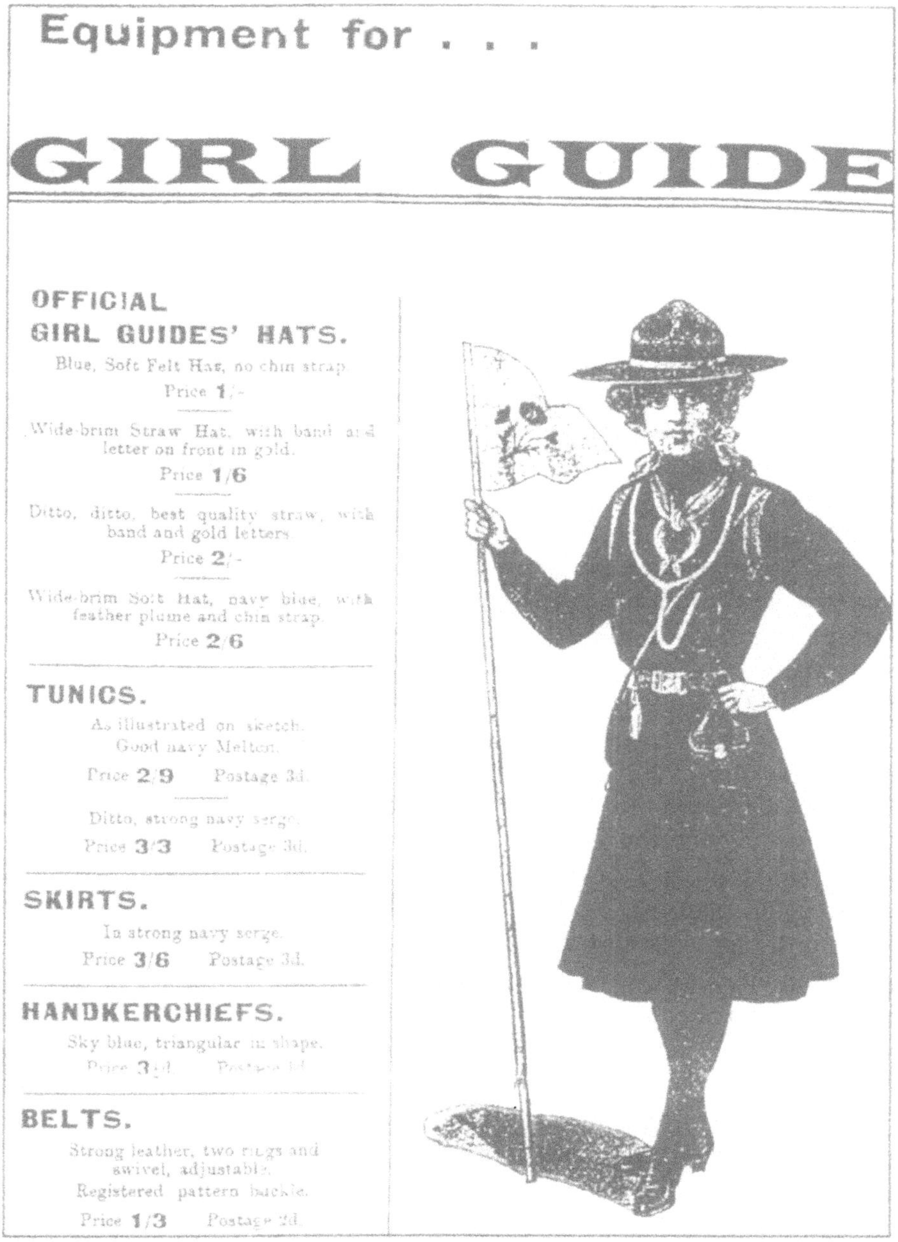

Equipment for . . .

GIRL GUIDE

OFFICIAL
GIRL GUIDES' HATS.

Blue, Soft Felt Hat, no chin strap.
Price **1**/-

Wide-brim Straw Hat, with band and
letter on front in gold.
Price **1/6**

Ditto, ditto, best quality straw, with
band and gold letters.
Price **2**/-

Wide-brim Soft Hat, navy blue, with
feather plume and chin strap.
Price **2/6**

TUNICS.

As illustrated on sketch.
Good navy Melton.

Price **2/9**   Postage 3d.

Ditto, strong navy serge.
Price **3/3**   Postage 3d.

SKIRTS.

In strong navy serge.
Price **3/6**   Postage 3d.

HANDKERCHIEFS.

Sky blue, triangular in shape.
Price **3**d.   Postage 1d.

BELTS.

Strong leather, two rings and
swivel, adjustable.
Registered pattern buckle.
Price **1/3**   Postage 2d.

FIG. 2 Gamage was an outfitter for Guides and Scouts. Note the price and quality variations in this 1911 advertisement. Courtesy of The Scout Association.

uniforms with other richer ones. Some suffered painful embarrassment over cheap or homemade uniforms. One Guide remembers a girl in her troop who did not have the official felt hat, but a blue linen cap. Imagine how she felt when during a rainstorm at camp, the dye in her hat began to run, turning her face blue.[56]

In addition to the uniform's pretensions as a leveler of class difference, the uniform also reflected the age distinctions of members. The movements added categories for children aged 8–11 and youth aged 16+ in response to demands for these branches during World War I. Age divisions had assumed an added significance in the interwar period, as school and work ages changed, military service was redefined, and youth was equated with regeneration.[57] As Scouts and Guides aged, their uniforms were transformed to reflect rites of passage. Brownies (8–10) and Cubs (9–11) gave way to Guides (11–15) and Scouts (12–16), who in turn became Rangers (16+) and Rovers (16+). In other words, children became adolescents, and adolescents were transformed into young adults. Each age level had different uniforms, badges, and accessories. Often the age indicator was as subtle as a different color of badge or tie or hat. As Nellie Priest wrote of her Guiding days in the 1930s, "I kept going [to Guides] till I was about 16. When you were 16, you had to go in the Rangers and wear a red tie."[58]

Uniforms also marked the separate sex structure of the organizations. The skirts and shorts of the two organizations point to the important role of uniform in maintaining the gender distinctions vital to Scouting and Guiding's ideologies. Initially, Guides wore long skirts and neat hair braids, with boots, heavy tunic tops, and wide-brimmed hats. Early skirts were designed to be wide and full, allowing girls greater movement and freedom in their outdoor pursuits. In the 1920s and 1930s, Guide skirts shortened to knee-length, but girls continued to be respectable with heavy, dark stockings. Skirts still forced girls to remember their feminine roles and to keep their tomboyish inclinations in check.[59] They could and did attach knives, haversacks, and other backwoods paraphernalia to their belts, but they were not encouraged to adopt trousers or Scout attire. In addition, Guide uniforms were dark blue because khaki was considered too military for girls.[60]

The Scout shorts served a similar function for boys and men. Scouts wore shorts, long socks, khaki shirts and wide-brimmed hats. The shorts, adopted by both men and boys early in the movement, set the Scouts apart from other youth movements and from soldiers. The reverse of the "lengthening" process that boys underwent when they moved from short pants to trousers,[61] the donning of shorts signaled a return to youthfulness. Shorts also reflected Scouting's imperial beginnings and the uniform Baden-Powell designed for the South African Constabulary, imbuing the movement with a serious purpose also.[62]

In short, the uniforms allowed the girls the freedom to be boyish and the boys the opportunity to be childish, but within the boundaries of proscribed societal and gender roles. The ambiguity of girlhood and boyhood as expressed in the Scouts and Guides created a space for experimentation for both adults and children in the movements, but also within safe parameters.

✠ CONSUMING AND COLLECTING

Two items of the uniform especially attracted Guides and Scouts: their hats and their metal Tenderfoot badges. These items required special care. Hats had to be soaked in sugar water and ironed carefully in order to achieve the stiff rim that was considered desirable and smart. The metal badges, received upon completion of first tests, had to be polished and rubbed frequently to retain their shine. The hat's visibility (it was very large for both girls and boys) made it key to the Guide and Scout public image, while metal badges assumed an important resonance for members within the organizations.

These metal badges were earned by learning the movement's promise and law and the special salutes, handshakes, and rituals of membership. They were worn for the rest of the member's career in the movement, and more than any other uniform piece they symbolized commitment. One Guide described in her diary the feelings she had for her metal "Trefoil" badge. It was a pre-1918 variety that had the letters BPGG inscribed upon it for "Baden-Powell Girl Guide." This Guide, Cicely Stewart-Smith, named her badge Beverly Percival Galahad Graham after her heroes. In the 1920s, she wrote about the badge: "He has been treated as a proud badge, as a bit of equipment, as a tie pin, as a safety pin, as a link of comradeship, and occasionally in my sentimental moments as a symbol"[63] [Figure 3].

Uniforms as well as badges functioned on a number of levels. They often were just an ordinary part of being a Guide or Scout, but occasionally they assumed symbolic importance as signs of membership, resistance, or responsibility. Members took their obligations seriously and the uniform functioned as moral raiment. Wearing the uniform was not enough, however, as one Guide wrote: "A Guide's honour is to be trusted and a girl whose honor is *not* to be trusted, is *not* a guide, however many times a week she may wear a uniform covered with badges" [emphasis original].[64] The Guide was suggesting that the purpose behind the uniform should not be forgotten, and she is implying that someone who did not live up to Guide principles was considered an impostor despite the uniform.

In addition to the metal badges described by Stewart-Smith, Guides and Scouts also collected a series of other uniform paraphernalia during

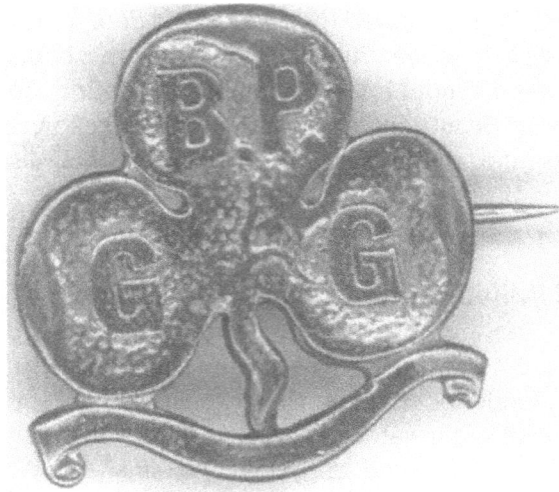

FIG. 3 Metal badges such as this early Baden-Powell Girl Guide pin proclaimed a girl's membership and obedience to the organization's promise. Author's collection.

their years of membership. In fact collecting Scout and Guide consumer items almost became as important a part of the movement as activities and ideology, especially for middle-class members who could afford the accessories.[65] Scouts and Guides bought whatever they could afford, borrowed and bartered for other items, and sometimes fashioned their own replicas of "official" pieces. These items included everything from uniform accessories to cameras to camping equipment to collectible ephemera. The most popular commodities seemed to be uniform accessories, either earned or bought. Scouts and Guides earned merit badges to sew on their arms and accessorized their uniforms with locally fashioned insignia, "official" cockades and plumes, whistles, knives, knapsacks, compasses, cameras, and whatever else they thought that a proper member needed.

By the 1930s, Scout catalogs like *Scoutannica* (Edward R. Buck & Sons, Manchester) were distributing catalogs that were more than 100 pages long, and whistles filled twenty pages of the Hudson and Company (Birmingham) catalog. They also had special editions for camping that did not claim to be "official," but which used drawings of Scouts liberally to illustrate their goods. Both the Scout and Guide organizations opened up their own shops in London to sell accessories, badges, uniforms, and equipment. Satellite shops opened in other parts of the country as well. If a Scout or Guide could obtain the funds, there were plenty of outlets for spending.[66]

An assortment of items attached to a small person in a uniform could present a very odd appearance at times. Katharine Furse, later a prominent

Guide leader, remembered her first look at the Guides during World War I. She described them as "little girls festooned with paraphernalia and carrying poles."[67] American Girl Scout leaders also noticed the excessive amount of items hanging from Guides in uniform. In her 1920 report on Guiding, U.S. Girl Scout Vice-President Helen Storrow compared the Guides and Girl Scouts:

> Our scouts look neater and smarter in their coats than the guides in their tunics, and the custom of wearing tabs and odds and ends of Christmas tree decorations detracts seriously from the otherwise good appearance of the guiders' uniforms. We should do well, however, to adopt as complete a series of insignia as they have in their cockades and hat cords.[68]

Like Guides, Scouts also had a fascination with baubles, whether official or otherwise. Yorkshire native Roy Hattersley remembered his collection of knives, including a jack knife, a buck-horn handled pen knife, and a Bowie knife. He wrote in his autobiography that for him Scouting was "irrevocably associated with knives."[69] Harold Wilson, later Prime Minister, remembered his fascination for knives in his Scout days as well. He told in his autobiography how he had asked his unemployed father for money to buy a sheath knife at a Scout function, but they could not afford it.[70] For Guides and Scouts both, money proved an obstacle to the consumer opportunities that the movements otherwise provided. In fact, consumerism helped further recognition of the movements' "hidden hierarchy."[71]

Other items that Scouts and Guides obtained were collectibles from events, such as souvenir programs, badges, and scarves. They purchased Guide and Scout postcards, publications, prints, statuettes, cameras, first aid kits, and sewing boxes. Scouts and Guides contributed souvenirs of their own to Scout and Guide collections. They crafted decorative items made out of leather, metal, fabric, and yarn, often selling them to other members as fundraisers. Some groups even created mascots; the 2nd Shipley (Yorkshire) Guide Company had a fully uniformed Guider doll named Dorothy.[72]

All of this paraphernalia served a two-fold purpose in the creation of Guide and Scout material culture. It allowed Scouts and Guides to personalize their uniforms and their particular groups and to set themselves apart from the larger movement. Each could create his or her own look, yet retain the uniformity and sense of belonging that was an attractive part of the organizations. The uniform functioned as a representation of the continuity of the movements, and it promised a connection between members and their hero, Baden-Powell.[73]

More importantly, however, this buying and collecting binge served to commodify the Scout and Guide ideology. The movements literally sold themselves to the nation and to the youth of Britain. Scouts and Guides sold, traded, and collected things that would legitimate, heighten, and validate their experiences in the movements. Just as the uniform functioned as a tangible symbol of belonging, commitment, and responsibility, the trappings of Scout and Guide life completed the process of belonging and identity. An 8-year-old boy might not quite grasp the responsibilities implied in the Wolf Cub Promise to serve God and the country, but he could surely understand the necessity of caring for prized possessions such as his uniform, his badges, his knives, his flags, and his whistles.

Guides and Scouts were taught to value upward mobility through hard work and clean living, and they were soon able to determine who had been successful in this mission by looking at the uniform. Scouts and Guides literally wore their accomplishments on their sleeves, sewing row upon row of merit badges onto their uniform sleeves after they had earned them. In addition to the merit badges, Scouts and Guides received special medals for courage or for merit, which they wore on the fronts of their uniforms or around their necks. Another outward sign of the success of a Guide or Scout could be determined by looking at the knots on the end of his or her scarf. If knotted, they had not performed their good deed; if loose, they had. Perhaps the most important indicator of status within the group, however, was "smartness." Personal cleanliness and starched, pressed, and polished outfits meant that Guides or Scouts had worked to make themselves creditable members of the organization.

The smartness of a Guide or Scout's appearance was taken very seriously in this period.[74] As one working-class Guide wrote: "There was no question of mother and grannies helping us. It was all part of the discipline and the fun to wash and iron our ties, press the uniforms, and polish belts and shoes . . ."[75] A former Cub Scout remembered the trouble he had convincing his mother that he wanted to clean his own boots and take care of his own clothing, writing: "My demands to do them were treated as a huge joke bordering on ridicule."[76] Caring for clothing could be used as a way of proving maturity and responsibility in a household, just as earning the money for the uniform itself was a responsible and self-sufficient act. Scouts and Guides often assumed the task of caring for their uniforms, and assiduously polished, mended, and ironed them.

Weekly meetings began with a uniform inspection, so they had to appear to good advantage each week, not just for special events. As one Guide log keeper wrote after a June inspection, "Many unfortunates were commanded to remove their emblems and sew them on correctly."[77] Cleanliness and "smartness" in the Scouts and Guides were often metaphors for order and self-control. Embedded in the language of "smartness" was a very real concern on the part of leaders to control sexuality in adolescents and young adults. Slovenly dress and poor uniform care were seen as signs of bigger character flaws, while cleanliness often meant respectability. Leaders believed that teaching members to revere and to care for their uniforms would encourage sexual morality and controlled behavior.

"Smartness" was not confined to uniforms and collectibles alone. The language of Scouting and Guiding reflected a concern with being "smart." Among the most famous of Scout and Guide maxims were "BYBM" and "TIB," which stood for "Brace Your Back Muscles" and "Tuck in your Back." BYBM-BOM was one of the Guides favorite marching songs, with the "bom" marking time as they walked. This special language accompanied a secret sign language as well. Guides and Scouts offered their **left** hands for handshakes, and they saluted each other with the Scout and Guide sign. Silence at rallies or meetings could be achieved easily and quickly by raising a hand, a signal to all Scouts and Guides to raise their own hands and to stop talking.[78] Scouts and Guides were invited to be insiders in the organizations by the signs and language.

✤ CONCLUSION

Scout and Guide rituals, language, and uniforms drew from and contributed to the building of a youth subculture in the interwar years. Unlike the youth subcultures of the post-World War II period that have been the focus of many studies,[79] Scout and Guide subculture was perceived to be a respectable, not a deviant, phenomenon. Scout style was expressed through regimented dress, secret rituals, and coded languages. Scout and Guide uniforms stood for responsibility, community, and service, but they also represented the desire of youth to carve out independent spaces for themselves in interwar society. These diverse goals were reflected in Scout and Guide "style."

Guide and Scout uniforms and accessories had complex meanings for members. The uniform assured membership in a mass movement that symbolized Guide and Scout participation in a postwar ideal of service and citizenship. However, the uniform and accessories also assumed personal meaning for each member, as boys and girls fought to obtain them and cared for them. They were worn, either with pride or shame, as symbols of the Guide or Scout's beliefs or aspirations. Leaders sought to use uniforms to establish a standard of conduct and respectability and to control difference, especially class distinctions. Yet youth themselves defined the uniforms to meet their own needs at home and in public. Members could attain "insider" status by wearing a uniform, but they could not ever attain equality in terms of wealth or skill.

Scouts and Guides created one modern youth subculture among many in this period, using uniforms, membership rituals, and collectibles. This subculture expressed group solidarity and a stated desire to transcend class differences, while reflecting individual identity and the realities of class within the movements. More attention needs to focus on the years following 1914, when transformations were taking place in definitions of youth, community, class, gender, and belonging.

ENDNOTES

[1] This chapter is a revised version of "(Uni)Forming Youth: Girl Guides and Boy Scouts in Britain, 1908–1939," *History Workshop Journal* 45 (Spring 1998): 103–134, ©1998 History Workshop Journal, reproduced by permission of Oxford University Press.

[2] See Violet Synge, *Royal Guides: A Story of the 1st Buckingham Palace Company* (London: Girl Guides Association, 1948). Incidentally, Queen Elizabeth is still one of the major patrons of the organization, and Princess Margaret served as President until her death.

[3] For good studies exploring the question of youth and politics in interwar Europe, see Victoria de Grazia, *How Fascism Ruled Women* (Berkeley: University of California Press, 1992); George L. Mosse, *Nationalism and Sexuality: Middle-class Morality and Sexual Norms in Modern Europe* (Madison: University of Wisconsin Press, 1985); Detlev Peukert, *Inside Nazi Germany: Conformity, Opposition, and Racism in Everyday Life* (New Haven: Yale University Press, 1987); Birgitte Søland, *Becoming Modern: Young Women and the Reconstruction of Womanhood in the 1920s* (Princeton: Princeton University Press, 2000); Mark Roseman, ed. *Generations in Conflict: Youth Revolt and Generation Formation in Germany, 1770–1968* (Cambridge/New York: Cambridge University Press, 1995); Susan Whitney, "The Politics of Youth: Communists and Catholics in Interwar France," PhD diss., Rutgers University, 1994.

[4] The most successful of the competing movements in Britain were the Boys Brigade and Girls Brigade for younger children and the club movements for older youth. John Springhall provides a good look at the comparative movements in *Youth, Empire, and Society: British Youth Movements, 1908–1930* (London: Croom Helm, 1977), 135.

[5] Two studies that have found membership estimates are: Paul Wilkinson, "English Youth Movements, 1908–1930," *Journal of Contemporary History* 4:2 (April 1969), 3; and Springhall, *Youth, Empire and Society*, 131. Wilkinson cites a study by Mass Observation in 1966 that claimed 34% of males born between 1901 and 1920 were Scouts. If Wilkinson's numbers are correct, the numbers of interwar Scouts were substantially higher since membership doubled from 1918 to 1930. Springhall cites a survey that says at least 60% of British women had been Guides at one time.

[6] On comparative youth movements, see the still useful studies by Springhall, *Youth, Empire and Society*, 135; and Wilkinson, "English Youth Movements." On the Jewish Lads' Brigade, see: Richard A. Voeltz, "'. . . A Good Jew and a Good Englishman': The Jewish Lads' Brigade, 1894–1922," *Journal of Contemporary History* 23:1 (January 1988): 119–127.

[7] Michael J. Childs, *Labour's Apprentices: Working-class Lads in Late Victorian and Edwardian England* (London: Hambledon Press, 1992), 142–151. See also David Fowler, *The First Teenagers: The Lifestyle of Young Wage-Earners in Interwar Britain* (London: Woburn Press, 1995).

[8] Jill Julius Matthews, "They Had Such A Lot Of Fun: The Women's League of Health and Beauty Between the Wars," *History Workshop Journal* 30 (Autumn 1990), 22–54. For information on young women and their leisure options in interwar Britain, see Claire

Langhamer, *Women's Leisure in England, 1920–1960* (Manchester: Manchester University Press, 2000).

[9] Figures are taken from the Annual Reports of the Guide and Scout Associations from 1917–1939. These reports are on file at the Scout Association and Guide Association Archives in London.

[10] The relative freedom that boys enjoyed echoed the prewar era. See, for example Anna Davin, *Growing Up Poor: Home, School and Street in London, 1870–1914* (London: Rivers Oram Press, 1996); Carol Dyhouse, *Girls Growing Up in Late Victorian and Edwardian England* (London: Routledge, 1981); and Deborah Gorham, *The Victorian Girl and the Feminine Ideal* (Bloomington: Indiana University Press, 1982).

[11] Figures used to compile this table are taken from the Annual Reports of the Scout and Girl Guide Associations and from the *Census of England and Wales* (London: HMSO, 1924, 1934).

[12] Roy Brook, *The Story of Huddersfield* (London: MacGibbon and Kee, 1968), 211; Noreen Branson, *Britain in the Nineteen Twenties* (London: Weidenfield and Nicholson, 1975), 82. Information on the occupations in Yorkshire was taken from the *Census of England and Wales 1931*, 280–295.

[13] David Hey, *Yorkshire from A.D. 1000* (London: Longman, 1986), 258–259, 303. For a brief look at the composition of Yorkshire's West Riding, see David H. Pill, *Yorkshire: The West Riding* (London: B. T. Batsford, 1977).

[14] Leslie Horsfall, interview with author, 7 May 1993, Huddersfield; 16th Huddersfield Warrant Records, Huddersfield North District, in the possession of Gwen Pearson, District Secretary; Ralph Whiteley, interview with author, 5 May 1993, Huddersfield.

[15] Ralph Whiteley, interview by author, Huddersfield, 5 May 1993, and oral history of male born 1 December 1907, Kirklees Sound Archive, Acc. #041CH, interviewed by Ilona Avotins 27 February 1986. Interestingly enough, both Whiteley and other people I interviewed mentioned the importance of Scout concerts in Huddersfield, and they especially cited the role of actor James Mason (a Huddersfield Scout) and his brothers in the success of these events. Each told a rags-to-riches story about Mason and Scouting's influence on his later success.

[16] Whiteley interview, 5 May 1993. Ralph Whiteley is still active in the Scout movement in Huddersfield.

[17] Kirklees Sound Archive, Huddersfield, Yorkshire: Female born 1904, interview by Gillian Greaves, 28 October 1986, interview #234; Female born 1911, interview by Allison Coulson, 2 December 1936, interview #257 CH; Female born 11 November 1918, interview by Sandy Smith 21 November 1986.

[18] Sheffield Warrant records for 1st Croft Hall. Warrant records are located in Group Folders at the Sheffield City Boy Scout Archive, Trippet Lane, Sheffield. My sincere thanks goes to Roger and Mary Sanderson, archivists, and to the staff of the Scout Association for their assistance in using these records.

[19] Sheffield Warrant Records for 7th Attercliffe and 10th Mount Tabor.

[20] Sheffield Warrant Records for 1st Croft Hall, 1944 testimonial.

[21] Still the best article on notions of respectability as defined in homes and neighborhoods is Ellen Ross, "'Not the Sort that Would Sit on the Doorstep': Respectability in

Pre-World War I London Neighborhoods," *International Labor and Working-Class History* 27 (Spring 1985), 39–59.

[22] The most famous early study of London remains the 5-volume study by Charles Booth, *Life and Labour of the People in London* (London/New York: Macmillan, 1902). For contemporary historical studies of London in the late nineteenth and early twentieth centuries, see Davin, *Growing Up Poor*; David Feldman and Gareth Stedman Jones, eds., *Metropolis London: Histories and Representations since 1800* (London: Routledge and Kegan Paul, 1989); Gareth Stedman Jones, ed. *Languages of Class: Studies in Working Class History, 1832–1982* (Cambridge: Cambridge University Press, 1983); Roy Porter, *London: A Social History* (Cambridge: Harvard University Press, 1994); Ellen Ross, *Love and Toil: Motherhood in Outcast London 1870–1918* (New York/Oxford: Oxford University Press, 1993); Judith R. Walkowitz, *City of Dreadful Delight: Narratives of Sexual Danger in Late-Victorian London* (Chicago: University of Chicago Press, 1992).

[23] *Census of England and Wales 1931*; David R. Green, "The Metropolitan Economy: Continuity and Change 1800–1939," in *London: A New Metropolitan Geography*, eds. Keith Hoggart and Green (London: Edward Arnold, 1991), 22–24.

[24] For boys, the numbers given represent those aged 11 and older; for girls, aged 14 and older. Hubert Llewellyn Smith, *The New Survey of London Life and Labour*, vol. IX (London: P.S. King and Son, Ltd., 1935), 190–191, 239. See chapters VII on Social Organizations for Adolescent Boys and VIII on Social Organizations for Adolescent Girls.

[25] Smith, *The New Survey of London Life and Labour*, 155, 190–191, 240.

[26] Smith, *The New Survey of London Life and Labour*, 220.

[27] Presbyterian Settlement Junior Guides Report of Members, Poplar, East India Dock Road, 1934–35; GA–London. These records show that life for working-class girls had not changed that much in London since the late nineteenth century. See Ross, *Love and Toil*, especially Chapter Five.

[28] T. S. Lukis to Archie Hogarth, 5 April 1908, March 1909, 21 June 1909; TC/93, SA–London.

[29] Tim Jeal, *The Boy-Man: The Life of Lord Baden-Powell*, (New York: William Morrow, 1990), 404–409.

[30] Much more work remains to be done on the local records of the Scout and Guide movements, kept at the county and divisional levels. For work that supports my finding about cross-class membership, see Michael Blanch, "Imperialism, Nationalism and Organized Youth," in *Working Class Culture: Studies in History and Theory*, John Clarke, Charles Critcher, and Richard Johnson, eds. (Birmingham: Centre for Cultural Studies, 1979), 102–120; and Charles Griffiths, "The Beginnings of the Boy Scout Movement in Reading, Berkshire, 1908–1914," unpublished project for Open University, 1996, on file at SA–London.

[31] For an interesting study of uniforms as devices for socialization and nationalization, see: Nathan Joseph, *Uniforms and Nonuniforms: Communication through Clothing* (New York: Greenwood Press, 1986).

[32] Grant McCracken, *Culture and Consumption: New Approaches to the Symbolic Character of Consumer Goods and Activities* (Bloomington: Indiana University Press, 1988), 60–61.

[33] Fred Davis, *Fashion, Culture, and Identity* (Chicago/London: University of Chicago Press, 1992), 5–9.

[34] Sally Alexander, "Becoming a Woman in London in the 1920s and 1930s," in *Metropolis London: Histories and Representations since 1800*, eds. David Feldman and Gareth Stedman Jones (London: Routledge, 1989), 256–257.

[35] Michael Budd's work on this subject suggests that a major transformation in the understanding and articulation of physical culture took place after World War I, especially in regard to youth (Michael Anton Budd, "Heroic Bodies: Physical Culture, Commerce and the Promise of the Perfected Self, 1898–1918," [PhD diss. Rutgers, October 1992]). For other works on the body and consumption, see Matthews, "They Had Such a Lot of Fun," 22–54, and Alexander, "Becoming a Woman," 262.

[36] Matthews, "They Had Such a Lot of Fun," 25, 35.

[37] For information on the movements for national efficiency and for worries about degenerated youth, see: John Gillis, *Youth and History: Tradition and Change in Early Age Relations, 1770–present* (New York: Academic Press, 1974); Harry Hendrick, *Images of Youth: Age, Class and the Male Youth Problem, 1880–1920* (Oxford: Clarendon Press, 1990); Michael Rosenthal, *The Character Factory: Baden-Powell and the Origins of the Boy Scout Movement* (New York: Pantheon Press, 1986); Springhall, *Youth, Empire and Society*; Allen Warren, "Mothers for the Empire," in *Making Imperial Mentalities: Socialisation and British Imperialism*, ed. J.A. Mangan (Manchester: Manchester University Press, 1990) and "Citizens of the Empire: Baden-Powell, Scouts and Guides and an Imperial Ideal," in *Imperialism and Popular Culture*, ed. John Mackenzie (Manchester: Manchester University Press, 1986); Wilkinson, "English Youth Movements."

[38] Ramsay MacDonald to Robert Baden-Powell, 20 April 1914. Interestingly enough, when MacDonald was prime minister in 1929, he arranged for a peerage to be awarded to Baden-Powell at the jamboree. Memo by Olave Baden-Powell, November 1950. TC/95, SA–London.

[39] Edward Ezard, *Battersea Boy* (London: William Kimber, 1979), 84.

[40] Almeria Stockdale to Rose Kerr, 2 November 1930; GA–London. For information on working-class hostility to the Salvation Army, see Pamela Walker, *Pulling the Devil's Kingdom Down: The Salvation Army in Britain* (Berkeley: University of California Press, 2001), 219–221.

[41] D. Allport to Mr. Middlemas, 30 November 1954. TC/271, SA–London.

[42] Ida Edwards to Rose Kerr, no date, GA–London. Quoted in full in Rose Kerr, *The Story of the Girl Guides* (London: Girl Guides Association, 1954), 64–68.

[43] Of course, street abuse, fights and territoriality were not uncommon experiences for children in Britain, whether they were wearing their uniforms or not. For a good discussion of some of these divisions, see Davin, *Growing Up Poor*, 204–208.

[44] May A. M. Rainer, "Emma's Daughter," unpublished memoirs, 1977. Brunel University.

[45] For a good example of this kind of bargaining, see Kathy Peiss, *Cheap Amusements: Working Women and Leisure in Turn-of-the-Century New York* (Philadelphia: Temple University Press, 1986), 70.

[46] William Tucker, *Autobiography of an Astrologer* (Sidcup: Pythagorean, 1960), 17, 24.

[47] Peter Kimpton, interview with author, 25 March 1993, Roland Philipps Scout Centre, London.

[48] Olave Baden-Powell, *Training Girls as Guides* (London: C. Arthur Pearson, 1917), 66.

[49] Winn Everett, interview with author, 24 March 1993, Bushey, Hertfordshire.

[50] G. V. Holmes, *The Likes of Us* (London: Frederick Muller Ltd., 1948), 97–98.

[51] Chaim Bermant, *Coming Home* (London: George Allen & Unwin, 1976), 37, 94–95.

[52] Molly Weir, *Shoes Were for Sunday* (London: Hutchinson & Co, 1970), 11, 46, 162–164.

[53] Alice Linton, *Not Expecting Miracles* (London: Centerprise Trust Ltd., 1982), 17, 56–57.

[54] "Scout! Get your 'Kit' from Gamage's: The World's Largest Scout Outfitters," (A.W. Gamage, Ltd., Holborn, E.C., 1911), 31. TC/84, SA–London.

[55] *Catalog* (1927, 1938), London: Girl Guides Association; GA–London. Advertisement in *The Scouter*, 21:5 (May 1927), 159; SA–London. These are representative selections from the large quantity of catalogs in the Scout and Guide archives.

[56] Winifred Renshaw, *An Ordinary Life: Memories of a Balby Childhood* (Doncaster: Doncaster Library Services, 1984), ch. 35. [Note: typescript document with no page numbers, just chapter divisions.]

[57] A good exploration of changing state and societal definitions of age divisions is Roger Cooter, ed., *In the Name of the Child: Health and Welfare, 1880–1940* (London/New York: Routledge, 1992). For the importance of "adolescence" as an age division, see Gillis, *Youth and History*. For information on expanded work opportunities for young women, see Diana Gittins, *Fair Sex: Family Size and Structure, 1900–1939* (London: Hutchinson, 1982). Militarization and its effects are usefully discussed in Michael Geyer, "The Militarization of Europe, 1914–1945," in *The Militarization of the Western World*, ed. John Gillis (New Brunswick: Rutgers University Press, 1989), 65–102.

[58] "Nellie Priest," in *The Island: Life and Death of an East London Community, 1870–1970* (London: Centerprise, 1979), 39.

[59] For a discussion of tomboys and sex-specific clothing in prewar working-class neighborhoods, see Davin, *Growing Up Poor*, 70–81.

[60] On the significance of being "in khaki" for women, see Susan Grayzel, "'The Outward and Visible Sign of Her Patriotism': Women, Uniforms, and National Service During the First World War," *Twentieth Century British History* 8:2 (1997): 145–164.

[61] On the lengthening process, see John Burnett, *Destiny Obscure: Autobiographies of Childhood, Education and Family from the 1820s to the 1920s* (Harmondsworth: Penguin, 1984), 305.

[62] For a further discussion of Guiding/Scouting and imperialism, see Tammy Proctor, "'A Separate Path': Scouting and Guiding in Interwar South Africa," *Comparative Studies in Society and History* 42:3 (July 2000): 605–631; "Scouts, Guides and the Fashioning of Empire, 1919–1939," in *Fashioning the Body Politic: Gender, Dress, Citizenship*, ed. Wendy Parkins (London/New York: Berg Publishers, 2002); and "Gender, Generation, and the Politics of Guiding and Scouting in Interwar Britain" (PhD diss., Rutgers University, October 1995), 168–236.

[63] Cicely Stewart-Smith, "The Log of a Loafer in the Guides" [unpublished handwritten diary] (1923–25), GA–London.

[64] J. Kerridge, "Honour," *Leader's Opinion* XII (August/September 1921), 14. Unpublished Guide magazine, GA–London.

[65] Susan Stewart has examined collections as "devices for the objectification of desire." She sees the acquisition of objects by a collector as the replacement of production with

an abstract form of consumption. Following Marx's theory of commodity fetishism, Stewart theorizes that "collection in general marks the final erasure of labor within the abstractions of late capitalism." Although Guide and Scout collecting was as much a response to as it was a part of mass consumption, Stewart's theories do fit with the frenzied collecting that characterized interwar Guiding and Scouting among members of all classes. Susan Stewart, *On Longing: Narratives of the Miniature, the Gigantic, the Souvenir, the Collection* (Baltimore/London: Johns Hopkins University Press, 1984), xii, 156, 164–65, 169.

[66] These catalogs and others like them can be found in TC/238, SA–London, and at GA–London.

[67] Katharine Furse, *Hearts and Pomegranates* (London: Peter Davies, 1940), 287.

[68] Helen Storrow, "Report on Girl Guiding, June 1920." Girl Guide Box, Girl Scouts of the USA–New York.

[69] Roy Hattersley, *A Yorkshire Boyhood* (London: Pan Books, 1990), 89.

[70] Harold Wilson, *Memoirs: The Making of a Prime Minister* (London: Weidenfield & Nicholson and Michael Joseph, 1986), 22.

[71] My thanks to Tony Peffer for this phrase and for his insights regarding this topic.

[72] 30 June 1934, 2nd Shipley Log Book (1930–1939), in possession of Sheila Marks, Ilkley, Yorkshire. The actual Dorothy doll, complete with full uniform and tiny metal and cloth badges, is on display at the Girl Guide Association in London.

[73] On the question of material possessions becoming signs of membership, see Eugene Rochberg-Halton, *Meaning and Modernity: Social Theory in the Pragmatic Attitude* (Chicago/London: University of Chicago Press, 1986).

[74] Smartness was inculcated in a variety of institutions, including the military, the nursing establishment, schools, and some workplaces. For example, on military nursing, see Anne Summers, *Angels and Citizens: British Women as Military Nurses, 1854–1914* (London: Routledge and Kegan Paul, 1988).

[75] Weir, *Shoes were for Sunday*, 162–163.

[76] Wally Horwood, *A Walworth Boy: Looking Back on Growing Up 1922–1939*, TS-282 pgs., (Southwark Local Studies Library, 1977), 83.

[77] 1 June 1925, Logbook of the 1st Chislehurst Company, 1924–1929. GA–London.

[78] Information on special handshakes, rituals, songs, and maxims may be found in any edition of *Scouting for Boys* and *Girl Guiding*.

[79] A rich literature on youth subcultures emerged from the work of the Centre for Contemporary Cultural Studies at Birmingham University, for example Phil Cohen, *Subcultural Conflict and Working-class Community* (Birmingham: CCCS, 1972); Stuart Hall and Tony Jefferson, eds., *Resistance through Rituals* (London: Hutchinson, 1977); Dick Hebdige, *Subculture: The Meaning of Style* (London: Methuen, 1979); and Angela McRobbie and Mica Nava, eds., *Gender and Generation* (London: MacMillan, 1984).

3

C H A P T E R

FIGHTING PETTICOATS

Between 1910 and 1939 in Britain, expectations regarding women's roles and responsibilities in society were redefined to reflect growing awareness of the needs of modern industrial production and militarized society. Women received limited suffrage in 1918, then full suffrage on an equal basis with men in 1928, and education and employment for females changed. Marriage and divorce laws were liberalized, and birth control became more widely available as books such as Marie Stopes' *Married Love* opened up discussions of previously taboo topics. As a result of these transformations, the war and interwar periods represented a time of great societal confusion over gender roles. At issue was nothing less than the moral and physical development of the nation and the proper training of children as future citizens of Britain.[1]

Before the war, suffragists battered at the walls of the male establishment, Voluntary Aid Detachments (VAD) and women's auxiliaries were formed to allow women to participate in the defense of the nation, and youth movements such as the Girl Guides were conceived to train the nation's future mothers. Yet these prewar movements functioned within the confines of Edwardian society, making it difficult for the organizations to conceive of roles for women that did not fit into Victorian categories of women as nurturer and mother. As Martha Vicinus has shown in her study of late Victorian and Edwardian women, females were expected to fulfill one of three roles: mother, celibate spinster, or prostitute.[2] Sexuality and childbearing were the prisms through which women's activities and desires were viewed. Caught between the emerging psychological discussion of sexual repression and the continuing reliance on Victorian morality, women (beyond a few notable exceptions) seemed unable to carve out public spaces for themselves in which they would have freedom of action and independence.[3]

After the war, women faced many of the same difficulties despite their new voting privileges and their laudable actions as workers contributing to the war effort. Women continued to organize, but in splintered groups working for different causes. A small group of equal rights feminists remained active, while the majority of the prewar suffrage movements shifted to a postwar concern with difference-based arguments. As Susan Kent has noted, the re-establishment of sexual difference and complementarity arguments pushed feminist rhetoric into the realm of anti-feminist speeches in an attempt to re-create order from the postwar anxiety over the perceived blurring of gender roles. The so-called "New Feminists" focused on endowments for mothers, widows' pensions, and other legislative advances.[4]

Despite divisions in postwar feminism, women had gained rights hitherto denied to them by the 1920s, and they responded with a new freedom in dress and public entertainment. British society was deeply fearful of what these changes and newfound freedoms meant for the family and women's lives. Relationships outside of society's narrow norm became open topics of discussion in the 1920s. For example, Radclyffe Hall's *The Well of Loneliness* sparked a highly publicized obscenity trial because of the lesbian relationships it described, while other intellectuals created controversy with their advocacy of free love.[5]

Above all, society worried about the single independent working woman. As Winifred Holtby wrote in the 1930s, women of her generation continued to hear a strong message regarding the dangers of independent life:

> Puritan morality taught unmarried women that the loss of virginity doomed them to the torments of Hell in the next world; twentieth-century morality teaches them that the retention of virginity dooms them to the horror of insanity in this one...I am an incomplete frustrated virgin woman. Therefore some time, somewhere, pain and regret will overwhelm me.[6]

Conflicting public opinions about feminist activities and about women's roles both before and after the war served to construct certain characteristics by which women were judged. Prior to the war, Guide leaders were conscious of the need to provide respectable chaperones and protection for girls who would be engaging in public activities. They wanted to liberate girls from some of the restrictions of home, but within the confines of womanly behavior. After the war, the organization realized that they needed to redefine their message of respectable adventure to include more autonomy and independence for a female population who would be future voters and leaders in the nation, while retaining some measure of protection for the girls in their charge.

While publicly touting their abilities to create fit future mothers for Britain, Guiding privately constructed spaces for same-sex friendships and relationships and for activities that promoted female independence. Young, single Guide leaders in their late teens and early twenties were especially drawn into the freedoms and the community that Guiding provided, but the movement also attracted young girls who became lifelong members. This chapter first traces the early development of Guiding and then explores the Guide movement's ability in the interwar period to use the rhetoric of companionate marriage and complementary sex roles while embracing activities that subverted traditional family and gender roles.

DEFINING WOMANLY FREEDOMS, 1910–1918

When the Guide movement was organized in 1910, leaders found themselves on the defensive, explaining a movement that to parents looked unfeminine and dangerously public. The first few years of Guiding's existence became an exercise in persuasion for leaders who needed to convince both parents and girls that the movement could combine Scout adventure with womanly pursuits. Agnes Baden-Powell explained the Guide philosophy in the first chapter of her 1912 handbook:

> Girls will do no good by imitating boys. Do not be a bad imitation. It is far finer to be a real girl, such as no boy can be. One loves a girl who is sweet and tender, and who can gently soothe when wearied with pain. Some girls like to do scouting, but scouting for girls is not the same as for boys.[7]

Baden-Powell concluded this explanation by explaining the difference between the manliness taught by the Scouts and the womanliness that the Guides promoted. Both girls and boys might experience adventure, but in different ways, and both should "be prepared," but for different roles in life. Part of the emphasis on "womanliness" expressed in early Guide writings stemmed from worries over the "hoydenish" tactics of women's suffrage activists in Britain, but especially in London. Pre-war British suffrage was a popular movement focused mainly in cities such as Manchester and London. Suffrage organizations were varied, but the two main branches were the National Union of Women's Suffrage Societies (NUWSS) headed by Millicent Fawcett and the Women's Social and Political Union (WSPU) led by Emmeline Pankhurst. Both organizations used spectacle to their advantage, holding mass rallies, marches, debates, and lectures. The difference between the two organizations was largely tactical; the NUWSS adhered to the laws while the WSPU used militant devices to make its point, such as harassing Parliament members, sending mail bombs, and destroying property. The WSPU wanted to shock the public, which they largely did.[8]

As Lisa Tickner has pointed out, the stereotype of "the womanly woman" permeated Edwardian propaganda both for and against suffrage. Suffragists were increasingly seen as "new women" or "militants" or "the shrieking sisterhood" by the antisuffragists and press, but suffragists saw themselves as "the true, the evolved embodiment of womanliness" in the public sphere.[9] Brian Harrison has discussed how bitter battles over public opinion were waged between the strong antisuffrage movement in Britain and the suffragists. Antisuffrage attacks centered on suffragists' neglect of their homes and families, on their unmotherly and therefore, unwomanly attributes.[10]

The Guide movement emerged while this social, political, and cultural struggle was taking place in the press, in Parliament and in the streets over the meaning of "woman." The question of girls' education was considered to be of vital importance because they would be training and caring for the women and men of the future. One of the greatest fears that fueled opposition to the women's suffrage movement was that women would neglect their homes and families if given political rights. Therefore Guide literature needed to promote the "mother training" aspects of their program in order to answer concerns about women's roles as reproducers of the nation.[11] An early Guide, Beatrice Swaine, expressed these difficulties:

> Our most difficult job was fighting the enormous amount of prejudice that existed against the Girl Guide idea. Most people were firmly convinced that we wished to turn all the girls of the British Empire into hoydens, who would run about with Boy Scouts all day long, and be a universal nuisance.[12]

With these prejudices in mind, Guide leaders attempted to distance themselves from any "unwomanly" activities. However, part of the fun of the organization was outdoor activities and ceremonies, so the Guides held rallies, demonstrations of skills, and pageants that closely resembled some of the suffrage events. The Guides used public spectacle for publicity in the same way that the suffrage movements did, whether tactics were consciously copied or not. The difference was that the Guides participated in controlled outdoor activities. For instance, at one 1914 rally at Richmond Green, the local Scout troop "kept the large square in which the girls drilled," by forming a human wall around the area.[13] This kind of male protection and maintenance of the girls' public display was quite removed from suffrage rallies, which often resulted in a different type of male protection, the police, dragging women off to prison. It seemed that the police protected society from the suffragettes, while the Scouts protected the Guides from society.

The Guides dabbled in new kinds of display and activities, while maintaining a respectable reputation because their rhetoric supported motherhood. They created a public middle ground for girls between fierce antisuffrage sentiment and militant suffragism in the years before the war.[14] The Guides sought to take a modern position and to reject the Victorian values of their parents, but to retain a certain level of respectability. Olave Baden-Powell wrote about her mother's reaction to Guiding in 1916: "She was so very Victorian in outlook. She condemned suffragettes and any form of 'Women's Lib' whatsoever—even the comparatively modest freedom Robin [Robert Bader-Powell] offered to girls through Guiding."[15] The phrase "modest freedom" aptly describes the first five years of Guide history as the movement placed itself and established a reputation in British society.

However, with the outbreak of war in 1914, the Guide program and concerns changed. As with many British voluntary and political organizations, Guiding embraced the war effort wholeheartedly. At first, most Guides helped by running errands, cooking, doing housework, nursing, and baby sitting. As the war progressed and Britain's need for workers increased, Guides volunteered for service as office clerks, munitions workers, and drivers. Guides in London served as messengers for the War Office and as orderlies in hospitals, while rural Guides joined the Land Army and various first-aid societies. Other Guides joined the Voluntary Aid Detachments (VAD) and the Women's Army Auxiliary Corps (WAAC), going overseas to serve the nation.[16] Guides even joined the Scouts in raising money for ambulances and entertainment huts for soldiers in France. Both the Guide Recreation Hut and the Scout Hut were opened near Etaples in early 1916.[17] The Guide War Service badge appeared in 1915, and girls flocked to the organization in record numbers after 1916, many of them hoping to be of use to the nation in its time of crisis. The war introduced Guides to a taste of independence and public freedom [Figure 4].

Although the emphasis remained on girls' duties as mothers of the new nation as in pre-war days, civic duty now became almost as important to Guide ideology as home-craft. Girls learned to be "splendidly useful" all the while enjoying themselves immensely. As one Guide wrote to her fellow members: "In such moments one did realize that it *was* War-time—and yet somehow it was rather jolly tearing about and managing everything for oneself. It gave you such a ripping feeling of independence. . . ."[18] Another Guide, Cicely Stewart-Smith, wrote that she refused to join the Guides until she heard that she could do war work:

> This decided me, previous persuasions and talks of the high aims of the Guides did not move me but the idea of doing proper war work was really thrilling. . . . Perhaps it was because the whole world was in uniform then and the idea that I could also help both the country and myself by being a Guide was thrilling.[19]

The war became a broadening experience for many women and girls, not just Guides. Many historians and women of the war period have recorded the feelings of liberation and change that they experienced. In her assessment of the war experience, Ray Strachey wrote that women "saw what the world was like for men; and neither Act of Parliament nor season of reaction, nor any other thing could thereafter take that knowledge from them."[20] Likewise, Vera Brittain, a VAD during the war, described the experience as

FIG. 4 Girl Guide messengers served the nation at the Paris Peace Conference, 1919. By kind permission of The Guide Association.

the end of the "struggle to escape from the tyranny of Victorian homes."[21] In almost all the accounts, women discuss feeling a freedom and a sense of purpose hitherto unknown to them. Beyond feeling liberated from the confines of home, girls and women also gained a new understanding of sexuality and the realities of physical relationships. Brittain noted this increased awareness in her memoirs, saying that she was thankful for the experiences of nude male bodies that came as part of her war nursing.[22]

During the war, the Guide movement attracted girls because of this sense of experience, purpose, and autonomy, yet it also appealed to their parents because it encouraged appropriate morality and contained, or at least seemed to contain girls' freedoms. One guide mentioned learning to play cards from soldiers in a hospital where she was working, a bit of worldliness that would have shocked her parents and Baden-Powell. Another report had older Guides, wearing "neither pads nor gloves," playing cricket with wounded soldiers. Sometimes Guides strayed even further from the respectable path. Three girls aged 14-15 from the 6th Clapton Company were dismissed from their Guide company after Armistice Day 1918 for "serious breach of laws and promise." Their particular misconduct was apparently too serious to record.[23]

The pleasure women received from their wartime experiences, beyond terrifying some parents, also alienated many returning soldiers who often felt anxious about the changing roles for women. Sandra Gilbert has explored how this anxiety assumed an angry and combative tone in literature of the period, while historians Angela Woollacott and Richard Voeltz have examined "khaki fever," the phenomenon where girls purportedly went mad over uniformed men. Woollacott found that girls desired men but also uniforms and independence for themselves, dangerously destabilizing the gender order both before and during the war. Voeltz takes this concept further by examining how Guiding functioned as a sort of "antidote" to the outrageous behavior of many young women classified as flappers or khaki-mad hoydens. Voeltz is right in saying that Guides created the appearance of a safe alternative for women, but Guiding also fashioned a space for girls and women to experience independence and freedom from the restrictions of home life during World War I.[24]

Ultimately, the war became a testing ground for the ideology and practices of the Guide movement. The war allowed adolescent girls to use skills that they had been learning for several years, such as first aid, child care, and ambulance. In fact, girls relished the opportunity to participate vicariously in the defense of the nation, and they readied themselves for action. Dorothy Scannell described her sisters' excitement: "Winifred was a tower of strength during the war because she was never afraid. A girl guide, she decided to get ready to 'be prepared,' and she stressed this necessity to Amy who was in happy agreement." The two girls made bags for their possessions and slept with them around their waists at night.[25] Suddenly the years of bandaging and tracking and preparing seemed to be paying off for girls.

In addition, Guide training in domestic duties and mothering skills served a symbolic function by assuaging fears that gender conventions turned topsy-turvy by the war could never be "normalized."[26] Guides became a sign that a woman could still reproduce the nation, despite the debacle of war. As Robert Baden-Powell succinctly wrote:

> The vast mass of our present girls will in the near future have a powerful voice in determining the affairs of the nation. Are they fitted for it or are they being fitted for it? They [women] are more important since it is the woman's influence that leads the man; it is the mother that develops the spirit of the child.[27]

Guides, who had proven their usefulness and respectability during the war, would be the future mothers of the nation. These girls would be called upon to raise the postwar generation and to help rebuild England. Of course, most members saw the Guides only as a grand opportunity for exercising new skills and for expanding their activities, not as a motherhood training school. Achieving a new level of personal freedom and independence was an extremely liberating feeling for girls, and they did not mind learning to cook and sew and care for children if it meant they could also learn Morse code, tracking and observation skills. The success of this program was evident by the vast boosts in Guide membership during the latter part of the war. In 1916, only about 50,000 girls in England were registered as Guides, but by 1919, that number had risen to more than 120,000. By the 1930s, Guide membership figures well exceeded half a million in Britain.[28]

Using gendered assumptions about citizenship, Guiding sought to create the perfect home, thereby creating the perfect postwar nation. Strands of national efficiency, racial purity, class harmony, and gender boundaries came together in the maxim: An efficient home yields an efficient nation. Although this maxim was not entirely new in Britain, the home and the nation had been irrevocably changed by the wartime militarized state, and civil society had been fundamentally redefined. The process of militarization blurred the lines between civilian/solider, male/female, and war/peace. Therefore, the pairing of home and nation in postwar Britain was intrinsically different from earlier periods.[29]

Citizenship in the nation was often represented to Guides as a personal experience. Actions in the home, in the camp, and in the workplace determined true citizenship and patriotism. Guides became citizen servants in the new nation, regenerating Britain through their youth and their service ethos in a variety of ways. A good citizen knew the meaning of personal responsibility and heroism. These traits were built into the Guide program from the movement's beginnings, but they assumed a new resonance with the advent of war. During the war, British homes were mobilized to fight in the same way soldiers were mustered. This connection between state and home was not severed in the interwar period, it merely changed roles. The wartime government had stepped into private homes in unprecedented ways; the interwar government controlled private lives even further through such programs as welfare provisions and educational reform.

With the broader opportunities that the war had provided, Guides and Guiders keenly felt the change of climate at the end of the war as men returned and women were encouraged to assume roles in the home and forego their jobs and public functions. Women experienced a backlash in the 1920s that forced them to redefine their role in society or go back to their homes. Women were under pressure to go back to "normal" after the war, which meant marriage and the re-establishment of a domestic ideal. As historians Susan Kent and Mary Louise Roberts found in their studies of interwar Europe, men and women tried to erase the sexual disorder of the war. Marriage and the affirmation of domesticity were posited as the answer to the anxieties and conflicts produced by the war. Both feminists and antifeminists embraced the ideology of motherhood in order to attain their goals, and the dominant image propagated by the media was again the housewife and mother, despite wartime changes. Single women did not seem to have a place in postwar society.[30]

Guide leaders responded forcefully to what they saw as postwar conservatism by stating the case for women, yet they too felt the contradictory forces shaping women's roles in the 1920s. At the Guide International

Conference in 1920, two older married leaders spoke on Guiding's role, illustrating the paradoxical program Guiding had embraced after the war. The first spoke on women's role as mothers:

> [T]he war had opened our eyes and shown us the true value of things. It has given us insight into a new fellowship and we recognize that we are all in a sense our brothers' and sisters' keepers, and that we cannot escape from our responsibilities. Woman has the strongest influence from the cradle upwards, and if she is herself trained in these high ideals she can use her influence and knowledge for the benefit of coming generations.

The second emphasized women's other roles:

> We have no right to let a girl think that to be a good wife and mother is the sole aim of women's existence, giving her indirectly the feeling that if she doesn't marry and have a family she is a failure.[31]

As early as 1919–1920 Guiding faced the necessity of defining their organization in a way that would empower girls and women without seeming threatening to a conservative postwar society seeking to rediscover the past and reproduce the future.

❖ CREATING NEW MOTHERS: 1917–1939

Guides after World War I found themselves seeking a new mission. Their challenge in the years following the war was to continue the tradition of independence and self-sufficiency that was instituted between 1914–1918. For Guides, meetings and events provided an important outlet for women and girls to enjoy single-sex camaraderie, without the constraints of male supervision. Camps became a place where women could be totally self-sufficient, and leaders and Guides enjoyed the bonds that they built with other women in the movement. Yet survival depended on the continuation of the Guide ideal of motherhood and character training. Guiding had to retain its service ethic, or it would degenerate into just another social club. Therefore, in the postwar period, Guiding combined an older service ideal with newer forms of leisure, integrating Victorian respectability with interwar modernity.

Also implicit in the Guide scheme was a central personnel paradox: the movement depended on single women who had chosen to forego matrimony and motherhood to lead Guide units, which taught training for marriage and parenting. Although married women were welcome, Guide leaders on the local level were almost always single, until well after the Second World War. For instance, at the 1924 World Camp, there were five single Guide leaders for every married leader. Of the married leaders, many were County Commissioners or headquarters staff members.[32] The irony of the situation reflects the realities of life for women in the 1920s, when they were caught in changing social and sexual roles.

Many women expressed ambivalence toward marriage and family relationships, resenting the media's labeling of unmarried women as "superfluous," yet longing for the emotional intimacy of "modern" companionate marriage. Statistically, women did outnumber men in the young-adult age category that had been decimated by the war, so there were women destined to remain unmarried. Former Guide and interwar feminist Winifred Holtby summed up the situation for unmarried women:

> During times like the present when females are in considerable excess of males in Western Europe, popular legend evokes a picture of several million 'superfluous' women—superfluous because each cannot have a husband, and in a monogamous society, is therefore mathematically destined to remain unmarried.[33]

Enid Bagnold echoed this sentiment, writing: "I'm twenty-six . . . a girl unmarried is a puzzle to men. They don't know how to take her . . . if she is a virgin she oughtn't to be at that age; if she isn't, well. . . ."[34] As single women struggling to lead independent lives, Holtby and Bagnold both experienced the constrictive atmosphere of postwar society, with its insistence on women's primary role as wife and mother.

In addition to anxieties regarding women's proper roles, a feeling of cynicism pervaded British society in the twenties. Some writers called it weariness, others apathy, some condemned it as outright immorality. In all cases, however, the sense is that a spiritual crisis had occurred in postwar Britain, and that a change could invigorate and revitalize the nation. One place to start this transformation seemed to be the home and the family by normalizing male and female relations.

Guiding faced the challenge of the postwar world by reinterpreting "traditional" female occupations and skills, and by providing spaces for women to pursue unconventional activities. They attempted to construct what I term the "New Mother" as an alternative to the "New Woman" or "Modern Woman" of the 1920s, who consciously rejected domesticity, motherhood, and traditional feminine pursuits.[35] The "New Mother" image promoted the importance of homemaking skills, while embracing new concepts of public activity and scientific management. This program was expressed in a two-pronged approach: official badge work stressing home/mothering skills and informal activities such as camps and hikes that provided girls with the thrill of adventure.

The core of the Guide program was weekly meetings to work on merit badges and on service activities. The Guides promoted badge work as a way to make girls useful citizens, and they surrounded this serious work with games, ceremonies and drills. A sample weekly program ran something like this one from Clapton in 1926:

7:15   Opening with prayer, hymn, renewal of Promise and Law
7:25   Marching, Physical Drill, Games
8:30   Patrol Work: badge work, tests, instruction

8:50   Inspection of Patrols, Notices
9:15   Fall-In for Closing Prayers, National Anthem, Dismissal[36]

Girls worked their way up in rank in the organization through tests and activities that were well-planned in the interwar period. After a month's attendance and a few simple tests, a girl could be named a Tenderfoot and wear a trefoil badge. Second-class and first-class rank was achieved through tests on intelligence, handicraft, health, and service. To be a first-class Guide, girls needed to earn the key badges of Cook, Needlewoman, Child Nurse, and Ambulance or Sick Nurse. Beyond these key home skills, girls had to know directions, knots, compass points, first aid, and Guide history, and they had to prove they could swim fifty yards and walk two miles in less than thirty minutes.

New badges created during or directly after the war included vocational badges such as Landworker, Printer, and Poultry Farmer. Also instituted were new activity badges such as Athlete, Health, and Sportswoman. Perhaps the most influential badge of the period was the Domestic Service badge, created in 1917, as a parallel to the War Service badge. This badge, one in a series of handicraft and professional awards, sought to teach Guides usefulness in their own or in others' homes. During the war, the number of women working as domestics dropped about six percent. Although this number was not great and the number of domestics actually rose during the interwar period, middle-class employers feared a mass exodus from service among working women, who could earn more in munitions and other occupations. Service had become increasingly unpopular among working women, who often left their jobs at the first hint of factory or shop work.[37] Guides, always attuned to the problems of domestic service, both paid and unpaid, tried to answer these middle-class fears. In addition to their worries about finding domestic help, leaders also thought girls had become far too interested in frivolous entertainment outside the home, like the cinema and dancing. Serious instruction for both middle-class and working-class girls was considered necessary to ward off disaster in the homes of Britain. The Guides tried to make Domestic Service an interesting and useful occupation for the girls they were training.

The Guide ran a series of articles on the badge in 1921 in an attempt to redefine domestic service as something more than the mere drudgery most girls thought it to be. In articles entitled "The Domestic Service Badge," "How to Dust and Sweep," and "The Spirit of Home-Making," the author tells the Guides to think of the word "servant" in terms of its Latin meaning, "ministers":

> We have ministers of Religion, ministers of State, and why not ministers of the Hearth? . . . it is [hard and tedious] to the ignorant, and the bad manager, but to the intelligent girl who can organize her work well, and who takes an interest in the scientific aspect of her duties, domestic service will prove very fascinating . . .[38]

Domestic service was Taylorized[39] to fit the modern postwar home, as Guides practiced domestic skills such as sweeping, scrubbing, dusting, and polishing, while also learning to construct domestic time tables, to create table appointments, and to absorb the spirit of homemaking. As Olave Baden-Powell wrote: "It is on the women in the homes that almost everything depends."[40] This strategy paralleled educational changes for girls in the interwar period. By the 1930s, domestic subjects centers that taught cooking, cleaning, and housework had become an important part of adolescent girls' education.[41]

This redefinition of housework as civic responsibility was promoted broadly in the movement, so that the domestic service badge was very popular in the 1920s and 1930s. As one Guide who joined in 1920 recalled, the Domestic Service was the first badge she attained, and when she was a Guider, the girls always seemed to begin their badge work with Domestic Service. The success of the Domestic Service badge was particularly interesting in that it was not easy, and it was not one of the badges required for initial advancement. In a sample district in West Yorkshire, the Domestic Service badge was the one most commonly earned after the required badges. Undoubtedly, Guide leaders promoted the badge and encouraged girls to work for it, but the numbers indicate that girls themselves were interested in the badge as well. Along with the required First Class badges, Domestic Service became a core of the Guide agenda in the interwar period.[42]

Beyond the weekly badge work, Guides also participated in local service activities and emerging leisure pursuits. Guides were encouraged to perform "good turns" for neighbors in the form of concerts and tea parties at orphanages, hospitals, and other charities. Guides tended war graves and performed public service in times of need, such as wartime and during the General Strike of 1926. These service activities were interspersed with group outings, usually to dance halls, the cinema, or sporting events. In the 1930s it became more common for combined Scout/Guide or Rover/Ranger (senior sections) activities, especially for socials, dances, or hikes.

Perhaps the most popular activity, however, and the thing that truly bonded girls together was camping. One Guide, Cicely Stewart-Smith, tried to explain why camping was "perhaps the most important part of Guides":

> I don't know why it is such fun, the tents are draughty, the palliasses are horribly hard, the food is very mediocrely cooked, and there are lots of dirty jobs one has to do, and lots more one usually does—yet if I were given the choice of a week at camp or a week at a Country House party, I would choose camp. I don't know why but I would and that's that.[43]

Stewart-Smith could not quite explain the attraction, but she recognized in her description that the hardships of camping played a part in its success. Camp life was exciting because it was an escape from the safe, but mundane world of home. Sleeping in tents, digging latrines, and eating half-cooked potatoes and burnt custard constituted fun because, as Alice Linton wrote, "all our food and drink seemed ten times as good having it out in the open air." Camping meant friendship and the liberation of open spaces. Marguerite de Beaumont summed up the excitement: "It was a week of rain and sun, of new joys and new wonders, of Scouting in its real sense because we were so entirely conscious of being Scouts and pioneers on a new trail"[44] [Figure 5].

Camp was a topsy-turvy world where conventions of class, gender, and even race could be manipulated, at least for a fortnight or a weekend. Camping fulfilled the desires of youth and adults and became a site for

FIG. 5 Dorset Guides enjoy the pleasures and chores of camping, 1924. By kind permission of The Guide Association.

rule-bending within increasingly bureaucratized organizations. In the imaginations of Guides, camp could be a fairy world, an African jungle, or the American frontier. They wove intricate fantasy worlds around their camp experiences, sometimes re-enacting favorite stories, and other times creating their own narratives of adventure. Marguerite de Beaumont wrote of a camp where the tent became Never-Never Land, and its inhabitants were Peter Pan, Captain Hook, Smee, the Crocodile, Tinkerbell, and Starkie. Others remembered the camp tradition in Guiding of the "Tribe," where Guides could be given names such as Minnehaha and Hiawatha after passing a series of tests.[45]

Camping became particularly important to single young leaders who valued the companionship and validation that camp offered. The center of the camp escape was Guiding's spiritual home, Foxlease, donated as a camp and training center in 1922. The eighty-acre estate and home in the New Forest became a retreat of immense practical and symbolic importance. Groups of Guide leaders recorded their impressions in log books, calling Foxlease "our home" and "Fairyland." With its wooded paths and secluded environment, Foxlease was an imaginative and romantic spot for a retreat. Here girls, but especially adult leaders, could oversee a Guiding "Herland" where anything was possible.[46] The estate was the ultimate expression of the camp spirit in the movement.

At Foxlease, leader training camps were always creative times for adults because the leaders "all became twelve and thirteen years of age" for the duration of the camp. Accounts of these adult camps demonstrate that a carnivalesque atmosphere reigned supreme, as leaders led ambushes and secret missions. At one Foxlease training course, Guide leaders ambushed the Chief Scout and the Chief Guide in their car. In another instance:

> In the afternoon we all returned to our second childhood and became Brownies. A perfectly delightful trail, haunted by dragons and gnomes, was laid by Miss Trotter and Miss Fripp. . . . Afterwards we played a thrilling game in which Boggarts pounced out upon unwary Brownies and hauled them off to deep dark dungeons if they could not answer a question on Brownie work.[47]

Camping represented freedom from convention for leaders and for youth. Camp was a place where Guides could test the bounds of propriety, while fending for themselves and being self-sufficient. They enjoyed the freedom from parental concerns regarding femininity, and they welcomed the opportunity to participate in same-sex communities of camp. Guides often employed poetic phrases when describing camps, and in log books, interviews, autobiographies, and illustrations, it is a pervasive image. The camp functioned as a symbol of the sense of belonging and community that Guiding could provide for girls. It was "utter bliss and a complete release" and the campfire "remind(s) us how the fire binds us."[48]

This freedom from convention provided a renewal of purpose for this increasingly bureaucratized movement, but also proved problematic at times to the serious ethos of motherhood and home training. Of most concern to some in the movement were the close relationships forged among female leaders. What if camp was teaching girls too much self-sufficiency and independence? What if girls chose to forego marriage for female companionship? Was camp helping or hurting the movement?

In the 1920s, a considerable number of Guide leaders did pursue close friendships and sometimes intimate relationships with other women in the movement. Lifelong members such as Marguerite de Beaumont and Doris Mason lived and worked together, purchasing a house near Newbury in 1934, where they lived until Mason's death.[49] Although such relationships are difficult to label without being presentist, it was quite common for Guide leaders to buy homes together, vacation together, and share each others' lives, whether as companions, friends, or lovers. In addition, it isn't uncommon to read of 'crushes' and 'raves' in Guide literature, private log books, and diaries. Cicely Stewart-Smith, who later married after travelling abroad to organize Guide units, wrote a poem to a beloved older Guide leader, who died when Smith was 21. Here is a stanza from that poem:

> (From "The Beloved Days" written for Mary Herbert in January 1926)
> I came in eagerness to help you
> Cut up bread and butter in a murky parish room
> Watching as I worked with my head bent downwards
> Your dear hands moving in the dust-grey gloom
> Fearfully I thought of the many years between us
> And the risk of cheap emotion with an overwhelming dread
> And I swore mid the clatter of the earth-ware teacups
> My love should be as loyal and wholesome as the bread.[50]

Smith wrote several other poems for Mary Herbert, and she ended her log book soon after Herbert's death in August 1925. Smith's experience was not unique, as Guides throughout Britain formed long connections with each other. Two guides interviewed in 1993 were still visiting their 97-year-old Guide captain in her nursing home on a regular basis, despite the fact that they were 89 and 90 years old. Other Guide and Ranger groups from the 1920s still meet two or three times per year, and the Trefoil Guild, a Guide section for older members helps foster these lifelong connections.[51] Guide leaders did not discourage close friendships and relationships among leaders, but did warn against allowing girls to get overly involved. In a lecture to Guide leaders during a training course at Foxlease, Miss Erskine spoke plainly on the subject in 1922:

> The ages of 12-16 are the idealising ages. It is a natural thing for the child to idealise someone—a Guide captain is often an obvious person—but be very careful not to play on it. Don't appeal to their emotions too much and use very great judgment according to their nervous states.[52]

Tim Jeal, in his biography of Robert Baden-Powell, discusses some of the conflicts that arose over personal relationships among leaders in the Guide movement. His work describes the romantic friendships that developed between members of the headquarters staff, such as Helen Whitaker (Head of Publications and Kindred Societies) and Ann Kindersley (a district commissioner). Although a bit scanty on evidence, Jeal's analysis is useful and persuasive in his argument that some in the highest leadership positions not only valued the female companionship that Guiding offered but countenanced intimate relationships between Guide leaders.[53]

Generally, the same-sex camaraderie of Guiding offered a comfortable atmosphere for both girls and women to engage in unconventional activities. In a society whose sexual mores, dress codes, and marital patterns seemed to be changing, Guiding offered a haven for those girls looking for meaning in their lives and for companionship. In the interwar, girls often showed their approval of the movement by remaining members well into their 20s and 30s.

❧ CONCLUSION

Guides in the immediate postwar period got a mixed education. On the one hand, they were encouraged to learn efficient home skills that would make them into good wives and mothers, the base for the reconstructed world. However, they were also encouraged to break free from constraining female roles and to play games, to learn self-sufficiency, and to value themselves as individuals and as women, not just companions for males. This paradoxical program was the reason for Guide success from 1916 up to World War II. Guiding had created its own female space and persona apart from Scouting, but had retained enough of Scouting's adventure and excitement to attract girls to the movement. Guides sought to fulfill their own goals and desires for self-sufficiency, to be active companions to men, and yet to remain true women by being mothers. The dilemma that women faced in the interwar was that of combining marriage and career, a task that few could achieve.

Guiding sought to teach girls motherhood and to inspire them to want marriages and families, but the movement also provided an "out" for those who chose to remain single. This program meant freedom from convention and a haven from a critical world for a whole generation of girls who were coming of age after the war. Guides themselves from the 1920s and 1930s recognize this experience as life changing, calling the movement "a sort of emancipation" and a means of "fighting petticoats." As one elderly Guide remarked in an interview, "I don't know what I would have done if I hadn't been in Guiding," and another expressed the sentiment even more strongly, "Without Guiding my life would have been nothing."[54]

❧ ENDNOTES

[1] A general history covering this period in the history of women is Martin Pugh, *Women and the Women's Movement in Britain*, 1914–1959 (Basingstoke: MacMillan, 1992). For more information on birth control, see Richard A. Soloway, *Birth Control and the Population Question in England*, 1877–1930 (Chapel Hill: University of North Carolina Press, 1982). On the impact of Marie Stopes, see Ellen Holtzman, "The Pursuit of Married Love: Women's Attitudes toward Sexuality and Marriage in Great Britain, 1918–1939, *Journal of Social History*, 16 (1982), 39-51.

[2] Martha Vicinus, *Independent Women: Work and Community for Single Women*, 1850–1920 (Chicago: University of Chicago Press, 1985), 4-5.

[3] For an interesting series of articles on the intersections of motherhood and sexuality, see Claudia Nelson and Ann Sumner Holmes, eds. *Maternal Instincts: Visions of Motherhood and Sexuality in Britain*, 1875–1925 (New York: St. Martin's Press, 1997).

[4] Susan Kingsley Kent, "The Politics of Sexual Difference: World War I and the Demise of British Feminism," *Journal of British Studies* 21:3 (July 1988). Two good accounts of the postwar new feminist agitation are Brian Harrison, *Prudent Revolutionaries: Portraits of British Feminists between the Wars* (New York: Oxford University Press, 1987) and Susan Pedersen, "The Failure of Feminism in the Making of the British Welfare State," *Radical History Review* 12 (1989): 86-110.

[5] A good overview of some of the sexual anxiety of the period is Jeffrey Weeks, *Sex, Politics and Society* (London: Longmans, Green and Co., 1981). Free love advocates ranged from members of the Bloomsbury group to couples such as Bertrand and Dora Russell. On Radclyffe Hall, see Michael Baker, *Our Three Selves: The Life of Radclyffe Hall* (New York: Morrow, 1985) and Lovat Dickson, *Radclyffe Hall at the Well of Loneliness* (New York: Scribner's, 1975).

[6] Winifred Holtby, *Women and a Changing Civilisation* (New York: Longmans, Green and Company, 1936), 132.

[7] Agnes Baden-Powell, *The Handbook for Girl Guides, or How Girls Can Help Build the Empire* (London: Thomas Nelson and Sons, 1912), 22.

[8] Lisa Tickner calls both suffrage campaigns an "agitation of symbol," and Susan Kent sees this "sex war" as an attempt by women to use and manipulate the public space to their advantage. Both suffrage campaigns collapsed at the outbreak of World War I as women threw their support behind the government, and only limited suffrage (for women over 30) was passed in 1918. Full suffrage for women was not achieved until 1928. Some excellent accounts of the suffrage campaigns in Britain have been written in recent years including Susan Kingsley Kent, *Sex and Suffrage in Britain*, 1860–1914 (Princeton: Princeton University Press, 1987); Jill Liddington and Jill Norris, *One Hand Tied Behind Us* (London: Virago, 1978); Lisa Tickner, *The Spectacle of Women: Imagery of the Suffrage Campaign*, 1907–1914 (Chicago: University of Chicago Press, 1988); Vicinus, *Independent Women*, 1985.

[9] Tickner, *The Spectacle of Women*, 226.

[10] Brian Harrison, *Separate Spheres: The Opposition to Women's Suffrage in Britain* (New York: Holmes and Meier Publishers, Inc., 1978).

[11] The classic work on imperial motherhood is Anna Davin, "Imperialism and Motherhood," History Workshop Journal 5 (1978), 9-65. A recent treatment of these issues is Nelson and Holmes, eds., Maternal Instincts. For specific work on the Guides and this concept, see Allen Warren, "Mothers for the Empire," in Making Imperial Mentalities: Socialisation and British Imperialism, ed. J.A. Mangan (Manchester: Manchester University Press, 1990), 96-109.

[12] Beatrice Swaine to Rose Kerr, 2 November 1930; Rose Kerr letters, GA–London.

[13] "Girl Guide Rally," Times (London), 4 May 1914, 5B.

[14] Guide records do not show an active link between the suffrage movement and the Guide organization, although some former suffragettes did begin Guide companies in the 1920s, most notably Norah Elizabeth Balls. Other women, such as Winifred Holtby, who had been Guides in the 1910s later became feminists in the interwar period. In many cases, however, the Guide movement's diversity and decentralization allowed for a variety of political viewpoints in its leaders and members in the early years.

[15] Olave Baden-Powell as told to Mary Drewery, Window on My Heart (London: Hodder & Stockton, 1973), 113.

[16] For an article on the British women's military, see Jenny Gould, "Women's Military Services in First World War Britain," in Behind the Lines: Gender and the Two World Wars, eds. Margaret Higonnet et al. (New Haven: Yale University Press, 1987), 114-125. On wartime nursing and the Guides cooperation with the VAD movement during the war, see Anne Summers: Angels and Citizens; British Women as Military Nurses 1854–1914 (London: Routledge, 1988), 279-282. On women workers in the First World War, see Gail Braybon, Women Workers in the First World War (London and New York: Routledge, 1989); Philippa Levine, "'Walking the Streets in a Way No Decent Woman Should': Women Police in World War I," Journal of Modern History 66 (March 1994): 1-45; Angela Woollacott, On Her Their Lives Depend: Munitions Workers in the Great War (Berkeley: University of California Press, 1994). Also useful in this context is Johanna Alberti, Beyond Suffrage: Feminists in War and Peace, 1914–1928 (London: MacMillan, 1989).

[17] Rose Kerr, The Story of the Girl Guides, (London: Girl Guides Association, 1954), 119, 125, 128. The Guide Recreation Hut, staffed by Guiders, opened in April 1916 for entertaining soldiers. Later, a billiard room, letter-writing room, and other extensions were added. The Scout Hut at Etaples opened in January 1916, and was one of the last huts during the war to close in November 1919. Log Book–Scout Hut, SA–London.

[18] Unpublished magazine of Marguerite de Beaumont, The Lone Trail, LI (December/January 1921/1922): 49; GA–London.

[19] Cicely Stewart-Smith, "The Log of a Loafer in the Guides," [unpublished handwritten diary] (1923-1925); GA–London.

[20] Ray Strachey, The Cause (London: Virago, 1978), 349.

[21] Vera Brittain, Lady into Woman (New York: MacMillan, 1953), 194.

[22] Vera Brittain, Testament of Youth (USA: Wideview Books, 1980), 166.

[23] M. P., "Guiding Light," Dundee People's Friend, 17 June 1989; Report on Girl Guide Officers' Training School Pilgrimage, 8-13 April 1918; 6th Clapton [Anglican] Company Register, 1916–1920s; GA–London.

[24] Sandra Gilbert, "Soldier s Heart: Literary Men, Literary Women, and the Great War," in *Behind the Lines*, eds. Higonnet et a , 197-226; Angela Woollacott, "'Khaki Fever' and Its Control: Gender, Class, Age and Sexual Morality on the British Homefront in the First World War," *Journal of Contemporary History* 29:2 (April 1994), 325-347; Richard Voeltz, "The Antidote to 'Khaki Fever'? The Expansion of the British Girl Guides during the First World War," *Journal of Contemporary History* 27 (September 1992), 627-638.

[25] Dorothy Scannell, *Mother Knew Best: Memoir of a London Girlhood* (USA: Pantheon, 1974), 56.

[26] For two excellent studies of the question of sex and gender disorder following the war, see Higonnet et al, *Behind the Lines*; and Susan Kingsley Kent, *Making Peace: The Reconstruction of Gender in Interwar Britain* (Princeton: Princeton University Press, 1993).

[27] Robert Baden-Powell, "Girls and the National Future," (n.d., about 1917); GA–London.

[28] Girl Guides Association, *Annual Report* (London 1916), 6; Girl Guides Association, *Annual Report* (London 1919), 6.

[29] This concept is explored in John Gillis, ed., *The Militarization of the Western World* (New Brunswick: Rutgers University Press, 1989). Particularly useful on the definition and effects of militarization are the introduction by John Gillis and the chapters by Geoffrey Best and Michael Geyer.

[30] See work by Deirdre Beddoe, *Back to Home and Duty: Women between the Wars, 1918–1939* (London: Pandora, 1989), 3, 48; Susan Kingsley Kent, "Gender Reconstruction after the First World War," in *British Feminism in the Twentieth Century*, ed. Harold L. Smith (Amherst: University of Massachusetts Press, 1990), 72-73; Kent, *Making Peace*; and Mary Louise Roberts, *Civilization without Sexes: Reconstructing Gender in Postwar France 1917–1927* (Chicago/London: University of Chicago Press, 1994).

[31] Speeches on "The Ideals of the Movement" by Lady Clinton and "The Training of Guides" by Mrs. Walter Roch in the Report of the Girl Guide International Conference at St. Hugh's College, Oxford 23-28 July 1920, p. 6, 12; GA–London.

[32] Foxlease Imperial Camp Leadership Roster, 1924, GA–London. Out of the almost 300 leaders present, 239 were single and 46 were married.

[33] Holtby, *Women and a Changing Civilisation*, 131.

[34] Enid Bagnold, *Letters to Frank Harris and Other Friends* (London: William Heineman Ltd., 1980), 26.

[35] A recent article that examines the "boyish" new woman is Laura Doan, "Passing Fashions: Reading Female Masculinities in the 1920s," *Feminist Studies* 24:3 (Fall 1998): 663-700. Also useful are the essays in Nelson and Holmes, eds., *Maternal Instincts*.

[36] 6th Clapton Co. Log Books (1926-1928), entry for Tuesday, Nov. 9, 1926; GA–London.

[37] See Beddoe, *Back to Home and Duty* 61; and Carol Dyhouse, *Feminism and the Family in England 1880–1939* (Oxford/New York: Basil Blackwell, 1989),108-109.

[38] "Domestic Service Badge," *The Guide*, 24 September 1921, 365.

[39] For an interesting article on Taylorism, scientific management, efficiency, and their effects on interwar Europe, see Charles S. Maier, "Between Taylorism and Technocracy: European Ideologies and the Vision of Industrial Productivity in the 1920s," *Journal of Contemporary History* 5:2 (April 1970), 27-61.

[40] Olave Baden-Powell, *Training Girls as Guides* (London: C. Arthur Pearson, 1917), 20.

[41] Beddoe, *Back to Home and Duty*, 38-39.

[42] Interview with B. Cobb in Bushey, Hertsfordshire, 24 March 1993; Annual Reports of the Yorkshire West Riding (North) District, 1928-1938, in the possession of Sheila Marks, Ilkley.

[43] Stewart-Smith, "The Log of a Loafer . . . ," GA–London.

[44] Alice Linton, *Not Expecting Miracles* (London: Centerprise Trust Ltd., 1982), 57-58; Marguerite de Beaumont, "Log of a Wanderer in the Woodland Way," account of Madingley Camp, 22 August 1922; J38, GA–London.

[45] Marguerite de Beaumont, "Log of a Lilywhite Cadet," account of Houghton Camp, August 1920; GA–London. Win Ritchie, interview with author, Huddersfield, 5 May 1993.

[46] This is a reference to Charlotte Perkins Gilman's utopian novel, *Herland*, first published during World War I.

[47] Log of the Greenfinch Patrol, Foxlease 1922-23, account of 29 August 1922. Log of the Rook Patrol, Foxlease 1922, accounts of 6 July 1922 and 11 September 1922; GA–London.

[48] Angela Rodaway, *A London Childhood* (London: B. T. Batsford Ltd., 1960), 137; B. Cobb, interview with author, Bushey Hertsfordshire, 24 March 1993.

[49] "Miss M. de Beaumont—an appreciation," *Newbury Weekly News*, 24 August 1989; Personalities file, GA–London.

[50] Stewart-Smith, "The Log of a Loafer . . . ," GA–London. The poem is entitled "The Beloved Days" and is dated 1/1926 and inscribed to Mary Herbert, who died August 30, 1925. The logbook is dedicated to Mary, and one other poem is as well (entitled "Loss").

[51] The Trefoil Guild was created in 1943 to allow members over 21 to stay in touch, even if they could not belong to a regular unit. Vronwyn Thompson, *1910 . . . and Then? A Brief History of the Girl Guides Association* (London: Girl Guides Association, 1990), 20. The Scouts have never created an "Old Scouts" organization on the same scale as the Trefoil Guild.

[52] Lecture on "Company Management" by Miss Erskine at the Foxlease General Training Week, Nov. 22-29, 1922. Recorded in the Girl Guides Association Training Book Log of Miss Doris Mason.

[53] Tim Jeal, *The Boy-Man: The Life of Lord Baden-Powell* (New York: William Morrow, 1990), 478-485.

[54] Interview with Jeanne Holloway in London, 27 January 1993; Interview with B. Cobb in Bushey, Hertsfordshire, 24 March 1993; Interview with Muriel Brown 28 April 1998 in Cudham, 28 April 1993. The quote cited here and used as title for the paper: "In the Guides we fight petticoats anyhow, don't we?" is taken from Alice Behrens' lecture on "Rules of Health" presented at the Foxlease General Training Week, Nov. 22-29, 1922. Recorded in the Girl Guides Association Training Book Log of Miss Doris Mason.

4

CREATING A
CLEAN MANLINESS

Just as World War I led to a redefinition of Guiding, it also created the need for changes in Boy Scouting. Before the war, Scouting was one in a multitude of service and character-building associations, dedicated to nineteenth-century ideas of imperialism and nationalism. The upheaval of the war brought a transformation in the definition of Scout service and focus. The postwar Scout espoused a personal commitment to the nation that he expressed through his healthy mind and body and through his stewardship of nature and striving for peace. The postwar citizen was no longer defined by his outspoken love of empire and nation or by occupation, but by his private life, his role in the family and his cheerfulness in the face of adversity.

Even before the war was over, contemporary observers began defining the war as a violent interlude between a comfortable old world and the frightening postwar world. In A War Imagined: The First World War and English Culture, Samuel Hynes explores this cleavage that the war created in English literature and society. Hynes notes a widespread feeling of loss, betrayal, and cynicism in the 1920s, and he identifies the war as the rupture that exposed the clefts in British society.[1] As Hynes suggests, the war became a frame of reference for Europeans in the 1920s and 1930s. War rhetoric suffused peacetime language and domestic and international disputes were interpreted through the filter of the Great War. The war did not simply end in November 1918; it lived on in the memories of the men and women who had survived. Historian Jay Winter has written: "The Great War brought the search for an appropriate language of loss to the center of cultural and political life."[2] In other words, the devastating experience of war caused many in postwar Britain to search for connections with the past, for stability, and for ways to memorialize the dead. Michael Adas has shown that many Europeans felt powerless in the face of the technological destruction unleashed during the war. They faced profound questions about the wisdom of being "civilized" and "modern," and they looked elsewhere for answers.[3]

Also, issues of masculinity and femininity became highly charged in the postwar backlash of the 1920s, a backlash that answered the alarming changes in the structure and function of British society. Politically, the feeble Liberal Party consensus had dissolved as Labour began its rise to power, and the role of the state changed with the advent of wartime censorship, expanded governmental offices, and rationing of goods. Economically, the 1920s were marked by unemployment and inflation. Socially, Britain experienced labor unrest, housing shortages and an unprecedented restructuring of land ownership. Overall, the numbers of war dead had been overwhelming, and with shortages and sacrifices at home, few in Britain remained untouched by the war in Europe. After the intrusiveness of the wartime state, people had trouble readjusting to peace.[4]

The redefinition of war was highly gendered as formerly "heroic" women in munitions works, hospitals, and civilian jobs were rapidly dismissed with a curt "thank you" for their time, whereas the men of the trenches were embraced and welcomed back to their homes and jobs. Both men and women felt alienation after the war, but in vastly different ways. Men who had fought felt disoriented and marginalized, while boys and men who had stayed at home felt a yearning for proof of their patriotism and valor. Women and girls had experienced the excitement of work, usefulness, and economic independence in unprecedented numbers during the war, but after felt constrained to abandon these new freedoms for the dubious and often unattainable pleasures of home and family.[5]

The war had demonstrated for Britons the dangers of aggressive nationalism and exposed fractures in the class system. Scouting tried to synthesize conservative concerns with order and a postwar need to "look back" with a growing identification of masculinity with healthy mind and body and the ability to "look wide" beyond the differences of class, party and nation. The vehicle for this transformation of young men and Scouting was a shift in the meaning of service from defense and preparation to love and humanitarianism. Rhetorically, aggressive nationalism had given way to international pacifism.

✠ CALLED TO HIGHER SERVICE: 1914–1924

At the outbreak of war in 1914, Scout headquarters received dozens of telegrams from County Commissioners who were answering Baden-Powell's call to Scouts for coastguard duty and other civilian occupations. After years of being prepared, Scouts were eager to use their skills in service to the nation. Those Scouts who were old enough, or looked old enough, joined the Army and Navy, while the younger Scouts rushed to offer their services to local authorities. Thousands of Scouts took part in harvesting and coast guard duties, while those who had bicycles registered for service to the nation as messengers. When Scouts passed their cyclist proficiency badge, they signed a form saying they would be willing to use their bicycles in service. In the final tally, almost 25,000 Scouts served on coast guard duty, and 30,000 earned War Service badges. More than 100,000 Scouts, former Scouts, and leaders became soldiers, 10,000 of whom died in combat.[6]

Scouting, already popular in 1914, was regenerated during the war period as boys rushed to find ways in which they could go to war as well. It was not uncommon for whole patrols of Scouts to join the army together in pal battalions, a practice which devastated membership and leadership of Scout troops, not to mention villages and neighborhoods. In autobiographies, many former Scouts mention being in camp when war broke out in August 1914, and they recount how the whole troop would march to recruitment centers to enlist in the army, navy, or civilian activities, depending on their ages. Many boys evidently lied about their ages, entering service at 15 and 16 years of age.[7] Likewise, "old" Scouts and Scoutmasters knew their duty when war broke out. To cite just one example, Dr. T. S. Lukis, founder of the 1st Toynbee (Hall) Troop in London's East End, enlisted along with 80 other "Old Scouts" in August 1914. When Lukis was wounded (fatally, as it turned out) at Neuve Chapelle in March 1915, two of his former East End Scouts carried him from the battlefield. Lukis' best friend and assistant Scoutmaster, Archie Hogarth, died at Neuve Chapelle as well.[8]

The practice of Scouts joining together provided a strong psychological connection for those Scouts still at home, allowing the young boys to live vicariously through their comrades' experiences at the front. Maurice Gamon, Scoutmaster and founder of the Wellington Scout Troop in Southeast London, continued a correspondence with his Scouts and others through individual letters, a diary that he made public, and articles written for Scout publications. In a letter to a Scout dated May 1916, Gamon outlined his experiences digging trenches and sending the "Boch" back to Germany, while commenting on troop news at home. In another letter written hours before his death on July 1, 1916, Gamon instructed Scout A. W. Wyatt to be cheerful under all difficulties (even imminent death, which Gamon implies that he is awaiting). He continued, writing:

> You Scouts cannot help out here. But you can help at home. And I hope that you and the other Wellingtons will always buck up and do your best to become brave Englishmen in the days ahead, fit and ready to take the place of those who fall today. Give my love to your comrade Wolf Cub Scouts, Your faithful friend and SM [Scoutmaster] . . .

Gamon even included a German coin, again feeding the vicarious thrills the boys at home must have experienced through these dispatches from the front.[9] In many Scout diaries and accounts, they record Zeppelin raids, encounters with soldiers, and letters from Scoutmasters or other Scouts, often bemoaning their own lack of action in this crisis.

Beyond the connection with local figures, boys could read in the pages of Scout periodicals about the mounting losses of national heroes from the early movement. These leaders included HQ staff and organizers, commissioners, and founding Scoutmasters throughout Britain. Perhaps best known of these Scout heroes (even today) was Roland Philipps, arguably one of the most important Scout officials of the early period. Commissioner for East and Northeast London, organizer of early Scoutmaster conferences, and author of an important Scout book on the patrol system, Philipps was an enthusiastic and influential proponent of Scouting. Robert Baden-Powell considered Philipps his right-hand man, especially because of his links with different classes of Scouts. Philipps, the son of an earl, attended Oxford and then took up philanthropic work at University House in London's East End. He could command the support of aristocracy, middle-class clerks, and slum boys, and he had expanded the movement's scope in his brief life as no other Scout official had. Despite his stated loathing for the war and his belief that, "Scouting is more noble in its aims and more permanent in its results than soldiering," Philipps entered the war and was killed at the Somme in July 1916. Just before his death, Philipps explained to a friend and fellow scoutmaster in Manchester: "I loathed joining the Army, but, having done so, made up my mind to give my best to the work."[10] His memorial was of his own making, and it fit perfectly with his Scout philosophy. In his will he deeded a house in Stepney to the Boy Scout Association for the creation of a Scout hostel and community center in East London, later named Roland House.[11]

As news of the losses filtered through the movement, Scouts seemed invested with new purpose, but leaders privately began to question the cost in lives. As the ranks of experienced Scoutmasters thinned, leaders were forced to re-evaluate the movement and its future. Before his death, Philipps commended Arthur Gaddum on his courage in remaining out of the war and continuing the Scout cause at home. Even Baden-Powell seemed to waver in his opinion toward the war, despite his continued support for a British victory. After Philipps' death, Baden-Powell wrote to Percy Everett: "The loss of Roland Philipps will be a very heavy one to us. It is a great blow to me personally and though I nominally expected it, I always hoped that he would get badly wounded and sent home!" Before the end of the war, Baden-Powell was even urging Everett to ask for exemption from military service "for the sake of the Boy Scouts and Girl Guides. . . ."[12]

As the war drew to a close and the Scout movement completed its rolls of honor, the pressure mounted to make this organization one that could memorialize the sacrifices of earlier Scouts while attracting a whole new generation of boys. Those who were left to lead the movement in 1919 were those who had been too young, too old or otherwise unable to participate in the war effort. They were joined by a group of war veterans who had spent most of their adult lives in the trenches. With this personnel, it is little wonder that the war figured so largely in the postwar ideology of the movements.

With the Armistice of 1919, a process of commemoration, redefinition and recovery began throughout Europe. Beyond the need for physical and economic reconstruction, people sought a spiritual healing and a return to normalcy that would not dishonor the dead. Above all, men and women wanted their wartime experiences to mean something, but the war itself provided only confusion and meaningless rhetoric about that for which they had fought. People sought reassurance that the deaths, the injuries, and the deprivations had meaning for Britain's future. The First World War ushered in a new era of memorialization that emphasized individual burials of war dead in "named" graves. These hundreds of thousands of names inscribed on stones throughout France and England partially assuaged fears that the dead would be forgotten and nameless.[13]

Scouts played an important part in the 1920s' redefinition of the war through the public discourse of commemoration as the meaning of youth assumed a new cultural resonance throughout Europe. Scouts acted out fantasies of national power and recreated male camaraderie, becoming banner-bearers in the cult of the dead. In articles, speeches, and pamphlets, Baden-Powell emphasized a new spirit in the Scouts, that of peace and cooperation. The memorial to the war dead should be "a living one, a reconstructed England, a better world to live in which war should be no more." Scouts fashioned themselves into what he called a "living memorial" of those who had fallen, a visible reminder of war and peace.[14]

At the same time, youth became an ideal and a force for change in postwar Europe, no longer limited to age, as youth organizations developed around religion, politics, nationalism, and militarism. These movements all sought to capture the spirit of youth.[15] Several scholars have examined the growth of uniformed youth movements throughout Europe, and most have developed an explicit connection between this concern with youth and the promotion of moral regeneration and ultranationalism that characterized the post-World War I period.[16] Healthy young male bodies were worshiped as a symbol of national fitness and virility, whether they were clothed in Scout uniforms or in black shirts.

Caretakers of the memory of the war, Scouts made memorialization part of their sacred service to the nation, thereby redefining youth's nationalist role in Britain. Scouts remembered England's dead by planting trees, providing caretakers for war monuments, and attending memorial services in vast numbers across England. In London, the Scouts became particularly connected with commemoration events, handing out programs, ushering guests, and forming guards of honor. These events continue up to the present with Queen's Scouts still given the honor every year of forming the guard of honor for the Queen and the Royal Family in the Remembrance Sunday services held at the Cenotaph in London.

From the early twenties Scouts staged remembrance rituals, but perhaps the grandest spectacles took place in the 1930s in the London Rovers' [Senior Scouts] "Pilgrimage of Remembrance." As the London Rover Commissioner eloquently intoned in his 1934 address at the Great Hall, Westminster Palace: "Can there ever have been an occasion more pregnant with power than this—THE ROVERS OF LONDON ACCEPTING THEIR HERITAGE OF SELF-SACRIFICE AND SERVICE?" Indeed it must have been a sight to see over four thousand bare-kneed young men marching past the Cenotaph with the aging soldiers of past wars.[17] Many saw the potential good in involving young men who might not remember the war in ceremonies designed to teach them to revere the dead and to understand sacrifice. Sir Fabian Ware, founder of the Imperial War Graves Commission, asked Robert Baden-Powell in 1933 if the Scouts might be allowed to participate in a summer camp with French Scouts: "The object would be to inspire the boys, by the war memorials there and in neighbourhood, with a fuller sense of Service and Sacrifice: also with a friendship for France."[18]

Scouts sought lasting ways to memorialize their own war dead as well as England's. Individual troops created rolls of honor, trophies, monuments, and special club rooms in an attempt to bring meaning to the deaths of fellow Scouts. For example, one troop had fifty-six members who served in the war, fifteen of whom died; the Scouts wore mourning for each of the dead. Scouts recorded pertinent information on a member's life, Scout work, war service, and death in their troop log books, often inscribing the tracking symbol for "Gone Home" over their obituaries. This symbol, widely used after the war, often was coupled with the phrase "Called to Higher Service."[19]

Commemoration, however, was only one aspect of the Scouts' mission of remembrance as Scouting sought to re-create a space for men to rediscover the male comradeship of the war. As Eric Leed and other historians have noted, many soldiers felt as if they had no place to return after the war. They were disillusioned by the abrupt move from the male community of trench life to a postwar British society looking for normality.[20] The Scouts provided an outlet for ex-soldiers to fulfill their need for male companionship. Ex-soldiers became scoutmasters and swelled the ranks of the older Scout branch, the Rovers, in the 1920s. Ex-soldiers and those who had not fought could come together in an attempt to redefine their masculinity around the campfires of Britain. Not only was there a social space for male comradeship in the Scouts, by 1919 there was a physical space. Gilwell Park, a large estate just north of London, became Scouting's spiritual home and camping/training center, when it was donated by W. F. de Bois Maclaren, a Scottish District Commissioner. Gilwell Park was a sixty-acre estate with an historic house, which opened in July 1919. Leader training camps, reunions, and socials were now held for both adults and for boys.[21]

The first Camp Chief at Gilwell was Francis Gidney, a war veteran appointed in May 1919. Gidney was a popular and innovative leader, who asked Scout leaders to recapture their boyhood during training. Gidney reigned over what was described by one Scouter as "controlled lunacy" at Gilwell, allowing experimentation whenever possible. The grounds were still covered with brush and trees, and the place resembled an untamed wilderness for Scouts. Gilwell and Gidney's unconventionality were a big success with war-weary veterans and eager young Scouts, but top administrators and older officials worried that Gilwell was setting the wrong pace. Colonel Alfred Acland complained to Baden-Powell about Gilwell, calling it "unkempt" and "ramshackle." Acland also attacked Gidney, saying that he had no business sense. Although uneasy about imposing too much form on the Scout organization, Baden-Powell eventually took action, forcing out Gidney in 1923 and replacing him with a retired member of the Imperial Indian Police, J. S. "Eelge" Wilson, who imposed a more formal program. Gilwell continued to function as a popular spot for camping and training, and in just over a decade, more than 40,000 leaders had participated in some part of the training program[22] [Figure 6].

Going "Back to Gilwell" was one source of community for Scouts, but like the Guides, the Scout movement created incredibly strong same-sex communities and male spaces in camps and gatherings. Camp allowed boys and men the freedom to indulge in male activities as well as more feminine pursuits such as cooking, singing, and handicrafts. Men and boys relished the lack of conventions and responsibilities, and for veterans especially, camp was an escape to and from memories of the war. It is this male

FIG. 6 Scout leaders at Gilwell, ca. 1919. Courtesy of The Scout Association.

intimacy without the accompanying fear and anxiety that made camp appealing for veterans but also for a later generation of boys. Two symbols of this all-male community mentioned over and over again in memoirs and accounts are bathing and campfires.

Swimming and/or bathing in the nude constituted a great joy for boys and a powerful signal of male prerogative. Free from the gaze of girls and from the restrictions of home, males could romp with no consequences. One such account, told with great hilarity, demonstrates this communal— and in this case, national—experience. When a troop from Eton visited the International Jamboree in the Netherlands in 1937, they found themselves in the middle of a controversy over their nude bathing. Scout Watkin Williams explained the situation in his diary:

> Apparently we've deeply shocked the Dutch scouts by having showers without "regu-lation pattern bathing drawers," and a regulation has gone out that costumes must be worn, even at 7 a.m. All sort of rumors have followed in its wake, and it's impos-sible to know what the current ruling is.

The British Jamboree Headquarters complained that this was their practice at home, so as Williams continued:

> When we got back from Harlen last night we found that a crescent of little cypress trees had been planted round the showers, so that we can now have our morning baths in offenceless seclusion, playing Malvolio in an arbour![23]

This humorous incident is only one that cites the public bathing rituals and nude swimming that went on at camp. Scouts enjoyed these pleasures because they marked camp as a topsy-turvy, male world, where conventions were different, and the real fun seems to have been the homosocial and multigenerational atmosphere. Although Tim Jeal does cite incidences of pederasty and improper sexual behavior at Gilwell in his book,[24] I found these to be isolated incidents. In fact, many of the Scout accounts and certainly the camp films in the Scout archives point more to a general worship of the healthy male body. They are, nonetheless, uncomfortably reminiscent of the healthy glowing bodies in the Nazi propaganda film, "Triumph of the Will," also produced in the 1930s.

The ultimate bonding time at camp, however, was the evening campfire, a sensual experience that evoked individual and communal feelings of belonging and pleasure. There is still a permanent Campfire Circle at Gilwell, which is the attraction of summer camps, training sessions, and yearly reunions held there. In the film version of the 1936 Scout extravaganza known as the Gang Show, one of the most moving scenes is a giant campfire singsong with Scouts packed in a circle swaying and singing. In fact, no national or international gathering was complete without a large campfire and many small ones in the individual camps. The campfire figures largely in the Rudyard Kipling verse adopted as the Scout (and Guide) alternative motto in the interwar years:

> Who hath smelt the woodsmoke at twilight? Who hath heard the birch-log burning?
> Who is quick to read the noises of the night?
> Let him follow with the others, for the young men's feet are turning
> To the camps of proved desire and known delight![25]

This verse captures the essence of Scout campfires and indeed the whole camping experience: desire and delight.

"A SENSE OF HUMAN BROTHERHOOD"

Beyond commemoration and male community, one further role of the interwar Scout was the ability to transcend petty differences of class, religion, and nation. Scouts were urged to be nonpolitical, humanistic and peaceful, and they were asked to rise above particular party politics. After the war, Scouting tried to portray itself as a multiclass and international brotherhood. In the late 1920s, a public debate arose that helped the Scouts define their "nonpolitical" stance and to articulate their rejection of traditional class politics. Perhaps the most visible event in this debate over the Scouts' international aspirations was the World Jamboree held in 1929 at Arrowe Park in Birkenhead, near Liverpool.

This celebration of the twenty-first birthday of Scouting was a two-week long Coming-of-Age World Jamboree, so-named because it coincided with the anniversary of the founding of Scouting in 1908. This literal and symbolic growth to maturity for the movement was an event that brought together thirty thousand Scouts from more than forty foreign countries and thirty-three British colonies. Organized as a self-sufficient camp with a post office, bank, shop, and tents, the jamboree even had its own newspaper, the *Daily Arrowe*, which was sold throughout camp for a penny. It was a grand undertaking to provide food, latrines, sleeping areas, and refuse disposal for so many young men, so that the camp resembled a small city when it was completed in late July. As the *Daily Mirror* recorded, "The 'self-contained' unit theory has been developed so thoroughly that there will be no need for any scout to go outside the boundaries of the camp for anything he needs."[26]

All was not rosy at the Jamboree, however, as the Scout promise to "smile and whistle under all difficulties" was tested by the weather. Torrential rains throughout much of the jamboree turned the grounds into a mud bath, prompting some to call the gathering a "mudboree." Despite the rain and the mud, curious onlookers flocked to the camp, especially on the August Bank Holiday, when an estimated 56,000 visitors entered the camp. Total attendance excluding uniformed Scouts and Girl Guides well exceeded 300,000 people, making the jamboree a huge emotional and financial success for the organization. The Scouts themselves seemed a little confused at the crowds, as the *Yorkshire Post* reported on August 6: "It has intrigued the Scouts all day that they were a spectacle at which people had come to gaze."[27]

Indeed the jamboree had become a national spectacle, with advertisements, news articles, and radio broadcasts of the speeches. The press followed the Jamboree closely, from the opening March Past of Nations for the Duke of Connaught to the Prince of Wales' recitation of King George V's welcome message. The Prince, who spent a night under canvas with the Scouts, read the King's message of congratulations on August 2 and informed the crowd of Founder Robert Baden-Powell's promotion to a peerage. Baden-Powell and his family were in attendance, and one of the highlights of the Jamboree was the presentation of "birthday" presents to the Founder. To his delight, Baden-Powell received a portrait of himself, a Rolls Royce and a caravan (camper), purchased with penny donations from Scouts around the world. As a special gift of the Scouts from the Irish Free State, he also received the pair of braces (suspenders) that he had requested.[28]

The official program of the jamboree included daily displays of Scout skills, rallies, receptions, and religious services, but the real attractions were the informal activities. The most popular pastime seemed to have been "swapping" as Scouts and visitors traded pieces of their uniforms, national memorabilia, addresses, postcards, and food. Language did not seem to be a barrier as boys spoke in what Scout leaders called "Jamborese," a mixture of hand signals, facial expressions, and swapping of items. The jamboree functioned as an international marketplace with groups of Scouts from Brazil making and selling coffee to visitors, French Scouts distributing chipped potatoes, and Americans hawking postcards. Girl Guides staffed food booths, infirmaries, and creches to help their male counterparts manage the crowds of visitors. Many international Scouts wore national costumes, displayed flags, and brought souvenirs of home to distribute, making the parades and rallies spectacular events for visitors.[29]

The movement had also branched out into the empire and into other countries of the world, making a significant impact in the United States, Chile, France, Poland, India, and Australia, to name a few. With all of the activity and growth of the post-World War I era, British Scout officials saw the need for an organized global association that would allow collaboration between national Scout organizations, while fostering a spirit of cooperation and education between boys. In truth, British leaders worried that unless a British-led coalition existed the movement could stray from the intentions and mission of the founder.

To inaugurate the international association that British leaders had in mind, an official international gathering was held in England at Olympia in 1920. At this gathering of Scouts, international leaders voted to create the Boy Scout International Bureau (headquartered in London) and to name Baden-Powell World Chief Scout. Later, it became policy to have international meetings every four years and to call them jamborees after the name given to the first Olympia meeting in 1920 by the Chief Scout.[30] These jamborees, although ostensibly a gathering of Scouts, became public spectacles over time. They were useful propaganda devices and recruitment tools, but they also provided legitimation for the Scout movement. I would argue that their greatest purpose in the 1920s and 1930s was as powerful cultural tools for the imagination of empire and of nation. The sight of 30,000 boys from nations around the world allowed spectators a vicarious peek at the empire and at foreign lands while simultaneously rearticulating and defining what was unarguably English.

The 1929 Coming-of-Age Jamboree served as a perfect opportunity for the Scout movement and the British nation to showcase their postwar ambitions. Throughout the two-week jamboree, the media highlighted the Scout world, which contained much of what Britain hoped to be in the late 1920s. As nationalist movements in the Empire and economic problems at home led Britons to question imperial power, the Jamboree showed a practical Commonwealth. Echoing the rhetoric of the international pacifism, the Scouts pictured themselves as leading the way to an international reduction of fear and hatred or as a "living Junior League of Nations."[31] The general celebration of the 1929 Scout jamboree in the British media focused on particular aspects of the gathering. These aspects reflected long-standing imperial and national sentiments, but also encompassed a growing pacifist ideal and internationalism in the wake of World War I. A close look at the media coverage of the jamboree uncovers the cultural ideas being both shaped and reflected by this spectacle of youth.

In many ways, the Jamboree functioned as an old-style imperial pageant, complete with royal splendor and the parade of imperial subjects. The first few days of the event highlighted appearances by the Duke of Connaught and the Prince of Wales, who even spent a night under canvas and wore Scout uniform. The jamboree looked like an imperial exhibition reminiscent of the British Empire Exhibition at Wembley in 1924 (in which the Scouts participated), with bands, displays, and pageantry. As David Cannadine has demonstrated, these pageants of British power reflected a need to emphasize Britain's continuing power and stability in the midst of the erosion of those powers.[32] The jamboree presented a whole empire and indeed a whole world brought together by British diplomacy and goodwill, reflecting a new discourse on empire that was emerging in the 1920s. Britons were encouraged to view the empire not so much as a sign of national power, but as a vast market held together with cooperation and mutuality rather than exploitation and aggression. To this end, the government funded the Empire Marketing Board to educate the British regarding imperial products, and Parliament also passed acts allowing for assisted migration to the dominions.[33] The Scout Jamboree was a visible sign that this kind of international cooperation could work. Baden-Powell explicitly tied the Scouts into this project of rearticulating the imperial project in his May 1929 Empire Day column for the *Scouter* magazine: "A tie which is greater than treaties is the spirit of goodwill. This we fortunately have in our Empire, and it is up to everyone of us Scouters at home and overseas to see that it is kept up and developed in the coming generations."[34]

Amidst the public idealism and approbation of the Scout jamboree were the less-promising realities of both Britain's and Scouting's international aspirations. Although Scouts had voted in 1924 at Copenhagen that they would allow "no discrimination as to admission to membership of fellow subjects or citizens for any reason of race, creed or politics," they were still admitting to a "thorny problem of 'minority' Scouts" in 1928.[35] The Scouts promised openness yet excluded non-Europeans in countries where racial tension existed. Especially problematic were British imperial holdings with significant white populations such as Rhodesia, Kenya, and South Africa. South Africa witnessed a particularly long battle for the inclusion of non-white boys into the Scout movement, setting off an international controversy over Scouting's real international goals. As the Chairman of the Indian Boy Scouts Association in South Africa wrote to Baden-Powell two weeks after the conclusion of the 1929 jamboree:

> As we understand it the whole purpose of the Scout movement is to inculcate the spirit of service to humanity and to develop the sense of human brotherhood . . . By

its decision the Transvaal Scout Association has gone back on these objects and has told Indian boys that the Scout Movement is not for them; that to the Scouts humanity means white humanity only; that brotherhood means the brotherhood of whites only; and that the privileges of the Scout Movement are restricted to the needs of white boys. We believe such an attitude is a complete misrepresentation of Scout ideals.[36]

His accusations focused not only on Scouting's inability to create a multiracial movement within South Africa but its contradictory policy in allowing so-called "coloured" Scouts from some countries to attend the jamboree while South Africans were excluded. His questioning of Baden-Powell exposed the biggest problem with the Scout project of international cooperation: did a "sense of human brotherhood" mean only white brotherhood with a few token exceptions?

The British government was also facing the difficult task of reconciling its public rhetoric regarding cooperation and the growth of a voluntary Commonwealth with its continued imperial control abroad and its racially exclusive policies at home. The growth of nationalist movements in imperial countries led to explicit calls for self-governance and economic change. The late 1920s and early 1930s were a time of civil disobedience campaigns in India, continued violence and unrest in Palestine, and eroding British local authority in many of its colonies. As the interwar progressed, the development of a Commonwealth seemed like a survival strategy for Britain's markets as much as a move toward international peace. At home, riots characterized as "race" incidents took place following the war in northern English cities such as Liverpool, and the government passed discriminatory legislation aimed at black British seamen in the metropolis. As Laura Tabili has shown in her examination of this legislation, the British government's racist laws could have been an attempt to perpetuate divisions between Britons and their imperial subjects in a society and an economy that was rapidly changing.[37] Whatever the motivations, it is clear that the interwar period in Britain witnessed the simultaneous rearticulation of empire as a goodwill enterprise and the perpetuation of older notions of British imperial privilege.

Another important part of the jamboree in British consciousness was as commemoration and reimagination of war. The years 1928 and 1929 saw the beginning of a new generation of war memoirs, novels, poetry, and plays as men began to try to make sense of the experience. In 1928 alone, one of the most famous of the World War I plays, *Journey's End*, was first performed, and memoirs and novels by Siegfried Sassoon, Edmund Blunden, and Max Plowman appeared.[38] In addition, the jamboree dates coincided with an important meeting of European leaders at the Hague, where World War I reparations payments were being renegotiated. The media was quick to point out that the gathering of males at Arrowe Park was quite different from those who had gathered at the Somme, and few missed the odd coincidence of the jamboree occurring while an older generation of European males met at the Hague to discuss the long-term results of the war.[39] As the St. James Messenger wrote: "The nations then united in war; at the Jamboree the men of the future, of every nation, kindred and tongue, clasped hands unitedly for peace." The Yorkshire Post picked up the refrain as well: "On the 15th anniversary of our entry into the war, the boys of Germany and France, Belgium and Austria, and two-score nations as well, gathered together here this morning. . . ." In some of the most touching coverage of the jamboree, the Times special correspondent recorded incidents of British ex-soldiers bringing wallets to the German scout camp. They had taken these mementoes off of dead soldiers a decade earlier and wanted to return them, full of photos, letters, and identification papers.[40]

This celebration of a gathering of males for peace rather than war is ironic given the events about to be set in motion, including the onset of world depression and the rise of nationalist aggression in Europe. Beyond a mere reflection on the ironies of history, the jamboree spectacle also reflected the power of nationalism, giving lie both to the stated internationalist and pacifist aspirations of the events. The variety of flags, uniforms, and languages illustrated an exotic and unusual sight of global youth for every Scout and visitor, but the "international brotherhood" was also institutionalized in a nationalist spectacle called the March Past of Nations. Each contingent carried flags and wore national costumes or uniforms and marched in military style past the grandstand, saluting for inspection. Camps were placed according to countries, and Scouts visited each other in national and regional contingents. At each public event, the national march-past occurred. In a description of the first of these national displays, the Times noted "an all-embracing solemnity" to the 45-minute procession, pointing out special cheers for the first "coloured" boys from Sierra Leone. Attempting to explain this mix of nationalism and internationalism for its readers, the Times reported:

> These parades . . . never lose their force in their emotional appeal. National pride, rightly enough, is symbolized as flag after flag, held high, passes around the arena and is dipped at the saluting base, but insistence of nationality begins and ends there. There is no challenge in the gesture, and the spirit of brotherhood suffers no violence.[41]

Scouts themselves were asked to reconcile the varying goals of the organization in their activities and ideals. In a resolution passed at the international conference in Copenhagen in 1924, Scout leaders described their goals:

> It is national in that it aims, through national organisations, at endowing every nation with useful and healthy citizens. It is international in that it recognises no national barrier in the comradeship of the Scouts. It is universal in that it insists upon universal fraternity between all Scouts of every nation, class or creed.[42]

Despite the rhetoric supporting the high-minded mix of internationalism and nationalism, Scouting reality did not always reflect the ideals it was promoting. Nations were excluded from participating if their politics did not match those of the Scouts (Germany and Italy were excluded in 1933), working-class attendance at jamborees was limited by monetary consider- ations, and many countries had erected racial and religious boundaries to full membership in the organization. Beyond these concrete realities of Scouting, the marching and saluting of the national contingents reflected a continued militarization and patriotic nationalism in society, and it mir- rored the youth spectacles and nationalist demonstrations that became common in the interwar. Young male bodies were a joyful sight to nations recovering from the physical and spiritual destruction of war, but massed in uniform, these youth symbolized the armies at the ready for any renewed conflict. Many scholars have written about the power of mass display, and in the case of the jamboree, what appeared in these gatherings was as much an aggressive nationalism as it was a benign internationalism.[43]

The last thing that the jamboree highlighted was the Scouts' stated goal of creating a classless society to complete its project of a combined "human brotherhood."[44] By holding the jamboree in the north of England and publicizing its schemes earlier in the year to help "distressed mining areas," Scouting was claiming a role as an organization of "everyman." Although it is true that Scouts were a multiclass organization in Britain by 1929,[45] few denied the bourgeois aspirations of the movement's law and activities, which called for loyalty to employers, God, and the king.

In fact, the events at the Jamboree served as an indication of Scouting's reputation for obedience to authority and national loyalty. On August 3, the newspapers were full of reports that four men were arrested by Scouts at the Jamboree for handing out literature "likely to cause dissatisfaction and discontent among His Majesty's subjects." The four men, all aged 23-28, were members of the Young Communist League (YCL) who had been attempting to expose the imperialist and militarist motives of Scouting by handing out literature exposing Baden-Powell and the Scouts. The news- papers, already avidly following the Jamboree with daily articles and photo spreads, pounced on this newest opportunity to display the honorable intentions of the Scouts in the face of antinational activities. Indeed, the arrest of the agitators made it possible for the newspapers to emphasize the cross-class culture of the Scouts once again, while pointing out Scouting's ability to attract the right kind of boys.[46]

The YCL's objections regarding imperialism were not unfounded consid- ering that in 1929 working-class lads were being trained at Scout farms for migration programs to the Dominions, where they would serve as little more than indentured servants. The Scouts had begun participating in migration schemes with an organized program in 1923, and in 1927 made sure that each Scout Troop had a "special migration card" describing the details of the program. At the Jamboree itself, factory owner T. H. Whitehead had made a public gift of £5000 to be used for migration of Scouts. Between 1923-1939, about 5000 Scouts migrated to the colonies and dominions.[47]

As to the charge of militarism, at the opening ceremonies, Scout service in the war had been mentioned as the numbers of those who had served and those who had won Victoria Crosses were read to the crowds. In fact, since its inception, Scouting had faced charges of militarism, and they were never able to silence critics entirely.[48] Antagonism from the YCL in particular arose after the General Strike of 1926 and earlier rail strikes of the 1920s, when Scouts engaged in strikebreaking activities. In addition, Scouting's success in attracting working-class members in the 1920s angered the YCL, who persisted in trying to point out Baden-Powell's support for the government status quo and disregard for workers and working-class politics. However, they lacked the numbers or the clout to get their point across. In a small victory, the YCL did manage through their arrests to demonstrate the spurious nature of the peaceful human brotherhood on display. In a description of the hearing at the County Police Court, the *Birkenhead Advertiser* recorded this exchange:

> Harry Wilson (Blackburn Scout): If it had not been for our intervention, I am sure the defendant's |sic| would not have been here today.
>
> William Rust (YCL): Do you mean to say that hundreds and thousands of Scouts would have lynched four men harmlessly distributing leaflets?
>
> Wilson: The coloured Scouts did not know who you were.[49]

This incident revealed the cracks and problems that remained in any concept of human brotherhood in Scouting, and it pointed to some of the difficulties that Britons faced in changing their notions of class, empire, and race in the interwar period.

The 1929 Coming-of-Age Jamboree was an extravaganza that allowed Scouting to assess and celebrate its progress in the interwar period. The Scouts put their handiwork on display, showing Britain how far they had come in making their brotherhood a reality in the twenty-one years since their founding. Reflecting a general move toward a stated internationalism, Scouting and also Britain itself retained a deeply entrenched sense of nationalism, imperial apologia, and class feeling. Although a minor incident in the overall history of the twentieth century, the Boy Scout jamboree provides one example of the need for scholars to re-examine how imperial imaginings defined metropolitan society and politics, reflecting a changing notion of British identity and imperial strength while reinforcing an earlier imperial paradigm of Britain as a cultural leader, bringing "civilization" and Pax Britannia to the world's youth.[50]

🏵 CONCLUSION

The Scouts inherited a memory of the war that was different from the Guides and from the rest of England. War symbolized the power of service, and Scouts experienced the benefits of honorable service through the memorial competitions, the public services and functions in which they participated, and fictional plays and books that valorized soldiering. Although Scouting shifted to a more peaceful ethos after the war, war still signified the ultimate service and sacrifice for nation that any Scout could make. The nation called for the blood of young men, and the Scouts were willing to provide it. In fact, London Rovers literally provided their blood to the nation in 1924, when they adopted blood transfusion as one of their main services. By 1934, more than one-third of all Red Cross blood donors were Rovers.[51] Ultimately, the Scout postwar heritage was bravery, sacrifice, remembrance, and community.

This memory of the war shadowed the Scout movement throughout the 1920s and 1930s. The interwar emphasis on "healthy" lives and outlooks was an attempt to recast national service as a personal event—an individual pledge. The Scout pledge of good deeds and service impressed upon children who joined that each person's actions could affect the nation as a whole. As Rovers pledged in 1926: "Our unity is not to be found in social functions but in our solemn pledge of Service—recreation has its very important place in our scheme, it has a great value, but it is not our object. . . ."[52] In the postwar period, Scouting shifted from an emphasis on defense of Britain to service for Britain. This shift enabled Scouts to pursue a more peaceful program in the interwar years, including international gatherings, cooperation with peaceful endeavors such as League of Nations committees, and mass leisure pursuits. Although troops might still play capture the flag and war games, they also participated in new activities like whist drives, dances, and gymnastic exercise. Badge changes after the war de-emphasized badges with military overtones such as marksman and bugler, instead introducing badges such as artist (1917), athlete (1920), and bird warden (1922), to name a few. The Scouts sought to create models of masculinity who understood their duty as servants to the nation, who could defend their country, but who also knew how to succeed in peaceful times.

Perhaps the most important of badges introduced following World War I was the Healthy Man (1918). Those Scouts who aspired to earn this badge worked on a four-part program. They could: (a) recite the importance of keeping the bodies functioning in a healthy way; (b) provide evidence that they had observed rules regarding cleanliness, sleeping, breathing, and exercise for at least 12 months; (c) explain the dangers of alcohol, tobacco, and unclean thoughts; (d) train others in exercise and explain its importance. In short, the badge promoted a "clean" manliness, both in body and spirit, and it encompassed the main message of inter-war Scouting.

Young Scouts became the New Men of reconstructed Britain, healthy and conscientious. Scouts often made nuisances of themselves by starting fires in private fields, tramping through fields during lambing, and creating a ruckus in public places, yet all seemed to be forgiven in the general cele-bration of youth. Into the cynicism of the postwar world came Boy Scout Jamborees where German, French, Indian, Australian, American, British, Malaysian, and many other nationalities met to create peace and under-standing. Like Guiding, Scouting was seen as a safe, worthwhile game for boys to play.

❖ ENDNOTES

[1] Samuel Hynes, A War Imagined: The First World War and English Culture (New York: Athenaeum, 1990).

[2] Jay Winter, Sites of Memory, Sites of Mourning: The European War in European Cultural History (Cambridge: Cambridge University Press, 1995), 5.

[3] Michael Adas, Machines as the Measures of Men (Ithaca/London: Cornell University Press, 1989), 365-369. Also see the discussion of "cult of the fallen soldier" in George Mosse, Fallen Soldiers: Reshaping the Memory of the World Wars (New York/Oxford: Oxford University Press, 1990), 7; and Robert Wohl, The Generation of 1914 (Cambridge: Harvard University Press, 1979), 121.

[4] For an interesting discussion of the multitude of ways in which the Great War endured in British society, see Paul Fussell, The Great War and Modern Memory (London: Oxford University Press, 1975), 315-317. For a dated but sound general overview of wartime Britain, see: A. J. P. Taylor, English History, 1914-1945 (New York: Oxford University Press, 1965). Other worthwhile studies of the period include: Noreen Branson, Britain in the Nineteen Twenties (London: Weidenfield and Nicholson, 1975); Modris Eksteins, Rites of Spring: The Great War and the Birth of the Modern Age (New York: Doubleday, 1989); Eric Leed, No Man's Land: Combat and Identity in World War I (Cambridge: Cambridge University Press, 1979); Susan Kingsley Kent, Making Peace: The Reconstruction of Gender in Postwar Britain (Princeton: Princeton University Press, 1993); and J. M. Winter, The Great War and the British People (London: MacMillan, 1985).

[5] For population figures that show the gap between men and women of marriageable age, see Statistical Abstract for the United Kingdom: No. 72 (1913-1927), (London, 1929), 10. For studies using literature to explore the effects of the war on men and women see Margaret Higonnet et al., eds., Behind the Lines: Gender and the Two World Wars (New Haven/London: Yale University Press, 1987); Leed, No Man's Land; Elaine Showalter, The Female Malady: Women, Madness, and English Culture (New York: Pantheon, 1985).

[6] Boy Scout Association, 11th Annual Report (London 1919), 15-17, SA–London. For a dis-cussion of "war fever" as propounded by prewar boys' magazines, see Robert MacDonald "Reproducing the Middle-Class Boy: From Purity to Patriotism in the Boys' Magazines, 1892–1914," Journal of Contemporary History, 24:3 (July 1989), 535.

[7] William Cotton, I Did It My Way: The Life Story of Billy Cotton (London: Harrap,1970), 24-28; William Holt, I Haven't Unpacked: An Autobiography (London: George Harrap and Co., 1939), 53-54.

[8] "The Passing of Dr. Lukis," Headquarters Gazette, 9:4 (April 1915), 95; Isabel Hogarth to Mr. Perrin, 4 April 1949, TC/93, SA–London.

[9] A. W. Wyatt letters (1916), Imperial War Museum, Dept. of Documents, 87/83/1.

[10] Typescript of Stanley Ince's Wireless Address, 7 July 1927. TC/168, SA–London; Roland Philipps to Arthur Gaddum, 13 February 1915. TC/248, SA–London. For more information on the role of university-educated, young male reformers such as Philipps and Lukis in the East End, see J. A. R. Pimlott, Toynbee Hall: Fifty Years of Social Progress, 1884–1934 (London: J. M. Dent and Sons, Ltd., 1935).

[11] "Captain the Hon. Roland E. Philipps," Headquarters Gazette, 10:8 (August 1916), 203. Roland House functioned as an East London Center until 1982, when restoration costs forced the Scout Association to sell the building. Interview with Peter Kimpton and Anthony Bolton, Tower Hamlets Scout Center, 25 March 1993.

[12] Roland Philipps to Arthur Gaddum, 13 February 1915, TC/248, SA-London; Robert Baden-Powell to Percy Everett, 16 July 1916 and 12 April 1918, Everett papers, SA–London.

[13] Thomas W. Laqueur, "Memory and Naming in the Great War," in Commemorations: The Politics of National Identity, ed. John R. Gillis (Princeton: Princeton University Press, 1994), 152-153. See also K. S. Inglis, "The Homecoming: The War Memorial Movement in Cambridge, England," Journal of Contemporary History, 27:4 (October 1992), 583-605; and Winter, Sites of Memory, Sites of Mourning, 78-116.

[14] Robert Baden-Powell HQ Memo, 1918. TC/38, SA–London. "What the Cenotaph asks for," St. Martin's Review (November 1925), TC/95, SA–London.

[15] Wohl, The Generation of 1914, 229; George Mosse, Nationalism and Sexuality: Middle-class Morality and Sexual Norms in Modern Europe (Madison: University of Wisconsin Press, 1985), 125-126. See the work on youth movements in France by Sian Reynolds, France Between the Wars: Gender and Politics (London/New York: Routledge, 1996), and Susan Whitney, "The Politics of Youth: Communists and Catholics in Interwar France," Ph.D. diss, Rutgers University, 1994. For work on the Communist Youth International, see Richard Cornell, "The Origins and Development of the Communist Youth International 1914-1924," Ph.D. diss., Columbia University, 1965.

[16] See, for example, Eksteins, Rites of Spring, 241-274; J. A. Mangan, ed., Shaping the Superman: Fascist Body as Political Icon (London/Portland, OR: Frank Cass, 1999); Mosse, Nationalism and Sexuality; and Detlev Peukert, Inside Nazi Germany: Conformity, Opposition, and Racism in Everyday Life (New Haven: Yale University Press, 1987), 145-183.

[17] Souvenir program from the London Rovers Pilgrimage of Remembrance, November 1934. TC/214, SA-London. Scouts first took up duties at the London Cenotaph in 1922 by distributing programs to the public. In 1927, King's Scouts first formed the Royal Guard of Honor; 1930 marked the first organized London Rovers Parade at the Cenotaph, with a record 4,000 in attendance. "For Rover Scouts," The Scouter, 24:12 (December 1930), 488; Remembrance Sunday card, SA–London.

[18] Robert Baden-Powell Memo to Percy Everett, Lord Hampton, and Hubert Martin, 29 November 1933. TC/43, SA–London.

[19] Log Books of the Mayfield & Clifton Troop, 2 vols. (1909–1919, 1919–1945). TC/267, SA–London. "Called to Higher Service" lists first appear in November 1914 in *The Headquarters Gazette*, the Scouts' official magazine. The phrase is attributed to that magazine's editor and Scout pioneer, H. Geoffrey Elwes. The symbol for "Gone Home," a circle with a large dot in the middle, was queried by a Scout in a letter to the editor in 1915. The editor wrote that the sign was possibly derived from an Old Irish symbol for "this is a safe home for you" that may have been used at the end of letters. In any case, the sign was widely recognized to mean death in the Scout movement by the time of this notice in *Headquarters Gazette*, 9:4 (April 1915), 89.

[20] See especially Leed, *No Man's Land*, and Joanna Bourke, *Dismembering the Male: Men's Bodies, Britain and the Great War* (London: Reaktion Books, 1996).

[21] SA, *Annual Report 1919*, 9-10; Jack Cox, "Back to Gilwell, Happy Land," *Scouting* (1977), 640-643.

[22] Robert Baden-Powell to J. S. Wilson, 29 October 1923; J. S. Wilson, "1933 Report on Training," 2, TC/269, SA–London.

[23] Watkin Williams, "Diary of a Dutch Jamboree 1937," TC/243, SA–London.

[24] The two most notorious incidents of pederasty cited by Jeal involved two successive "doctors" at Gilwell, Robert Patterson (who wasn't even a medical doctor) and H. D. Byrne. Together, the men spent almost twenty years at Gilwell. For information, see Tim Jeal, *The Boy-Man: The Life of Lord Baden-Powell* (New York: William Morrow, 1990), 509-510.

[25] Inscribed on much of the Scout and Guide memorabilia of the interwar period. Quoted in Marguerite de Beaumont, *The Wolf That Never Sleeps: A Story of Baden-Powell* (London: Girl Guides Association,1944; reprinted 1984), 59. The verse comes from "The Feet of Young Men," according to Hugh Brogan, *Mowgli's Sons: Kipling and Baden-Powell's Scouts* (London: Jonathan Cape, 1987), 36.

[26] "The World Jamboree of Boy Scouts 1929," reprinted from the *Times* July 31-August 7, 1929, 5-6; "50,000 in Camp of Nations," *Daily Mirror* 22 July 1929, TC/259, SA–London. Scout Association, *Annual Report* (London: Scout Association, 1930), 21.

[27] "The World Jamboree . . ." *Times*, 7–11, 20, 38-40; "Lighter Side of the Jamboree," *Yorkshire Post* 6 August 1929, TC/259, SA–London.

[28] "The World Jamboree . . ." *Times*, 7; "The Future of the World Depends on You," *Daily Express* 3 August 1929, TC/259, SA–London; "Last Day of the Jamboree," *Times* 13 August 1929.

[29] "Lighter Side of the Jamboree," *Yorkshire Post* 6 August 1929, TC/259, SA–London; Eileen K. Wade, *Twenty-Seven Years with Baden-Powell* (London: Blandford Press, 1957), 121. On jamborese, see J. S. Wilson, *Scouting Round the World* (London: Blandford Press, 1959), 11.

[30] Scout Association, *Annual Report* (London: Scout Association, 1928), 7; The History and Organisation of World Scouting (London: BSA, n.d.), 2-3; *Resolutions* [passed by Boy Scout International Conference 1922-1955] (London: BSA, 1956), 6-7.

[31] The phrase "living Junior League of Nations" comes from a published report. Robert Baden-Powell and Olave Baden-Powell, *Report on the Boy Scouts and Girl Guides in South Africa* (London: Boy Scouts Association, 1927), 9.

[32] See Eric Hobsbawm and Terence Ranger, eds., *The Invention of Tradition* (Cambridge: Cambridge University Press, 1983), esp. the article by David Cannadine, "The Context,

Performance and Meaning of Ritual: The British Monarchy and the Invention of Tradition, c. 1820–1977," 101-164.

[33] On the Empire Marketing Board, which functioned as a governmental department from 1926-1933, see Stephen Constantine, *Buy and Build: The Advertising Posters of the Empire Marketing Board* (London: HMSO, 1986). For a good view of the politics and realities of the Empire Settlement Act and interwar migration, see Stephen Constantine, ed., *Emigrants and Empire: British Settlement in the Dominions between the Wars* (Manchester: Manchester University Press, 1990). See also Alex G. Scholes, *Education for Empire Settlement: A Study of Juvenile Migration* (London/New York: Longman, Green & Co., 1932) and Gillian Wagner, *Children of the Empire* (London: Weidenfeld and Nicolson, 1982).

[34] Robert Baden-Powell, "B.P.'s Outlook - Empire Day," *Scouter*, 23:5 (May 1929), 162.

[35] *Resolutions*, 7; *Annual Report 1928*, 8-9.

[36] Chairman, Indian Boy Scouts Association to Robert Baden-Powell, 29 August 1929; Yale South African Institute of Race Relations records, AD843/RJ/Pp1.2.

[37] Laura Tabili, "The Construction of Racial Difference in Twentieth-Century Britain: The Special Restriction (Coloured Alien Seamen) Order, 1925," *Journal of British Studies* 33 (January 1994), 54-98. See also Paul Rich, *Race and Empire in British Politics* (Cambridge: Cambridge University Press, 1986).

[38] Fussell, *The Great War and Modern Memory*, 109.

[39] For a description of the Hague Conference of August 1929, see Charles Mowat, *Britain Between the Wars, 1918–1940* (Chicago: Chicago University Press, 1955), 374.

[40] Clipping from St. James Messenger pasted in William Macadie, "Hiking Through the Past," MS, 62 pp. Spring 1981, TC/316, SA–London. "Scouts Bond of Brotherhood," *Yorkshire Post* 5 August 1929, 10; "Last Day of Jamboree," *Times* 13 August 1929.

[41] "Scouts of the World," *Times* 1 August 1929, 14; "Chief Scout Honored," *Times* 2 August 1929, 12.

[42] *Resolutions*, 7.

[43] See the work by George Mosse and Detlev Peukert on Nazi spectacle, Victoria de Grazia on Italian fascist organizations, and Michael Geyer on the militarization of interwar society. Also useful here are theoretical works by the Frankfurt School, especially essays by Walter Benjamin, Theodore Adorno, and Siegfried Kracauer.

[44] The goal of creating a spectacle of brotherhood that would bring together Scouts from around the world continues to have resonance as regional and national Jamborees are held yearly across the globe and in 1999, the international jamboree was held in Chile.

[45] Tammy Proctor, "(Uni)Forming Youth: Girl Guides and Boy Scouts in Britain, 1908–1939," *History Workshop Journal* 45 (Spring 1998), 103-134.

[46] "Jamboree Arrests," *Daily Mail* 3 August 1929, TC/247, SA–London; "Four Arrests at Jamboree," *Liverpool Daily Courier* 3 August 1929, 4; "Boy Scouts Arrest Communists," *Yorkshire Post* 3 August 1929, 12.

[47] "Hands Across the Sea. Scout Migration," *Annual Report* (London: SA, January 1928), 23-24. "Peopling the Vacant Spaces," *Annual Report* (London: SA, 1931), 48. Wilson, *Scouting Round the World*, 82. Migration figures are drawn from annual reports and quarterly migration statistical reports, TC/215, SA–London.

[48] For a good analysis of charges of militarism, see Martin Dedman, "Baden-Powell, Militarism, and the 'Invisible Contributors' to the Boy Scout Scheme, 1904–1920," *Twentieth Century British History* 4:3 (1993), 201-223.

[49] "Boy Scouts Avert Lynching," *Birkenhead Advertiser* 10 August 1929, 13.

[50] Particularly useful works that connect imperial imagination with metropolitan concerns are Shula Marks, "History, the Nation and Empire: Sniping from the Periphery," *History Workshop Journal* 29 (1990), 111–119, and Ann Stoler, *Race and the Education of Desire: Foucault's History of Sexuality and the Colonial Order of Things* (Durham and London: Duke University Press, 1995).

[51] Pamphlet of British Red Cross Society, 1934. TC/330, SA–London. For more information on the motivations of blood donors in England, see the following study of post-World War II blood donation: Richard Titmuss, *The Gift Relationship: From Human Blood to Social Policy* (New York: Pantheon Books, 1971).

[52] C. Lisle Watson, The London Rovers Book 1926, 17. TC/214, SA–London.

5

C H A P T E R

CONSTRUCTING AN INTERWAR FAMILY

Keeping pace with the ideological shifts and the change in public perceptions that followed World War I, Guiding and Scouting underwent massive reorganization, especially the Guides, as both movements tightened their structures and bureaucratized their administrations. The war losses forced some of the leadership changes, but more importantly the climate surrounding the war period affected how the organizations functioned. Just as leaders saw the war as a break between old and new civilizations, they saw a need for a new outlook. Some of these changes were quick and violent, with the displaced members feeling betrayed and forgotten. As one Guider wrote to her friend, who had just lost her position in the Guides:

> How curious it is isn't it how the war has altered people's taste, the strain and push and nerve racking of the war has made people like all those queer futurist pictures, they genuinely like the dischords, and I suppose they will go on liking them till they get back into harmonious balance perhaps a generation hence.[1]

Postwar society felt the same disillusionment and confusion that the Guider above expressed when faced with the fragmentation of modern society and the destruction of the war. Scouting and Guiding sought to combat these feelings by creating progressive yet controlled movements that filled a need for modernist renewal and vigor while simultaneously expressing a conservative nostalgia for the past.

The ideology that held together the postwar movements was a complicated familial model with the Baden-Powell family as its symbolic head. This family metaphor functioned on two levels as both a heterosexual model of companionate marriage and cooperative family life and a homosocial world of brotherhood and sisterhood that allowed an escape from the responsibilities of home. In one program, Scouting and Guiding addressed opposing postwar needs for a restabilized family and for an empowering homosocial retreat for men and women. Tapping into fears of gender disorder following the war, Guiding and Scouting assured society that their members knew their places in the order of things, yet paradoxically they allowed boys and girls to break free from the confines of prescribed behavior.

In addition, the movements provided a space for the negotiation of emerging mass leisure activities and changing standards of morality. Scouting and Guiding mixed a traditional concern with service and civic responsibility with new activities such as cinema, radio shows, and coeducational events. The movements walked a fine line between modernist and Victorian codes of ethics in the 1920s and 1930s.

MARRIED LOVE

The creation of a heterosexual familial model in the Scout and Guides necessitated and accompanied a reinvention of the Guide movement. From its beginning as a hastily constructed parallel movement under the leadership of Robert Baden-Powell's sister, Agnes, Guiding evolved into a highly structured movement run almost entirely by a young generation of women. In 1914, Robert Baden-Powell had expressed interest in reorganizing the Guides to fit the Scout structural model, and by 1918, the Guides had a charter of incorporation, a new executive council, and a revised organization. Basically, the new Guide structure imitated Scout lines with a strict hierarchical model of leadership. This arrangement allowed for flexibility at the local level, while maintaining control at the national level over badge/uniform distribution and general ideology.

Along with this restructured organization came a new leadership philosophy. Members of the former executive council, now criticized as too old, were forced into honorary positions, retirement, or unimportant jobs. The new guard, led by Robert Baden-Powell's young wife, Olave, ushered in the changes. Olave was young (only 23 when she married the 55-year-old Baden-Powell in 1912) and ambitious to join her husband in his activities for the two movements. As she wrote in an article for *Home Chat* in 1930, "During the first years of our marriage I could not do much to help my husband, apart from the home duties to which any woman must attend, for I had my babies to bring up." Despite this depiction of herself as a mother tied to the home, she also admitted that she could visualize her part in her husband's work almost as soon as they met.[2]

Olave Baden-Powell began offering her assistance to the Guides in 1914; she became a County Commissioner in March 1916, and by October of that year she was Chief Commissioner. In early 1918, she was named Chief Guide to match Robert Baden-Powell's role as Chief Scout and was responsible for overhauling the training program and replacing its leaders. Both Robert and Olave wrote new handbooks, in 1918 and in 1917 respectively. The original handbook, written by Robert and his sister Agnes, was dismissed by Olave as "The Little Blue Muddly," and Olave portrayed her sister-in-law as old-fashioned and out of touch with the younger generation. Agnes was forced out as head of the Guides and into an honorary position; later, she was virtually expelled from the movement entirely.[3]

At first glance, Olave's new guidebook *Training Girls as Guides* did not differ substantially from the original in tone. She called for attention to mothering and for "true womanliness" to repair the ruin of war and to stave off social upheaval. The crucial difference in the new ideology, however, lay in its emphasis on complementarity and its concern with self-control and patriotism. Largely gone were the guides for defense of Britain, instead the instructions now focused on becoming citizen mothers.[4] The aim of the Guides was "to make efficient future citizens, good home keepers and mothers."[5] Olave depicted the Guides as a movement appealing to "the more adventurous girl," yet not too adventurous. Looking fearfully to the threat from within—the new woman—and the threat from without—Bolshevism—Olave Baden-Powell promoted the Guides as directing girls' energy in a positive, constructive direction. The Guides would train women to be companions to men but would safeguard and regulate their sexuality as well:

> Familiarity with freedom is apt to make a girl blasee. When she has learnt the ABC of sin, it is but a step toward the primer of vice. And because war has played battledore and shuttlecock with so many of our ancient codes of morality the young girl is easily caught.[6]

Robert Baden-Powell's handbook, *Girl Guiding* (1918), followed a similar line, but was less theoretically based and contained more practical information for implementation. He laid out requirements for badges, instructions for games, and information Guides should know. Guides learned the story of the Brownies and the origins of the name "Guide," while memorizing laws, codes of ethics, war cries, chants, secret handshakes, and salutes. For instance, the Brownie war cry was "We're the Brownies. Here's our aim! Lend a hand and Play the Game." After singing this, they were to dance in circles singing "LAH, LAH, LAH" to signify lending a hand.[7] Girls were encouraged to fantasize and to sing and perform in rituals and spectacle, but in a controlled environment only, and under a constituted authority.

In addition to concern with the handbooks, training was crucial to Robert and Olave Baden-Powell's reorganization of the Guide movement, and the head of training was in a particularly powerful position in both organizations. Scouting, as the more developed movement before the war, began exploring training programs earlier than the Guides. By 1914, they had instituted a six-month correspondence course for scoutmasters, which drew almost eight hundred participants before it had to be postponed by the war. Ideas for training camps and diploma courses had also been suggested, but none of these ideas were implemented until the war ended. So many Scout leaders had left to fight that Scouting had to struggle to find volunteers. They could not worry immediately about training qualified scoutmasters.[8] After the war, they were able to develop a training program centered at Gilwell Park.

The Guides, unhampered by the loss of leadership that plagued the Scout organization, created their training program in 1915 and ran it almost continuously through the war. The Guide Officers' Training School (GGOTS), fondly dubbed the "Goats", had correspondence courses in place by 1916 and a diploma program by 1917 [Figure 7]. GGOTS, managed out of a large house in London by Agatha Blyth, had an exciting program for leaders. The school followed the patrol system as Scout and Guide groups themselves did because Blyth believed that officers should train by "practising the same rules the children observe." GGOTS held training camps, administered correspondence courses, and held less structured hikes and events. Blyth, by all accounts, was a popular and interesting trainer/leader for the school.[9] One Guider sent her memories of the training school and of Blyth to Rose Kerr, who included them in her official history of the Guides:

> She [Blyth] was a real dreamer of dreams, and see-er of visions, and she had the child's imagination, and the child's way of playing seriously any imaginative game. . . . To those of us who worked with her, Mrs. Blyth stands for the incarnation of the real spirit of Guiding with its mixture of idealism and fun.[10]

GGOTS was successful but also too limited for the growing movement, so in 1917, two other training centers were created. One was founded in Manchester to serve the north of England, the other was placed in Malvern for southern and western England. The London school continued to service the southeast. By 1918, officers had to pass written, oral, and practical exams in order to earn diplomas from the Guide training centers. These exams tested Guide subjects such as hygiene, home-craft, and mother-craft, as well as examining knowledge of the "psychology of the girl" and company administration.[11]

Despite the success of these training programs, change was on its way and Blyth was vulnerable to attack from the beginning as a member of Agnes Baden-Powell's committee. Blyth (whose sisters founded the elite girls' public school, Roedean) was an educated, competent, and popular leader, but she would not have easily fallen in with Olave's ideas for the

FIG. 7 Agatha Blyth runs a leadership training course under the auspices of the Girl Guide Officers' Training School during World War I. By kind permission of The Guide Association.

training program. Although Robert Baden-Powell had praised Blyth's program and asked her to author an official training manual in July 1918, by the end of August he was calling the "spirit of the school out of harmony with the movement." This attack from the Chief Scout coupled with his wife's negative comments about Blyth at a Commissioners' Conference at Swanwick led to an upheaval as Blyth resigned along with her entire committee. Olave Baden-Powell, backed by her husband, moved to change the training program almost immediately, despite continued protests from Blyth's supporters. The committee was replaced, and Agnes Maynard was installed as the new head of GGOTS. Headquarters had decided the school should no longer be independently administered by October 1918, and by December GGOTS voted to dissolve itself after the Chief Scout wrote threatening to sanction the school no longer.[12]

The fierce but short battle over training had immediate effects on some of the members, with Blyth resigning and others becoming disillusioned and bitter about Guiding. One Guider, Edith Moore, summed up the frustration and anger that Blyth's supporters felt in a letter to the new head of the school, Agnes Maynard:

> To allow such a woman as this to leave the organisation must seem—to everyone who has the welfare of our girls and not just a movement at heart—an act of extraordinary stupidity as well as shabby treatment.[13] [emphasis original]

Moore went on to accuse the leadership of looking for the "glamour of name and prestige." As Moore so astutely pointed out, Olave Baden-Powell was chasing a larger vision of Guiding. Moore herself recognized the Chief Guide's plan in a letter to Blyth over a decade later. While reflecting on what the movement could have been she wrote, "Perhaps this cruder [vision] was necessary to awaken a popular response."[14]

Olave Baden-Powell bureaucratized the movement, and in the process, attracted a diversity of members that had not been anticipated in 1918. This organization that she shaped in the 1920s was not only more successful than the Scouts in terms of membership, but it was run almost entirely by women. The only men in positions of authority in Guiding in the interwar period were Baden-Powell and Percy Everett, who handled the finances of both Scouting and Guiding. Bureaucratization was Olave Baden-Powell's route to success, and this process made Guiding more than a "ladies'" social reform movement. Guiding was transformed into a modern, structured, female-led youth movement.

The Guides moved on after the destruction of the London training school to a vast organization of training and licensing. Guiding acquired a spiritual home and training center in 1922, with the donation of Foxlease Park near the New Forest. Foxlease, an eighty-acre estate with a grand house, became a center for camping and all training programs. Another Guide home was acquired for Northern England in 1927, with the opening of Waddow Hall, an estate in Lancashire. By the mid-1930s, Waddow and Foxlease were training close to 2,000 leaders per year, and the demand greatly exceeded the supply. Supplemented by local and regional programs, the training structure was highly organized and smooth-running by the end of the 1920s.[15]

In fact, once the training battles had been won, other structural changes followed. It now became routine for Scout (1931) and Guide (1923) leaders to acquire camping licenses and permits for taking their groups on holidays. Insurance and indemnity programs were created. The staff at the two headquarters expanded with the addition of new departments such as the office of International Commissioner (1918) and the Scout Publicity Department (1925). A new Guide Headquarters, paid for by a massive fundraising campaign, opened in 1931. Publications were flourishing, with the *Guide* and the *Guider* having a total of more than 60,000 subscribers by 1930. Scout magazines also seemed to be on sound footing, with the *Scouter* selling about 26,000 copies a month by 1931. Since these publications were often shared among the members of a troop or company, the figures speak to their success.[16]

Bureaucratization was a priority in both movements after World War I, but for different and gendered reasons. Scouting appealed to men and boys looking to escape the structures and responsibilities of the work place, so a move toward professionalization was in many ways a threat to Scout success. However, after the early battles over control of ideology with competing movements, it was also necessary to maintain the Scout movement's reputation and membership. The process of restructuring reined in the creativity that had inspired the early explosion in membership, but it also solidified Scouting's image as a respectable and modern mass movement. For Guiding, reorganizing along more professional lines was a necessity. Girls and women wanted to escape the dependent roles that were often assigned to them in marriage, family life, and the work place. Guiding, by bureaucratizing, created a space for them to assume positions of power within an organization and provided Guides with the thrill of autonomy and power.

Accompanying the bureaucratic changes was an emphasis on constructing a Scout and Guide tradition that would tie members together. Although already rich in a culture of songs, rituals, and artifacts, Scout and Guide leaders sought a spiritual connection in the interwar period. Christianity could not necessarily bring the movements together because of divisions between varying sects and because of the influx of non-Christians in England and in the Empire. The traditions of Scouting and Guiding emerged in the early years but were solidified in the interwar period in the construction of a familial metaphor centered on the relationship enjoyed by the Chief Scout and the Chief Guide.

Just as the Chief Guide and Chief Scout maintained a companionate marriage, so should boys and girls aim to cooperate and complement each other's skills. The Chief Guide not only functioned as the ideal companion for the Chief Scout but her presence defined the movements' familial metaphor, and she set the boundaries of women's roles by couching her success in terms of her role as helpmate. Calling herself and her husband "twin souls," she told readers that "the woman who learns to help her husband really does succeed in helping herself."[17] Olave Baden-Powell knew her role was more than that of her husband's helper as she quietly assumed responsibility for the Guide movement and for many Scout events and appearances as well.

The Baden-Powells placed themselves at the heads of the organization as Chief Scout and Chief Guide, serving as parental figures, role models, and guidance counselors. Robert Baden-Powell functioned as an ideal of Christian manliness, and Olave Baden-Powell became a female exemplar for the movement, as the Chief's comfort and his strength. Rose Kerr records this familial myth in her official history of the Guide movement: "Altogether, it was the greatest good fortune that the Chief Scout should have found a woman so fitted to help him and to carry on his work. The greatest thing which she did for the Guides was that she united them all into a big friendly family."[18]

As Kerr indicated, the process of reorganizing the Guides with Olave as their leader created a new ideology that gave added importance to the organization. The symmetry of having a married couple leading coexisting male and female movements seemed to work beautifully. In his introduction to the official history of Guiding written in 1932, Baden-Powell explained how this relationship worked for members of the organizations:

> But, Just as that rib [referring to Adam/Eve] grew in the end to become the important partner of the man (apart from the incident of nearly wrecking his career), and to be mother of the human race, so, too, the Girl Guide Movement has grown up automatically, in equal strength with the Boy Scouts, to develop individual character in the girl hood, not only of our own race, but of our neighbor nations about the world.[19]

In this vision of complementary roles, the boys and girls were "equal," but all knew their sex-assigned roles and followed them, answering many of the public gender anxieties aroused by the topsy-turvy nature of wartime society and the postwar period.

In addition to Olave and Robert's roles as models, the chiefs' three children became symbols of the vast Scout and Guide family, often being pictured in uniform and submitting their lives to public scrutiny. For instance, in 1916, a "Heather Empire" competition was set up to award a prize for the patrol earning the most badges. The prize was the accolade "Heather" and special badges for the patrol in honor of the birth of the Baden-Powell's daughter, Heather. Similarly, Peter Baden-Powell, the chiefs' son, had a namesake Wolf Cub pack. The 1st Westminster (Peter's Own) Pack was registered in 1914 (right after Peter was born), and Robert Baden-Powell took his 6-month-old son to visit the pack in May of that year.[20] Again, the Baden-Powell family functioned as a microcosm of the Scouting and Guiding family as a whole and provided a sense of generational continuity. Members of the movement received family Christmas cards, and they were encouraged to celebrate great events in the lives of the Baden-Powells such as weddings and births (usually by contributing toward a gift). Olave and Robert's joint birthday of February 22 even became the official Guide holiday of "Thinking Day," still celebrated each year with a grand ceremony at Westminster Abbey and other cathedrals throughout the country.

Beyond the Baden-Powells' role modeling of family life for the movements, the introduction of wider age categories in the last years of the war also supported the emerging familial metaphor. By 1918, a child could enter the Wolf Cubs or the Brownies at age 8, could advance to the Scouts or Guides, and then move up to the Rovers or Rangers. In this way, Guiding and Scouting almost covered a person's whole life and had the possibility of making members feel like they were part of a vast family. Leaders were trained to recognize and nurture this feeling, and they were encouraged to "above all, see that family relationship of all three branches is preserved."[21]

Because there was no upper age limit on Rover and Ranger membership until after World War II, sometimes men and women stayed in the movements as members, not leaders, into their 40s. In addition, it was common in the 1930s for Rover and Ranger groups to have membership from 16 to 40 years old meeting together. One Guide remembered starting her own Ranger group in 1924 at age 21 when more than half of the members were older than she was. The 15th Tunbridge Wells Rangers, formed in the 1920s, met up to the war and they still meet twice a year [Figures 8 & 9]! Angela Rodaway recounted a similar situation in her autobiography, writing, "When it was proposed, in the Girl Guides Association, that there should be an upper age limit of twenty-one, there was dismay in our Ranger Company, for this would have made nearly all of its members ineligible."[22]

The interwar period also brought an increase in Scout and Guide cooperation, with the advent of coeducational hikes, socials, and even camping in some areas. Some isolated incidents of Guide and Scout cooperation had occurred before World War I, but they were usually accidental and/or painful. As Mrs. Janson Potts remembered from her days with the 1st Rusthall company, "On one occasion we went for a trek to a neighbouring heath where we fell in with a Troop of Scouts who came back with us and helped to push our cart up the hill. We enjoyed this very much but found that we had apparently committed the unpardonable sin of fraternizing with the Scouts."[23] In other examples, Scouts helped provide security for Guide rallies and Guides provided "service" in the form of serving food or babysitting for Scout events. During the 1920s and 1930s, cooperation between the two movements became more acceptable, with the most common combined activities being Church Parades, fundraisers (such as concerts), and occasional parties

This cooperation in the 1920s and 1930s arose as much for practical reasons as for ideological ones because the two movements often needed to share facilities and/or leadership, especially in poorer areas. In her autobiography of life in East London, Nellie Priest described a common experience in which children found that church was the center of all activities outside of the home, including Cubs, Brownies, Scouts, and Guides. Other locations were shared, such as meeting halls, Scout huts, schools, or popular camping areas, so sometimes cooperation was a necessity.[24]

Cooperation between Scouts and Guides sometimes provided an extra measure of security, especially for Guide companies. As one Guide related in an oral history, "As you know, Guide camps are magnets for boys." She took a patrol of hand-picked Scouts with her each year to camp in order to protect the Guides from such outside attacks.[25] It was common for Guide camps to be plagued by village children who flattened tents by cutting guy lines, or who knocked over latrines. Occasionally village "hooligans" might throw vegetables at Guides or call out abuse. The presence of Scouts could deflect this kind of abuse at rallies or camps.

Another practical consideration that led to the cooperation of the two movements was the shortage of male Scout leaders during and just after the war. Women were recruited to be Lady Scoutmasters and to lead Cub packs in increasing numbers, and they have never lost their presence in the movement's leadership ranks. Wherever possible, Baden-Powell and other leaders tried to steer women into the leadership roles associated with younger boys, and the emphasis was on women as Cubmistresses. This use of women fit well with the familial metaphor since popular wisdom dictated that women had well-developed mothering instincts for dealing with small boys, but they weren't equipped to instruct older boys in manliness, especially when they were "usually entirely uninstructed in sex matters."[26] These restrictions did not eliminate women from the ranks of Scoutmasters, however, because some women refused to give up their positions working with older boys.

In addition to these practical considerations, Scouting and Guiding began promoting cooperation because they felt they needed to keep pace with the times. Although some worried that combined activities might worry parents or turn off boys, joint activities and conferences became acceptable in many areas of the country by the 1930s. Usually these activities varied according to local restrictions, and combined activities seemed to have been more common in London and its environs. Many Yorkshire members recounted stricter guidelines for the separation of the two movements in their districts, citing only an occasional combined Church Parade or public concert. George Herridge, a 36th Sheffield Scout, said "If there was a Girl Guide within two miles, we had to move the camp." Marjorie Yonwin agreed, saying that she found her Guide experiences in Salford, Lancashire, to be stricter and "more old-fashioned" than her later Guiding in the London suburbs, while Win Ritchie attributed the lack of Scout/Guide cooperation in Huddersfield to lack of interest and Scout leaders' misogyny and fear. Other Guides and Scouts mentioned that combined events did not always work because older members might head for the pub and younger members might head for opposite walls.[27]

Even though all combined activities were not a success and some regions still frowned on these joint events, Scout and Guide cooperation became a regular part of interwar operations. Many members recalled combined concerts, hikes, debates, and parties, especially for older Rovers and Rangers. Perhaps most popular in the 1930s was the Rover/Ranger Social, which either took the form of an informal party or a fancier dance. These could be local gatherings of a couple of groups or larger entertainments such as the London Rover Social or the Holborn Rovers Ball.

FIG. 8 The 15th Tunbridge Wells Ranger Company pose with the Kent County Shield and Cup, which they won in 1935. Author's collection, gift from Jeanne Holloway.

FIG. 9 The 15th Tunbridge Wells Ranger Company were still meeting in 1986. Author's collection, gift from Jeanne Holloway.

These events were one reason for the longevity of members' participation in the movements in the 1930s because men and women saw the Scouts and Guides as opportunities to meet and socialize with members of the opposite sex outside of the home. May Rainer described her Guide years in a meeting hall in which both Scouts and Guides held their meetings. Rainer wrote that she expected a certain measure of freedom in the Guides and was disappointed. She explained, "Having had so many restrictions at home, the thought of constantly being told you must not talk to the young men in the Scout Hut by a prejudiced old maid" led her to quit the movement. However, she continued to socialize at the Scout Hut. Likewise, Alice Linton remembered the thrilling camp (and first real vacation) that took her away from home and her job at a laundry for a week. There she met Scouts who were invited to join in cricket matches and even a campfire/concert on the final evening: "Most of the girls, especially the older ones, had made friends with some of the Scouts." The girls were reluctant to part from the boys, and Linton remembers her sadness at returning home to "rows of dreary looking houses."[28] In another humorous incident, a Guide leader recalled a girl from her company falling in a stream and being rescued by Scouts. A Scout loaned her some shorts so she could change out of her wet clothing, and he stood guard while she changed. The leader was amused when the next day all of the Guide company wanted to go together to return the shorts to the Scouts.[29]

The combination of this socialization and a common ethic meant that Guide and Scout relationships and marriages were quite common in the interwar period. The boy and girl would meet at a Ranger/Rover Social or some other official activity, and they would continue to meet through organizational events. These marriages were sometimes among high-ranking members, such as the marriage of Alice Behrens (Head of Training and longtime Guide leader) and Arthur Gaddum (Commissioner and early organizer for the Scout movement) in 1929, or they could be among less exalted members who got write-ups in the local newspapers. William Macadie of the 177th North London Scouts met his future wife, Janet Downie, when he gave a lecture at her Ranger Company in 1931. They dated and she became his assistant in the Cub pack that he ran, and they were married in 1934. Both continued to be active Rover/Rangers and leaders. Guide clippings, books, and logs are full of marriages and engagements, and one elderly Guide leader reported that nine or ten Guide/Scout marriages took place in her companies alone.[30]

In addition to such marriages, the weddings themselves sometimes took on a distinctly Scout-like flavor. Weddings were sometimes performed in which the whole wedding party was garbed in Scout and Guide uniforms, including the priest or parson. Jeanne Brown, a Brownie, Guide, and Ranger since 1922, met her husband Edward Holloway, while singing at hospitals and running whist drives with a Rover group. When they married in December 1939 both wore their uniforms as did the Scout padre and the whole wedding party. They entered and exited the church through a Scout/Guide color guard, which had created an arch made up of raised staves. Jeanne wrote to Guide headquarters for special permission to wear light-colored silk stockings rather than the opaque uniform tights, and they even had a wedding cake that was decorated with tiny merit badges.[31]

These relationships became part of the mythology of the movements and did much to support the familial metaphor promoted by the Baden-Powells. Scout/Guide marriages created whole families that were tied up into the movements' ideologies, and some Scouts and Guides extended the movements' definition of family into their private lives by having family photos taken of parents and children in Scout/Guide uniforms. Others recalled how all family members participated in the movements, and many members interviewed mentioned how their children and grandchildren carried on proud traditions. Harold Wilson (Labour Prime Minister from 1964 to 1970 and 1974 to 1976) recounted his Scout days in his autobiography, mentioning that his father was a Rover leader, his mother a Guide captain, and his sister a Guide. It was no wonder that he became a Cub as soon as he could and later an enthusiastic Scout in Huddersfield.[32]

In short, Scouting and Guiding created intergenerational male and female space, uniting its members with a variety of activities and a unified familial ethos. Britain was depicted as a huge family, brought together by grief, war, and hard times, so Guides and Scouts adopted a similar metaphor to describe their community of members. This image of complementary male and female roles in a vast family won the two movements validation in the years following the war, when parents worried that their children might not be learning to be true men or women. This concern with male and female complementarity also reflected the "New Feminism" of the interwar period, that concerned itself more with male and female difference than with prewar equality arguments.[33]

This intergenerational family also provided a context for coping with the emerging consumerism and mass leisure pursuits of the interwar period. As class connections and neighborhood ties began to disintegrate with the introduction of new technologies and ideas, Guiding and Scouting filled a void by providing an alternative identity and a safe space for experimentation.

THE GANG'S ALL HERE

Not only did wider age categories and changing societal mores create a heterosexual family model in organizations, they also facilitated Scouting and Guiding's role as venues for the rearticulation of the communities of the war period. They perpetuated the single-sex model of comradeship that had cemented wartime friendships, allowing Scouts and Guides to fashion a space for rediscovering these bonds. Men and women, boys and girls, could relive the best part of the war—single-sex comradeship and community—without the violence and fear and without societal repercussions. However, it was sometimes confusing for members when they attempted to discover what roles ought to be paramount and where their loyalties should lie. Were members to revel in the brother/sisterhood of the organizations, or lay the groundwork for marriage? When should activities be single-sex, and when should they be coeducational?

Evidence suggests that this was indeed a puzzling dilemma for Scouts and Guides, especially for those in leadership positions. Many members wrote to Baden-Powell in the 1920s and 1930s asking him to clarify this thorny issue. Vincent Jackson, one such Rover from Southgate, got to the heart of the matter quickly in a letter from 1929. His Rover Den was associated with a church that also had Rangers, and these Rangers had helped finance and build the Rover Den. He understood that Rover Dens were supposed to be for men and boys only, and he and his Rovers saw themselves as "still boys" in need of this male retreat. Yet the Rangers wanted to use the den and Jackson's wife was one of the Rangers (and the Guide captain).[34] Others were even more specific in their requests for guidance. Lambeth Scout Albert Partridge wrote to Baden-Powell in 1923, asking, "Should Scouts go with girls, or not?"[35] Baden-Powell replied to this letter and to hundreds of others, by urging chivalrous relationships with girls and late marriages. As he wrote to another Scout, "a man should only marry a woman many years younger than himself, otherwise there will be differences."[36] Once again, the Founder is using his marriage as a model for Scouts.

Perhaps one of the most useful records of the tension between single-sex community and coeducational experience is the logbook of Tony Heap, logkeeper of the Coeur de Lion patrol of the Holborn Rovers from 1927 to1936. For almost nine years Heap recorded experiences, observations, and editorial comments.[37] The Holborn group was a cosmopolitan and somewhat unruly one, but their concerns echoed a struggle emerging in Rover Dens and Scout troops throughout Britain. In early entries, Heap records activities such as debates and outings. However, even in 1928, a division is apparent within the group. On one cinema outing, the group split with one faction going to the Tivoli to see "Napoleon" and the other going to the Palace for "The Girl Friend." The following week, two Rovers attended a Ranger social and were dubbed "Sheiks!" by Heap. That autumn, Heap's writing is full of the activities of the group, and he especially notes a weekend camp, which he describes as the epitome of Scouting's masculine culture: "The little glowing pyramid of fire was at its best, as though in complete satisfaction with the worship that was made by the brotherly circle which surrounded it."[38] This moment of male community was for Heap the essence of the Scout experience.

Trouble, however, was on the horizon in the form of a debate in April 1929 on Rover/Ranger cooperation. Although Heap and a couple of others spoke against the idea, a motion to try cooperation passed 8-3. The first combined meeting, a political debate, took place in May with 20 Rangers and 30 Rovers. Heap's anger is readily apparent in his description of the debate:

> The rangers sat herded together, occupying all the seats, while the rovers, whose meeting it should have been exclusively, either stood about or sat on the floor. It proves, I think, the utter stupidity of inviting the rangers. They're no ornament and were not needed there. We should have enjoyed it much better if we had had comfortable seats and been able to argue in the manly way amongst ourselves.[39]

After this initial cooperative event, a few combined dances and parties took place in the next few years, but Heap mostly concentrated on "manly" activities, such as games where "the object . . . seemed to be to tear each other's uniforms to shreds. Black eyes and red noses were not infrequent either." He also made mention of the important moment that the group went together to the theater to see *Of One Blood*, E. R. Hougham's play about the trenches.[40]

Heap again addressed joint Ranger/Rover activities in 1931 in his description of a cooperative hike. "Some of us diehards have held out, flatly refusing to go on these hikes, scornfully dismissing them as mere 'petting' parties." But Heap adds later, after attending such a hike, he found it unobjectionable and even met a Ranger who was an "agreeable surprise." Events escalated from here as Heap's 1932 and 1933 entries increasingly address socials, balls, dances, and late-night revels. In fact, one entry records a New Year's party in January 1934, where all of the Rovers brought girlfriends (some of whom were Guides). At this party, Heap was disrobed until nearly nude in a game. Later that same month, Heap records the consumption of "strong liquor" at many activities, a distinctly un-Scoutlike pastime. Entries become sparse after this until 1936, when Heap announced that "apathy has won the day" and monthly meetings will be discontinued due to lack of interest. Although the Holborn Rovers were different from more traditional groups, their experiences mirror those of other interwar Scouts and Guides, who record a similar mixture of single-sex meetings and coed "special" events.[41]

In addition to this compromise between the increasingly coeducational world of mass leisure and the single-sex model of "respectable" youth service, Scouts and Guides combined modern style entertainments with more traditional class-based activities. The organizations mixed service and merit-badge activities, cinema outings, sports and dating, functioning as a combination of modern entertainment, civic duty, and preparation for marriage. Countless former members described this mix of fun and purpose as the reason for Scouting and Guiding's appeal. Jill Julius Matthews has examined a similar phenomenon in the 1930s in her examination of the Women's League of Health and Beauty. As she noted of this fitness organization, there was a clear "tension between an older, class-bound, service-motivated femininity and a more modern, mass, commercial style" in the period before World War II.[42] Likewise, Lizabeth Cohen's important work on the response of the working-classes to mass culture in Chicago suggests that modern institutions such as the cinema were mediated by community standards, class activities, and peers.[43] The experience of Scouts and Guides in this period supports this research, as members used the "local" company or troop to negotiate the emerging mass culture and modernizing influences.

The movements provided a clear mix of "insider" activities and outside pursuits. Some popular activities within Scout and Guide organizations included sponsoring intellectual debates and inviting speakers. For instance, the 1st Chislehurst Guide company held debates on subjects such as "lifts v. moving staircases" and "Eton v. Harrow." Likewise, the 6th

Clapton had a debate between 'Miss Worldly Woman and Miss Christian."[44] Other groups debated political issues, international development, or film. In one of the most heated of the Holborn Rover debates, they discussed in 1935 whether women should be allowed to be in paid employment during times of severe unemployment.[45] Dances, socials, and parades were also popular, as were annual competitions in counties and regions.

Scouts and Guides did not just sponsor their own activities, however. They often attended other events, especially the cinema, dances, and gramophone recitals. Mentions of the cinema and films abound in the logbooks and diaries of Scouts and Guides from this period. Not only did they go to the cinema, but they often attended local theaters in groups or they had a film brought into a hall for their use. For instance, Cicely Stewart-Smith wrote in her logbook that when her Guide company disbanded in 1919, they "celebrated the breaking up by going to the cinema on the remains of the company funds." Coventry Scout A. E. Hughes recorded in his diary in 1921 his cinema trips either once or twice a week with his fellow Scouts or with his girlfriend, who met him after Scout practice. As another Cub wrote in his account of "The Party" in the troop log: "After tea we had a sing song. And then we had a ciman. The man showed us such pictors a mickey mouse and feelics and other things. That lasted for about an hour."[46]

In addition to such use of commercial cinema, members also featured Scout and Guide films at their meetings. These films could be borrowed from the organizations, or they sometimes were shown at local theaters. For example, the newsreel "Girl Guides and Work" (1917), the fictional film "The Woodpigeon Patrol" (1930), and the propaganda film "Boy Scouts—Be Prepared!" (1917) were featured at cinemas throughout Britain, either alone or with other programs. Often these films concentrated on the bravery and ingenuity of either an individual Scout or Guide or a patrol in the face of mysterious circumstances, wrongdoing or disasters. These stories have a strong moralistic overtone and often feature a conversion experience of some kind that is reminiscent of nineteenth-century Sunday schools and Victorian prescriptive literature, but they also feature fantastic adventures.

"When Scouting Won," filmed in Minehead in 1930, follows the adventures of brave Patrol Leader Alan Dale. The main story line concerns Dale's advocacy of a man who is being forced to sell his coal-rich land. Dale fights gypsies and other social undesirables, escaping dramatically from near-death situations. In "Trail of Youth," another Minehead production from the 1930s, a whole group of Boy Scouts saves a scientist's invention from evil interlopers. Such heavy-handed fare had limited appeal to members, who were often skeptical.[47] As one Guide in the 2nd Caversham wrote about a film her company saw at a theater in Reading:

> We witnessed some very thrilling episodes in the life of a girl guide in a foreign country (we all wondered if there ever had lived a girl who was such and [sic] ideal Guide as the one shown on the screen).[48]

Despite such doubts, Guides and Scouts continued to view these films, as well as British and American commercial films, whether they were viewed in the clubroom or the cinema.

In addition to participating in the coeducational mass culture of the cinema and the social whirl in the 1920s and 1930s, they also began participating in a series of events that helped define the movements for Britain—the Gang Shows. These events echoed nineteenth-century music halls yet incorporated the modern idea of the mass spectacle, and most importantly for the movements, they displayed uniformed Scouts in performances. The Gang Show began as a small local revue staged by the Holborn Rovers, Tony Heap's group. The driving force behind the show was "A Holborn Rover," who in 1935 revealed himself to be Ralph Reader, a West End producer and Scouting enthusiast. The first revue, entitled "Good Turns," drew a disappointing crowd because it conflicted with the London Rover Social. Reader persevered, however, creating "A Good Night" in 1931. He continued speaking to the Rovers about entertaining, while building material through these local shows. Finally, after the London Scout Commissioner asked Reader to produce a larger show, 1932's "The Gang's All Here" became a reality. As Tony Heap observed, this production was a mix of earlier Holborn shows with new material and a larger cast. It played to crowded houses all three nights at the 1100-seat Scala Theatre.[49]

Tickets were sold out virtually every year after that in the 1930s, and many theatergoers had to be turned away from the box office. By the late 1930s, the Gang Show had become an institution in English society, creating substantial revenue for the Scout movement.[50] Reader and his gang gained the approbation of the entertainment industry in 1937 when Herbert Wilcox created a film of the Gang Show, and when BBC's Coronation Variety broadcast featured the gang. More importantly, however, the Gang received official recognition when the Gang Show was the first amateur show ever selected to appear in a Royal Command Performance.[51] The Gang Show eventually spread to different mediums, including television, film, and radio, but it never lost its focus on the Scout community. Most of the show was performed in Scout uniforms, and the profits went to the Scouts.

The Gang Shows served as fundraising and propaganda tools for the Scout movement, reinforcing the Scout and Guide image in public perception. More importantly, however, the shows functioned as the ultimate expression of group identity. They institutionalized the secret language, the uniforms, the collectibles, and the culture.[52] For instance, the material from the shows was renovated and used nationally and locally. At large annual gatherings, Scouts would gather around the campfire singing favorite songs and acting out scenes from the shows. In local and regional areas, Gang Show material was used to stage fundraising and charity events, with proceeds going either to the Scouts and Guides or to local children's charitable organizations. The Gang Shows in London were well-known and widely copied phenomena in the Scout and Guide movements by the late 1930s. Gang shows became a feature of London theatre life that spread throughout Britain and created a whole network of amateur theatricals in the movements, while gang show songs and dialogues became part of the Scout and Guide language.

As a companion to these modern and more-expensive Gang Shows, the Roland House annual pantomimes achieved moderate success as well. Begun in 1927 as a project to raise money for Roland House, the East End home of Scouting, the annual pantomimes were entertainments that mimicked music hall shows. Often they were paired with a Ball and were performed by a troupe of players that contained both men and women. Pantomimes were based on older popular forms of entertainment and contained elements of melodrama and burlesque performances. They dramatized favorite fairy tales or children's stories, and they were usually characterized by slapstick-style comedy and topical jokes. Also, the performers parodied gender boundaries by cross dressing men and women and acting out silly sexual intrigues. The Roland House pantos consisted of well-known shows that had familiar plots and songs such as Cinderella, Ali Baba and the Forty Thieves, and Dick Whittington's Cat.[53]

Like the Gang Shows, the Roland House pantos enjoyed the patronage of the Royal Family. Edward, Prince of Wales, and later, the Earl of Athlone and Princess Alice served as patrons of the shows. The pantomimes were copied throughout the country as local troops and companies performed their own versions of the popular stories. In London, performances were generally successful at earning money for Roland House, although they could not command the prices and the crowds that the Gang Shows did by the 1930s. In 1929, 4500 tickets were sold for "Dick Whittington," and Roland House received £300 profit.[54] The shows, which were not produced during World War II, continued to create funds that were steady if not spectacular into the 1970s.

Unlike the calmer, family-oriented entertainment of the Gang Shows, the Pantomimes were opportunities for the older Scouts and Guides to exercise their freedom. Rover Tony Heap described the fun of the post-Panto excitement in January 1933. A crowd of about forty Rovers and Rangers stayed out until three a.m., holding "revels" at Marble Arch, walking to Piccadilly, then marching down to Victoria, where the group split up.[55] Perhaps this kind of license was not the norm among Scouts and Guides, but the story illustrates a couple of important points about these pantomimes. These were group entertainments, not individual endeavors. The crowds were composed of Scout and Guide acquaintances, and the Panto Balls were opportunities to meet new friends. The panto was assuredly a theatrical event, a spectacle, but it was as important in its related activities as in the show itself. Scouts and Guides who attended Gang Shows and Pantomimes could feel a sense of pride and belonging in the performances of their peers. They could vicariously experience the fun of performing by participating in the parties, balls, and informal post-performance discussions that characterized both the pantos and the gang shows. Most importantly, they could reproduce these entertainments in local amusements, area fundraisers, and camp frolics.

One such local pantomime held at a Guiders' party in Sheffield in 1931 parodied cinema, Guide activities, and the panto itself all in one show. The production, entitled "Dick Pickering and his Cat," apparently brought down the house with its original humor. In the last scene, the Guides build a house for Dick. As the author noted, the scene started "with a burlesque of the Matinee we had had at the Empire towards the building of London H.Q." This short matinee was a promotional film asking Guides to contribute bricks toward the building of a new headquarters for the organization. After the funny scene of Guides building a house with bricks, the panto ended with a bride in Guide uniform marching through signalling flags to meet her groom, Dick.[56]

CONCLUSION

In a study of working-class youth in interwar Britain, David Fowler discussed the existence of a "distinctive teenage culture" by the 1930s. Using evidence culled from club, employment, and official records, he argued for the development of the "teenager" in the interwar period.[57] Scout and Guide history suggests a slightly different story in the development of the interwar youth culture. Instead of a unified and identifiable "teenaged" culture, Scout and Guide activities point to a continuation of an ambiguously defined period of time between school-leaving and marriage. This youthful part of a man or woman's life could and did extend to those in their twenties, blurring the lines between "teens" (in a modern sense) and adults.

Also, unlike the subcultures of the post-World War II period,[58] Scout and Guide subculture exemplified respectability not deviance. The movements attempted to define themselves "against the fragmentation of class communities and growth of hedonistic pursuits," allowing members to sample emerging mass pursuits, while maintaining community ties and a service goal.[59] Scouting and Guiding provided an opportunity for youth and adults to develop homosocial and heterosocial relationships in the 1920s and 1930s and to participate in the new leisure activities of the period. Yet, the real value of the Scout/Guide experience lay in its ability to invest these activities with meaning, providing a sense of responsibility and purpose that was lacking in other organizations and in the activities themselves. Guides and Scouts expressed this unique quality time and again in oral histories and memoirs. According to Jeanne Holloway, "If they took away the Promise, the Guides would be just another youth club." Ralph Whiteley thought Scouting was different because "We had a promise and that was a challenge," while Hazel Harrison and Marjorie Yonwin both pointed to the sense of purpose that Guiding provided.[60] It was this combination of progress and tradition, service and entertainment that drew over a million British youth per year into these organizations.

ENDNOTES

[1] C. Anstruther-Thomson to Agatha Blyth, 31 March 1919; GA–London.

[2] Olave Baden-Powell, "A Successful Wife," *Home Chat* (27 September 1930), 663; TC/219, SA–London.

[3] Olave Baden-Powell as told to Mary Drewery, *Window on My Heart* (London: Hodder and Stockton, 1973), 108, 111-112.

[4] For a discussion of the shift from defensive imperialism to multinationalism in the Guides in the 1920s and the idea of the citizen mother, see Allen Warren, "Mothers for the Empire," in *Making Imperial Mentalities: Socialisation and British Imperialism* (Manchester: Manchester University Press, 1990), 96-109.

[5] Olave Baden-Powell, *Training Girls as Guides* (London: C. Arthur Pearson, 1917), 22.

[6] O. Baden-Powell, *Training Girls as Guides*, 13-14.

[7] Robert Baden-Powell, *Girl Guiding* (London: C. Arthur Pearson, 1921), 22.

[8] Scout Association, *Annual Report 1913*, 26; SA, *Annual Report 1914*, xix. The Scouts used Senior Scouts aged 16/17 as well as women to fill the leadership gap during the war. For a discussion of the Lady Scoutmaster controversy, see TC/33, SA–London.

[9] Girl Guides Association, *Annual Report 1916*, 11. Agatha Blyth to members of the Elder Patrol (Commissioners) 14 January 1917; OTS Timetable 1916; Reports on GOATS Pilgrimages 1917, 1918; GOATS box, correspondence and reports, 1916-1917; GA–London.

[10] Rose Kerr, *The Story of the Girl Guides* (London: Girl Guides Association, 1940), 228.

[11] Girl Guides Association, *Annual Report 1917*, 7; Girl Guides Association, *Policy Organization and Rules 1919*, 75.

[12] Robert Baden-Powell to Agatha Blyth, read to the meeting of the GOATS executive on 18 July 1918, GOATS Minute Book; Agatha Blyth to Olave Baden-Powell, 1 September 1918; Robert Baden-Powell to GOATS Executive, read to the meeting of the GOAT Executive 7 December 1918, GOATS Minute Book; GA–London. Tim Jeal, *The Boy-Man: The Life of Lord Baden-Powell* (New York: William Morrow, 1990), 477.

[13] Edith Moore to Agnes Maynard, n.d. (late 1918/early 1919); GA–London.

[14] Edith Moore to Agatha Blyth, 6 January 1932; GA–London.

[15] Foxlease was donated by an American in 1922, and Princess Mary donated £6,000 of her wedding gift for the upkeep of the estate. She later donated £4,000 more. Waddow was purchased by the Guide Association. For information on these acquisitions, see the Girl Guides Association, *Annual Reports*, 1922/1927, and Kerr, *The Story of the Girl Guides*, 182-184, 192.

[16] Henry Collis, Fred Hurll, and Rex Hazlewood, *B-P's Scouts: An Official History of the Boy Scouts Association* (London: Collins, 1961), 263-273; SA, *Annual Report 1931*, 28; Girl Guides Association, *Annual Report 1930*, 32; Camping chronology, card file at GA–London.

[17] Olave Baden-Powell, "A Successful Wife," *Home Chat* (27 September 1930), 705; TC/219, SA–London.

[18] Kerr, *The Story of the Girl Guides*, 116-117.

[19] Robert Baden-Powell, "Introduction," (to 1932 edition and reprinted in subsequent editions) in Kerr, *The Story of the Girl Guides*, 5.

[20] "Heather Empire," *Times*, 3 June 1916, 12F. J.F. Colquhoun, "Peter's Own: The First Pack," *The Scouter* (February 1935). TC/276, SA–London.

[21] *The Akela Leaders Handbook* (London: Boy Scout Association, 1924), 30.

[22] Interview with Lady Marjorie Stopford in Bushey, Hertsfordshire, 24 March 1993. The amazing 15th Tunbridge Wells Ranger Company had a meeting of 15 Rangers in 1986, and the youngest in the group is now in her eighties. Angela Rodaway, *A London Childhood* (London: B. T. Batsford, 1960), 135.

[23] Quoted in Marjorie Campbell, comp. *The Story of Guiding in Kent*, 1910–1960 (Dartford: Perry Song & Lack, Ltd., n.d.), 14; GA–London.

[24] "Nellie Priest," in *The Island: Life and Death of an East London Community*, 1870–1970 (London: Centerprise, 1979), 34-35.

[25] Interview with Margaret McMillan in Tunbridge Wells, Kent, 13 April 1993.

[26] Baden-Powell note, 21 December 1927; F.S. Morgan [Kent] to R. Baden-Powell, 7 April 1922, TC/33, SA–London.

[27] Interview with George Herridge in Sheffield, 12 May 1993; Interview with Win Ritchie in Huddersfield, 5 May 1993; Interview with Marjorie Yonwin in Cudham, 28 April 1993; Interview with B. Cobb, in Bushey, Hertfordshire, 24 March 1993.

[28] May Rainer, "Emma's Daughter," TS, 165 pp., Brunel collection, 1977, 56-57; Alice Linton, *Not Expecting Miracles* (London: Centerprise Trust Ltd., 1982), 58-59.

[29] Interview with B. Cobb, in Bushey, Hertfordshire, 24 March 1993.

[30] I draw here on a variety of news articles and photographs deposited at Scout and Guide headquarters in London, and on interviews with former members. William Macadie, "Hiking Through the Past," MS, Spring 1981; TC/316, SA–London. Interview with Margaret McMillan in Tunbridge Wells, Kent, 13 April 1993.

[31] Interview with Jeanne Holloway in Tunbridge Wells, Kent, 13 April 1993.

[32] Harold Wilson, *Memoirs: The Making of a Prime Minister* (London: Weidenfield & Nicholson and Michael Joseph, 1986), 17.

[33] For more information on the postwar feminist movements, see: Brian Harrison, *Prudent Revolutionaries* (New York: Oxford University Press, 1987), Susan Pedersen, "The Failure of Feminism in the Making of the British Welfare State," *Radical History Review* 12 (1989), 86-110; and Susan Kingsley Kent, "Gender Reconstruction After the First World War," in Harold L. Smith, ed., *British Feminism in the Twentieth Century* (Amherst: University of Massachusetts Press, 1990), 66-83.

[34] Vincent Jackson to Robert Baden-Powell 4 January 1929; TC/29, SA–London.

[35] Albert Partridge (16th Lambeth) to Robert Baden-Powell 18 October 1923; TC/194, SA–London.

[36] Robert Baden-Powell to P. Curnow 14 November 1932; TC/194, SA–London.

[37] The logbooks, authored by Anthony Heap, cover several volumes: Vol. I (1927-1929), Vol. II (1930)—both for the Coeur de Lion patrol; Vol I (1931) for the Wayfarers patrol; and Vol. I (1930-1933), Vol. II (1934-1936) for the whole troop. Holborn Rovers and 8th Holborn Scout Troop, TC/239, SA–London.

[38] Heap logbooks, TC/239, SA–London.

[39] Ibid., TC/239, SA–London.

[40] Ibid., TC/239, SA–London.

[41] Ibid., TC/239, SA–London.

[42] Jill Julius Matthews, "They Had Such a Lot of Fun: The Women's League of Health and Beauty between the Wars " *History Workshop Journal* 30 (Autumn 1990), 22-54.

[43] Lizabeth Cohen, "Encountering Mass Culture at the Grassroots: The Experience of Chicago Workers in the 1920s," *American Quarterly* (March 1989), 6-33.

[44] Logbook of 1st Chislehurst Guide Company (1924-), 12 June 1926; Logbook of the 6th Clapton Guide Company Scarlet Pimpernel Patrol (1929-1932), 10 February 1929, 3; GA–London.

[45] Holborn Rovers Troop Logbook, 2 (1934-1936), 110-112. TC/239, SA–London.

[46] Cicely Stewart-Smith, "The Log of a Loafer in the Guides," [unpublished handwritten diary] (1923–1925), GA–London. Boy Scout diaries of A. E. Hughes (1920-1921), TC/85, SA–London. Logbook of 6th Streatham Wolf Cubs (1937); SA–London.

[47] Films, brochures, descriptions, and memorabilia are located in two file boxes (TC/166 and TC/275) at SA–London.

[48] Logbook of 2nd Caversham Guide Company (1918-1924), 12 December 1922; GA–London.

[49] Coeur de Lion Patrol Logbook, 2 (31 January 1930); 1st Holborn Rovers Troop Logbook, 1 (31 March 1931 and 2 November 1932), 80, 235. TC/239, SA–London.

[50] In the Gang Show Silver Jamboree program, Reader is credited with raising more than £500,000 over the years. Gang Show history folder, TC/173, SA–London.

[51] Gang Show—General and Gang Show—History folders. TC/173, SA–London.

[52] For more information on the importance of uniforms and memorabilia in the movements, see Tammy M. Proctor, "(Uni)Forming Youth: Girl Guides and Boy Scouts in Interwar Britain, 1908–1939," *History Workshop Journal* 45 (Spring 1998), 103-134.

[53] Letter from PB Nevill to Chips, 2 July 1960 and pantomime programs from 1928-1973; TC/169, SA–London.

[54] Roland House "Down East" Magazine (Spring 1929), 11; TC/294, SA–London.

[55] 1st Holborn Rovers Troop Log Book, 1 (14 January 1933), 268.

[56] Logbook of Miss Swann, Sheffield Divisional Commissioner (W), collection of Margaret White, Sheffield.

[57] David Fowler, *The First Teenagers: The Lifestyle of Young Wage-Earners in Interwar Britain* (London: Woburn Press, 1995).

[58] There is a rich literature on youth subcultures that has emerged from the work of the Centre for Contemporary Cultural Studies at Birmingham University. Some of the most useful of these studies include Phil Cohen, *Subcultural Conflict and Working-class Community* (Birmingham: CCCS, 1972); Stuart Hall and Tony Jefferson, eds., *Resistance through Rituals* (London: Hutchinson, 1977); Dick Hebdige, *Subculture: The Meaning of Style* (London: Methuen, 1979); and Angela McRobbie and Mica Nava, eds., *Gender and Generation* (London: MacMillan, 1984).

[59] Proctor, "(Uni)Forming Youth," 129.

[60] Interview with Jeanne Holloway in London 27 January 1993; Interview with Ralph Whiteley in Huddersfield 5 May 1993; Interview with Hazel Harrison and Marjorie Yonwin in Cudham, 28 April 1993.

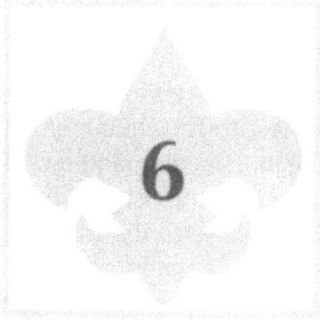

6

C H A P T E R

"LOOKING WIDE"

Capitalizing on their newly won legitimation after World War I and their phenomenal expansion in Britain, the Scouts and Guides moved onto the international scene in earnest in the 1920s and 1930s. Using the language of pacifism, cooperation, and assimilation, Scouts and Guides pictured themselves leading the way to a more peaceful and humane world. The movements hoped to create a feeling of goodwill among nations in Europe and to foster a cooperative spirit in the Empire. International expansion looked promising for the movements and spurred them to "look wide," as Baden-Powell often exhorted them. In particular, Baden-Powell and his organizations looked to the United States for the construction of a British/American alliance to "peacefully penetrate" countries and instill British values. As Baden-Powell said in a speech in the United States in the 1930s:

> If the World War did no other good, indeed it did mostly harm, it did, I think, open our eyes to the fact that patriotism is only a narrow patriotism if it confines itself to getting to the top of one's own country—we want to look beyond that. It wants to look beyond that and see how we can help in the world to bring about peace, and that is a special responsibility for great nations . . .[1]

The responsibility of great nations that Baden-Powell emphasized in his speech is the assumption that white Europeans made up a "natural community," whether they lived in Europe or in the colonies and that they had a duty to "civilize" and "educate." The Anglo coalition that Baden-Powell imagined could bring peace to the world on British terms, by spreading the values Scouting and Guiding espoused. The emphasis on the redeeming qualities of Anglo-Saxon culture was by no means new. In the nineteenth

131

century, imperialism had been justified by theories of white racial superiority. Imperialism was constructed as a duty and a destiny for white men, in particular. Fed by emerging ideas of Social Darwinism, eugenics, and moral reform, imperial apologists such as Cecil Rhodes and Frederick Lugard built their fortunes and careers on theories of Anglo-Saxon superiority. The construction of the dominant Anglo-Saxon race was a reinvigorated and powerful myth by the late nineteenth century, which encompassed thinkers from Fabians to Tariff Reformers.[2] As anthropologist Ann Stoler has found, colonial authority was based on this notion of a homogenous colonizing community, which shared class backgrounds, racial attitudes, and a common culture. This imaginary community of settlers should have then been easily identifiable and separate from the colonized. Of course, neither of these categories reflected the colonial reality of colonizers and colonized because both of these groups were deeply divided by issues of class, religion, and political affiliation, and homogeneity was merely an illusion.[3] This myth, illusory though it might have been, permeated British society until World War I, and it continued to have cultural resonance in the interwar period.

Despite the continuation of such myths, the international brotherhood/sisterhood aspirations of the Scout and Guide movements pointed to a new articulation of empire in post-World War I Britain as well. Apparently Guide and Scout leaders and members in the interwar period could reconcile their conceptions of white supremacy with their stated nonracial policies by erecting boundaries within countries. Indians could be Scouts, but in a separate division. Catholics could be Guides in Malta, but in closed companies. Modifications, accommodations, and assimilation determined the character of Guide and Scout companies.

In addition, the movements embraced an Anglo-American coalition in the post-World War I period both for practical and ideological reasons, despite policy disputes. Concerned with segregation and older notions of British supremacy and white power, yet drawn to the language of international cooperation espoused by agencies such as the League of Nations, Scouting and Guiding used their newly founded World Associations and the funds from U.S./European associations to create a movement with a multiracial membership that became the largest youth organization in the world. By the 1980s, the Scout and Guide movements had a combined world membership of more than twenty million extending across the globe.[4]

In short, Scouting and Guiding did not want to eliminate the British Empire in the interwar period. They wanted to revitalize it with new bonds and relationships that would lead to a peaceful and fundamentally gendered community. Whether it was a debate over the inappropriate name "Girl Scout" or the mixing of racial groups within the movement, gendered constructions of sexuality were major concerns. Guides and Scouts had different obstacles to overcome in their quest for global prominence, yet they also seemed to need each other for defining themselves. Scholarly work has shown how notions of gendered boundaries and sexual control legitimated imperial rule and established boundaries.[5] In order to maintain their boundaries of respectability, the Scouts and Guides had to reconfigure their gendered message of nationalism and adventure as they expanded.

✦ THE CALL OF EMPIRE

Although movements had developed in countries outside of Britain as early as 1910, the most sustained and organized expansion of Scouting and Guiding came in the post-World War I period with the creation of international departments in the organizations. Concerned with the uncontrolled development of programs in other countries, British and American leaders felt the need to provide leadership for fledgling movements, especially in non-white and non-English speaking regions. These same leaders saw an opportunity to create a postwar atmosphere that encouraged cooperation among those of European ancestry around the world—whether in the United States, Britain, Australia, or South Africa, just to name a few.

The Guide International Council was founded by Olave Baden-Powell in February 1919, "for the purpose of carrying assistance and inspiration to those countries newer and consequently smaller and less experienced in the world of Boy Scouting and Girl Guiding." At first, this council was considered advisory and mostly functioned as a means of organizing biennial conferences beginning with the first at Oxford in 1920. This council was dominated by U.S. and British personnel from the beginning, with its headquarters and financial backing coming from London.[6] At the 1926 World Conference at Camp Edith Macy in the United States, Guide and Girl Scout leaders decided to create a more substantial international organization, to accommodate the expanding movement. The World Association of Girl Guides and Girl Scouts (WAGGGS) was formed at the World Conference in Hungary in 1928, with twenty-eight founder member countries. WAGGGS consisted of a World Bureau in London and a World Committee made up of nine elected members from various countries. The British woman chosen to direct this vast world organization was Dame Katharine Furse, former head of the Voluntary Aid Detachment and the Women's Royal Naval Service during the war.[7]

Like the Guides, the Scouts set their sights on an international organization at their first Jamboree, held at Olympia in 1920. At this meeting, Baden-Powell was proclaimed World Chief Scout, and a unanimous vote heralded the formation of an International Bureau and Committee. The former International Commissioner for British Scouting, Hubert Martin, was chosen as the first director, and the International Bureau was established in London with funds from an American donor, F. Peabody. As with the Guide organization, biennial international conferences were held beginning with the Paris Conference of 1922.[8]

These organizations began small, but were prospering by the late 1920s when general optimism about Britain's imperial strength was beginning to wane. The only vital and expanding part of the empire after the war seemed to be the white Dominions, and they became the focal point of government officials, social reformers, and imperial apologists. The Dominions appeared to represent a place where Britain could create a "mythical white community" and regenerate its empire, so it became a political imperative to populate the Dominions to save them from encroachment by non-white peoples. Also, some legislators and social observers saw overseas settlement as a viable solution to Britain's problem with postwar unemployment. British imperialists, concerned with postwar economic and social reconstruction, sought a solution to problems at home that might ensure stability in the empire and Commonwealth as well. Partially shaped by the advent of the U.S. Quota Law in 1921, British emigrants shifted their focus away from the U.S. toward the white Dominions. Officials in voluntary associations and in positions of power within the British government created the Overseas Settlement Committee in 1919 and then passed the Empire Settlement Act in 1922. This legislation allowed for free or assisted passages for ex-servicemen and women, while providing training facilities and grants for groups encouraging emigration of other British citizens, including single women and children.[9]

In practice, the Empire Settlement Act and related governmental initiatives helped more than two million Britons emigrate from 1920 to 1938. Empire settlement was a reaction to domestic economic problems (especially unemployment), but more importantly, it pointed to a new direction for the imperial impetus. As Keith Williams has argued, the Empire Settlement Act reflected a new ethic of imperialism that sought the creation of a "Greater Britain" with the settlement of white Britons in the Dominions. This ethos mirrored earlier concerns with the health of the imperial race and with the protection of overseas colonies, but it went further by advocating the creation of new Britains abroad. As an island, Britain could not expand its boundaries at home, but by creating an ideological and a racial connection abroad, Britain could forge new frontiers.[10]

This concern with forging bonds in the empire appealed to the Scout and Guide associations, with their new emphasis on internationalism. Along with twenty other associations such as the Salvation Army, the YMCA, and the Girls' Friendly Society, the Scout and Guide movements became strong advocates of juvenile migration in the interwar period, setting up their own structures to encourage emigration. Although they had dabbled in migration before the war, Scouting and Guiding never seriously embraced migration as a goal until the early 1920s.[11]

The interwar impetus for juvenile migration was a reflection of a larger program for the migration of children that had begun in the late seventeenth century and continued up to the 1950s. In this long period, most children left Britain for the United States and or the Dominions and only for a couple of decades were substantial numbers of children sent to other countries. From the 1870s to the 1920s, more than 100,000 children moved from Britain to Canada alone, and large numbers also emigrated to Australia, New Zealand, and other parts of the empire. Most of these children were sent under the auspices of orphanages, churches, and reform movements, most notably the Salvation Army and Dr. Barnardo's Homes.[12]

Even with their programs in the 1920s, the Scout and Guide associations never played more than a small role in the overall history of child migration programs in Britain. The Guides operated only a modest migration scheme, probably because the emigration of single females in general was problematic, and few volunteered for the domestic service that they knew awaited them in the Dominions.[13] The Guides sent some girls and young women to the colonies under the auspices of the Society for the Oversea Settlement of British Women (SOSBW), but the numbers were quite low. For instance, in 1930, only about 100 Guides emigrated. Those who did emigrate went as "home-help" with the promise of a choice of occupations after a year of domestic service. Finding a husband was also hinted at in the literature, but the reality was that most girls and young women who emigrated remained in paid domestic service.[14]

Although Guide migration numbers were low, the Scout movement had been encouraging possible migration since 1910. Scouts were told to contact the proper authorities to volunteer to emigrate, and then were often connected to Scout troops abroad when possible. Scouts engineered an efficient migration method: boys left with a Scoutmaster, they were entertained by local Scouts upon their arrival, and they became members of a new Scout troop at their place of employment, if possible.[15] An early example of Scouts who volunteered to emigrate was a group of thirty-two boys and young men en route to Australia in 1913, who formed a Scout troop on board their ship, the *Beltana*. This group planned to keep in touch in Australia and to publish a newsletter. All the members had been Scouts in England, and most came from working-class or lower middle-class urban areas. When the Beltana Troop got to Cape Town, they were shown around town by local Scoutmasters. On board ship, they held three concerts and two afternoons of sport.[16] The Beltana Troop illustrated why Scouting was a useful organization for encouraging migration. Scouts could form connections with members of the organization in other countries, and they might feel more at home in the new environment with the network of peers that Scouting could provide.

These early attempts were sporadic, and most of them ceased with the advent of World War I. However, by 1923 the Scouts had constructed an extremely successful migration program. The movement had always encouraged Scouts to consider themselves pioneers and adventurers, and they had perfected the outdoor ethos through camping, hiking, and nature study.[17] Since land settlement and the hardships and rewards of outdoor life figured largely in the Empire migration programs, Scouting had little problem adapting this message for its own use. The movements publicized migration schemes by issuing a "call of the open" or a "call of empire" to its members, telling Scouts that moving to the dominions would be like one long camp. This call was an "echo of the cry of the early pioneers," and Scouts emphasized the danger, hardship and romance of moving to the colonies in the footsteps of the builders of empire.[18]

The Scout Migration Department participated in a variety of external migration programs, such as the Fairbridge Farm School in Canada and Australia's Big Brother scheme. Along with these external schemes, the Scouts created their own migration programs as well. The Te Poi project was a farm in New Zealand staffed by Scouts and their families that had mild success in the mid-1920s. Scouts trained for the Rhodesian and South African Police forces, and they trained as apprentices in fur trading companies in Canada. The largest number of Scouts went abroad as agricultural workers. A large annual scholarship fund for migration and agricultural training from T. H. Whitehead, an aircraft factory owner, reinforced this emphasis on farming. The Whitehead scholarships for Scouts and Guides began in 1929 with a small grant of £5000, which expanded when the Scouts became residuary legatees of his estate upon his death. From 1929 to 1932, more than seventy Scouts went abroad on Whitehead scholarships.[19] Altogether, more than 5,000 Scouts emigrated to Canada, New Zealand, South Africa, Rhodesia, Australia, and other parts of the empire from 1923 to 1939. The largest numbers went to Australia (more than 3500) and Canada (more than 1000).[20] To put these numbers in context, only about 25,000 unaccompanied male juveniles migrated under the auspices of the Empire Settlement Act in the 1920s.[21]

Perhaps the most ambitious, if not the largest, Scout migration scheme was the Scout training camps for the migration of pit lads. This program took boys aged 14 to 18 from areas that the government had deemed "distressed," and trained them in England for three months before assisting them to migrate to the Dominions. The Ministry of Labour's schedule of Distressed Areas in 1929 included parts of Gloucestershire, Derbyshire, Staffordshire, Durham, Northumberland, Yorkshire, Cumberland, and

Lancashire: all northern counties. The Scouts targeted these areas, and chose boys to travel to the Migration Training Farm in Oxfordshire and the Domestic Training Scheme in Essex. The migration scheme was run as a camp by Doris Mason at Eynsham Hall near Witney. Mason, an enthusiastic Guide, Scoutmaster, and later commissioner, was only 25 when she assumed responsibility for the 'overseas troop" of boys slated to emigrate.

The first camp ran from April 13 to July 16, 1929, and consisted of twelve boys aged 14 to 18 from County Durham. Training consisted of Scouting supervised by Mason and her staff, and each boy had a day job on a nearby farm. Discipline was a problem from the beginning with the boys going to the village without permission and refusing to play cricket. The week of April 23-26 was a crucial one, with some of the boys going on strike. Mason gave them the ultimatum: "To Work, or else, Clear Out." By Friday, April 26, only eight boys remained, and these were still being insubordinate and idle. Four new boys arrived the next week to make up the numbers, and Mason joyously recorded: "Every single one to work—for the first time! Getting more like Scouts." By July, the boys were working, playing cricket, and obeying orders. Eight passed the medical exams for Australia, and seven migrated to Queensland in August.[22]

The Eynsham scheme is important for its intimate look at the goals and methods of the Scout migration programs. Scout authorities sought to train boys not just in agricultural skills, but they also wanted to instill a Scout work ethic as well. The Scout games, badge work, cricket matches, and patrol organization of the Eynsham training camp taught character, and boys learned to be backwoodsmen and pioneers. As one report stated, the poor boys learned the duties of "an Empire-building citizen" and Scout training prepared each boy for the "responsibility he will carry on as an Empire-builder."[23] Encoded in the program was a strong emphasis on British manliness and the responsibilities of the British man in the empire. As Robert MacDonald has persuasively argued in his study of the Scouts, the frontiersman myth functions as a particularly "potent symbol of masculine fantasy" because through this myth, boys could escape into a world "where pure masculine character could be shaped."[24]

The records of the Eynsham scheme also provide some insight into how successful these migration programs were. Boys wrote to Mason about their experiences in Australia and Canada, often asking advice or just reporting progress. These letters show that Scouts often had mixed feelings about emigration when faced with the realities of life in the Dominions; it was not just one long camp as they had been led to believe. Of course, in some cases life had elements of camping and adventure. One Scout, aged 18 when he went to Australia, was not allowed to sleep indoors at his new home, and he milked sixteen cows and slept in a tent in the paddock. He wrote to Mason that he hoped to leave soon because he did not feel settled. Another Scout enjoyed the hardships of work at a fruit orchard, calling the experience "stalking in real life."[25]

In general, though, the Eynsham Scouts had trouble settling into their new environments. Some worked twelve- to fourteen-hour days on isolated farms. Others ran into financial difficulties because they were working only for their board during the first few years. The Scouts felt trapped in dead-end occupations and homesick for their families and friends. Charles Whiting, after three years in Australia, sent a plea to Mason for her assistance with his family. His brother had died and his father was chronically unemployed. Whiting could not come home or send money because of the poor wages he was earning at a farm near Brisbane. Another Scout wrote to Mason in 1933 requesting assistance to come home from Canada to help out his mother.[26] It seemed that Scouting had not prepared the boys for the loneliness and isolation of Dominion life because it was too busy training them to be empire builders. The irony was that the boys worked too hard ever to have a chance to build the empire.

Emigration undoubtedly realized Scout (and Guide) fantasies of living on the frontiers, building up empire, and pursuing adventures. Also, the Scout movement was always eager to capitalize on new ideas, and the well-publicized Empire settlement schemes were creating some enthusiasm. With the advent of economic depression in 1929, Scouting wanted to alleviate the pressures of unemployment at home by training poor boys for agricultural work abroad. However, the most important reason why Scouting and, to a lesser extent, Guiding, established themselves as emigration agencies was because it fit their new ideology of nationalism and imperialism. The two movements were opening up national boundaries and attempting to form an international brotherhood/sisterhood that went beyond empire and consolidated white leadership and power outside of Europe. In effect, the Scouts and Guides in the interwar period sought to create a mythical white community that would be "Greater Britain."

This desire for white community echoed the ideas of many leading proponents of empire migration in the interwar period. At the Ottawa Conference in the early 1930s, the question of empire migration was discussed by a Joint Committee of the Parliamentary Migration Committee and by the Migration Committee of the Royal Empire Society, made up of representatives from migration organizations such as the Scouts, YMCA, and the Boys' Clubs. At this conference, these committees drafted a resolution, writing:

We are of the opinion:

1) That a redistribution of our white population is of urgent importance; it is at once a political and economic necessity, vital to the stability and future well-being of the Empire . . .

2) That the concentration of one-half of the population of the world in and around the Eastern Pacific is a factor which cannot be ignored. . . . There is a risk that other races may not be content to continue only to cast envious eyes on the vast empty spaces of the Southern Continent.

The resolution pointed out that migration relieved unemployment and encouraged trade and stability because "every successful settler in the undeveloped parts of the Empire is a potential customer."[27]

In a way, Scouts and other migration proponents hoped to reconquer the Empire through settlement and dispersal of the white population. The crumbling British Empire might be revitalized through the hardy stock of Britain, especially its vital youth. Just as youth functioned at home as a promise of national revitalization following the war, youth going abroad could also serve this function. As Scout officials wrote in one of their appeals for migration volunteers,

Life is poor without adventure, meaningless without enterprise and endeavour, and the time is much nearer than many people realise when young eager blood will be called once again by the Dominions to lend a hand with Empire building. This is no idle dream. Youth must take its place in the Empire and it is to virile youth that the call will come.[28]

NATURAL SELECTION

With the international expansion and consolidation of the 1920s, Scout and Guide leaders sought to prove that the "fundamental needs of young people are much the same all over the world."[29] This vision was not totally new. From the movements' beginnings, leaders sought religious and social harmony among classes in Britain, and racial harmony in the Empire, but of a particular variety. Baden-Powell apparently hoped to create a truly popular movement, albeit one that would allow white elites to train others to meet the responsibilities of their particular station in life. Non-whites were admitted to the movements to be trained to fulfill their potential within the constraints of their birth. To realize these goals within international Scouting and Guiding, leaders realized that they would have to come up with a flexible program that would help them avoid the potential problems that they would face. The movements had some success in their development of programs that could be adapted to meet the needs of different religions, languages, and social classes, but the issues of race and gender remained obstacles throughout the interwar period.

In Britain, Scout and Guide officials had fought over the place Christianity should have in the movements from their beginnings before World War I. Scout and Guide religious expression was focused on and mediated by Baden-Powell and his ideas. Religion meant good deeds, pure thoughts, service to nation, and an occasional Church Parade. As one clergyman Scoutmaster described it, Scouting was "applied Christianity."[30] How did this application work? From the beginning, Scouts and Guides pledged their faith to God and to the King. They were encouraged to attend a worship service regularly, and often companies and troops went on "parade" at a sponsoring church. If a group was of mixed denominations, then prayer and services were to be simple, general, and voluntary.[31]

Baden-Powell promoted a simple religious message: "Love and serve God. Love and serve your neighbor." The definition of religious observance was purposely "left elastic," so that groups could use Scouting and Guiding to meet their own ends. The only guidance offered to leaders was to emphasize the "heroic side" of religion and to use nature and camp life to illustrate God's work.[32] Members were also encouraged to use Baden-Powell for inspiration and guidance in a Christian idiom, looking to him much as they would Christ. As Eileen Wade wrote in her 1924 biography of Baden-Powell:

> There can never be another discoverer of Scouting, any more than there can ever be a second Founder of Christianity. . . . [Baden-Powell was] a baby whose future career was destined to have perhaps more widely reaching effect than that of any man since the founder of Christianity. No 'star in the East' heralded his coming.[33]

Wade's testimonial echoed that of Scouts and Guides who were using Baden-Powell as an exemplar. An anonymous author spelled out these ideas in an article entitled "Scouting and the Church," which was rejected by the *Manchester Guardian* but kept by Baden-Powell. The author compared Scouting and Christ's teaching, saying that the Scout Law was a "boys' version of the Ten Commandments," and the Scout motto, "Be Prepared," was not unlike Jesus' "Be ye also ready." The author even went so far as to equate Jesus and his disciples with a Scout camp:

> Is it unlike Jesus and His little Troop, as He wandered over the fields and hills of Palestine, noticing the lilies and their colours, the fig tree and the mustard-seed, the foxes and the birds-nests, drawing lessons from them and imparting all the time to His little flock that Divine Life which was in Him. . .[34]

This kind of reinterpretation of Christian ideas happened over and over in the two movements. Scouts and Guides learned lashing and knots by making crucifixes out of sticks and rope, with the Christ figure consisting of a knotted piece of rope. Catholic Girl Guides prayed to "Our Blessed and Immaculate Mother, who is the Guide of all Guides," while a Protestant Guide wrote of being "inspired I am sure with the Guide spirit, which being interpreted is God's spirit."[35] As historians have shown in recent years, formal and orthodox beliefs declined, but religiosity did not in the period surrounding World War I. Spiritualism was popular in the 1920s, and people worshiped by listening to services on the radio in the 1930s. They provided "imaginative and emotional focus in their lives" by creating civil religions surrounding socialist beliefs, imperialism or nationalism.[36] Therefore, theological ambiguity in the Scout and Guide movements did reflect a more general trend in British society in the period.

Perhaps the best and most enduring expression of this melding of Scout and Guide ideas with religion were the "Scouts' Own" and the "Guides' Own." These ceremonies, introduced at the Crystal Palace Rally of 1909 and subsequently developed, were devised as simple, interdenominational religious celebrations. Often consisting of songs, prayer, and a yarn, the "Scouts' Own" encouraged quiet times of reflection and were used at camp and in Scout and Guide meetings. Although invented by "Uncle" H. Geoffrey Elwes, these ceremonies increasingly mirrored Baden-Powell's ideas about individual development and expression. Scout and Guide lore was blended with religious stories and ideas in writing and in practice. Emphasis was on good deeds and upright character, not on salvation after death. As Baden-Powell wrote before his death, "You will find that heaven is not a kind of happiness somewhere up in the skies after you are dead, but right here and now in this world."[37]

This is not to say that all Scouts and Guides followed Baden-Powell's ideas on religion. There were many members with deeply held formal religious convictions, some of whom kept their religion separate from their activities in the two movements. Most controversy, however, arose in the Scout movements over the inclusion of non-Christian members in the movements, especially Hindus, Muslims, and Buddhists. The Jewish population, leaders believed, could be more easily included in religious celebrations because they believed in the same God as the Christians. With the expansion of the movements outside of Britain, however, the inclusion of non-Christians and non-Jews became an issue. At a conference held in East London in 1930 on the issue of Scouting and the Churches, Rev. Colin Carr, a rector from Spitalfields, voiced the objection that many Christians in the movement shared. He accused Scouting of carrying "comparative religion" too far, and he called this policy "anti-Christian." Carr continued, saying, ". . . we cannot put our hearts into a movement which inculcates into boys at the most impressionable age that it does not really matter whether they follow Jesus Christ, Buddha, or Mahomet."[38]

Baden-Powell maintained a predictable stance on the issue, saying any religion was better than none at all. He continually spoke of the "realisation of God in Nature," as more important than a dispute over particular beliefs and practices. To one earlier complaint, he answered:

> So far as having an Arab and Hindu at our "Scouts Own" at Gillwell, we could easily have driven them away by keeping the service to a strictly Christian line. We preferred to take the wider view of recognizing our brother Scouts as being also sons of the same Father with ourselves. They were broad minded enough to listen to our Scriptures; it was not very much for us in return to listen to a chapter from the Koran. You probably know the Koran yourself and will agree that it contains very fine ideas and inspiring words, and I am positive we did ourselves no spiritual harm but good from what we heard that day.[39]

Baden-Powell here suggests not only that strictly Christian services be sensitive to non-Christians but that other religious traditions be welcome in mixed gatherings. He asks for a tolerant and open approach to religious practice. Although Baden-Powell preferred to sit the fence on the matter of religion offering vague expressions of religious tolerance, he still had to contend with a vocal Christian presence in the Scouts that disagreed with his policies.

The most important of these critics was "Uncle" H. Geoffrey Elwes, founder of the 1st Colchester Scout Troop and editor of the Scout magazines, *Headquarters Gazette* from 1911 to 1922 and *Scouter* from 1923 to 1926. A lawyer and a devout Christian, Elwes had begun work with youth in the Boys Brigade movement in 1899 and with the Scouts in 1908. Through his editorial control of the Scout magazine for leaders, and his visible presence at conferences, rallies, and meetings, Elwes had a profound influence on early Scouting. Although confined to a wheelchair after 1922, Elwes continued to work tirelessly for the Scout cause until his death in 1936.[40]

In general, Elwes enthusiastically supported Baden-Powell and his ideas, but they did clash rather seriously over the question of religion. In 1921, Baden-Powell wrote to Elwes to object to his use of Jesus in a speech to Scouters of various faiths. Elwes wrote a scathing reply, obviously upset over the issue. In a long and articulate letter, Elwes laid out his beliefs and his criticisms for Baden-Powell:

> We are quite willing to meet and welcome as Brothers Jews and others who sincerely acknowledge the Fatherhood of God, and to let them go their own way;—but a vague sort of indefinite woodcraft God of Nature is no help to us, and if we may not mention Christianity when we want to help each other because of the possibility of a Jew etc. being present, it makes it impossible for us to have any religious observances, or to touch on what to us are the only things that really matter.

Elwes went on to cite instances when he spoke of Jesus at large rallies in 1909 and 1914 and was praised for it. He warned Baden-Powell that "if Christianity is to be left out for the sake of embracing non-Christians, there will come a great split" in the Scout movement.[41]

Baden-Powell backed down immediately from this challenge by Elwes, writing:

> It was only a minor question of courtesy towards men of other beliefs. These as a rule show broad minded courtesy to us Christians, especially the Mohameddans who, as you know, make it a capital offence for anyone to abuse the name of Christ. We are strong enough, in our Faith, to meet them with an equal courtesy. The ideas you imply other than this never entered my head, so please dismiss them from your mind.[42]

Baden-Powell successfully quieted the fears of leaders such as Elwes, defending his actions as mere courtesy, while pursuing a policy in the international realm that did encourage the development of flexible religious programs.

Although other challenges occurred throughout the 1920s, by the early 1930s individual religious expression was the order of the day and prayers, sermons, and publications carefully reflected the inclusion of non-Christians. In adult training notebooks, trainers were adjured to "inculcate reverence, whatever form of religion the boy professes." They were also taught to use nature to teach the kind of interdenominational spirituality that Scouting and Guiding espoused: "Not nature study as a form of worship or substitute for religion, but [a] step towards gaining humility and reverence." Prayers also reflected the religious policy with vague references to deities: "Do Thou raise our thoughts and purify our aspirations; Strengthen our wills on the side of what is right and good, and against what is wrong and evil."[43]

Despite disagreements and controversy, Scouts, Guides, and leaders accepted and used the odd mix of God, Baden-Powell, and Britain that the movements offered in the interwar period. Members used the flexibility of the policies to fit their own needs, changing the rules to suit their beliefs. Abroad, the importance of this religious policy cannot be underestimated, as members who would have been excluded from many international social organizations because of their non-Christian beliefs were welcomed to worship as they pleased. The thread that held this tenuous flexibility together both in Britain and in the Empire was the emphasis on reverence of nature. Camping and nature-craft were the dominant spiritual ties in the movements, and fit splendidly into most religious belief systems.

Despite the popularity and flexibility of this policy, however, more complicated problems arose in the global Scout and Guide communities over the accommodation of religious beliefs and the solution of disputes in areas with more than one dominant religion. Accommodating various religions was one of the easier problems for the international movements to solve, but the issue of countries with several religious traditions was sometimes a more insoluble difficulty. Scouts and Guides provided separate worship facilities at camps, events, and training, and they encouraged generic prayers for peace in mixed gatherings. In addition, the Scouts and Guides were lenient with the rules in individual countries. For instance, in Malaya, a large multiracial and mixed-religion national Guide movement arose in the 1920s, led at first by white missionaries. As Janice Brownfoot has demonstrated, Guiding achieved success in the Muslim community because of its nonsectarian pronouncements and because Malay Guides were allowed to design their own uniform. The khaki uniform was modified to meet restrictions on Muslim girls that required them to cover their limbs. Just a small change in uniform such as this could smooth a difficult situation.[44]

Likewise, the question of recognition of only one national movement could often be a tricky situation for the Scouts and Guides. Their policy was to require affiliation of different divisions under the aegis of one national organization. This could sometimes be problematic in countries where different religious groups had separate movements. For instance, in France two groups existed side by side: the Scouts and the Guides (Catholic) and the Eclaireurs/Eclaireuses (Protestant). In Malta, where Guiding began in 1918, "Trouble arose between the Maltese Roman Catholics, and the English Protestants, and they had a 'crisis' every few weeks." Eventually, two divisions were formed that reflected the religious divisions, but also the racial divisions in Malta.[45]

In addition to questions of recognition, Scout and Guide officials were called upon to deal with regional and local disputes within countries over religion. In the Caribbean, one Guide leader wrote, ". . . we are all mixed up, our greatest difficulty being class and degrees of colour." She illustrated her difficulties by listing the six companies in Trinidad and Tobago:

> Co. 1 - middle class black co with equally divided religion; leader Anglican
> Co. 2 - middle class white co, 2/3 Roman Catholic; leaders Anglican
> Co. 3 - high class black and few white Anglican
> Co. 4 - very poor black co, 1/3 Roman Catholic; Roman Catholic leader
> Co. 5 - poor black Anglican co, with 2 Scotch Church leaders
> Co. 6 - poor black Anglican co, with Roman Catholic leader[46]

For the leader in Trinidad and Tobago, class and race were more important distinctions than religion, when deciding how to divide the companies. On nearby St. Lucia, the opposite was true, as nuns protested when a Protestant leader tried to take over a Catholic Guide company.[47] This problem arose in many countries with nonhomogenous populations, especially in the United States, the Caribbean, and British/French colonies.[48] In countries such as Ireland and Canada, distinctions between Catholics and Protestants were of paramount importance because of the political resonance of religious identities. Religion was tied to culture, politics, and language, and separate Scout and Guide groups were the rule.

As indicated in Trinidad and Tobago, perhaps more divisive than religion was the question of race. The Scout and Guide white global community was continually threatened and compromised by the large numbers of nonwhite youth who wanted a part in the movements. Officially, the two movements maintained a nondiscrimination policy that prohibited exclusion of youth because of race or color, but in reality that policy was problematic. In Bermuda, Guides were designated "white only" until 1930, and in the Bahamas, nonwhite Guides were prohibited throughout the interwar period. Even in countries that had mixed organizations, nonwhite groups were often subject to "special," or simplified Guide activities and rules.

Olave Baden-Powell and other leaders made their position on race clear in notes and correspondence on the companies at St. Helena. The Guides and Scouts there were run by a "native" clergyman, L.C. Walcott, and his white wife. Baden-Powell could not fault Mrs. Walcott's abilities, calling her the "prop and stay" of St. Helena Guiding and "perfectly splendid." However, she considered her unsuitable as a Guide leader in many ways, describing her as "a very pathetic person" because of her marriage. A Guide leader seconded this opinion in a letter to Olave Baden-Powell regarding Walcott in 1936, "She has, of course, grave limitations, one of which is the fact that she is married to a native."[49]

In British colonies, race was a special concern because of the growth of nationalist movements. Just as colonial authorities were often ambivalent toward missionaries, who often as not created revolutionaries rather than docile workers in their mission schools, they also treated youth movements with some suspicion, figuring that they could perform a similar function.[50] "Belge" Wilson, Deputy Commissioner of Police and Scoutmaster of a mixed troop of Anglo-Indian youth in Calcutta, remembered struggling mightily for the admittance of Indian boys into the Boy Scouts Association after World War I. Wilson noted that there was a Government of India Act forbidding the movement on the grounds that "Scouting might train them to be revolutionaries." Finally, in 1921 the various official and unofficial Scout groups in India were amalgamated into one association, which the government sanctioned. Janice Brownfoot found a similar reluctance in Malaya to accept Guiding at first. Colonial officials seemed to see the movement as subversive at first but they embraced the Guides by the late 1920s.[51]

Implicit in these concerns over race and revolutionary activity was the question of nationalism or patriotism. Both Scouts and Guides had always encouraged loyalty to one's country as well as an international ethic of friendship, but in the interwar period, the line between positive and negative nationalism did not seem clear. Following the violence of World War I, balancing loyalty to nation and international brotherhood/sisterhood was difficult for some. For example, at the 1937 Jamboree in Holland, British Scouts learned about the delicacy of international peace. While building a bridge, a Dutch farmer interfered and stopped their activities by taking away their staves. They threw mud-clots and shouted at him. As one Scout, recorded, "How easy it must be for 'international incidents' to arise . . ."[52]

The balancing of nationalist loyalties and international aspirations became increasingly difficult with the rise of ultranationalist youth movements in places such as Italy and Germany in the 1920s and 1930s. At the 1933 Jamboree in Godollo, Hungary, members of Balilla (Italian youth organization) and the Hitler-Jugend (German youth organization) attended uninvited as visitors. They were received unofficially and "in a friendly fashion," but their refusal to embrace internationalism meant their exclusion from any "official affiliation" with Scouting.[53] This was a contentious issue in the movements, however, with some leaders proposing alliances. Katherine Furse wrote in the Guide World magazine in 1938:

> I have long felt that we should be able to find some way of co-operating more with the youth movements in countries like Germany and Italy, if they were allowed to co-operate with us on a free and equal basis. Our reason given for not admitting them now, should they wish to join us, is that they are political and that Guiding must maintain its non-political status. But is Guiding really non-political in fact?[54]

Furse contended that Guiding was used for political purposes in many countries and always would be, no matter what the pronouncements from headquarters. She advocated an open policy toward other youth organizations. Few leaders agreed with her sentiments, and most recognized that Scouting and Guiding had to retain a nonpolitical image to maintain their reputation and members.

Nationalism was a problem on the local level as well, especially in the empire. For example, Afrikaans Scouts in South Africa did not want to pledge allegiance to the British king; in India, Bluebirds (Indian Brownies) had to pledge to the King-Emperor. Scouts and Guides had to consider their promises, which were taken very seriously, and figure out their own feelings on the subject. Some wrote to London for advice, as this eleven-year-old Jamaican Guide wrote to Olave Baden-Powell:

> Please may I be enrolled as a Lone Guide? I am 11 years old but I will be 12 June 27th. My grandmother says I may and so does Daddy. I can make up beds and take care of babies, and set tables and all that sort of thing. We are going to New York this fall, but if I became an American Girl Scout I would have to pledge allegiance to the American flag, and that wouldn't be honourable if I love England best, that's why I must be an English guide.[55]

As this Guide pointed out, a promise was a serious thing, and Scouts and Guides often worried about their patriotic loyalties. The International Bureaus did all that they could to create exceptions for those who needed to change the promise or the uniform or the activities in order to be loyal to their countries, religious beliefs, or families. This flexibility was one of the reasons for the successful expansion and longevity of the international movements.

Beyond concerns with race, class, nationalism, and religion within the movements at home and abroad, the issue of the appropriate inculcation of sexual identity remained central. Complicating this problem of how to train both boys and girls in a variety of religious and cultural settings was the fact that leaders themselves had trouble agreeing on how this should be done. From the founding of the Girl Scouts of the U.S.A. in 1912 by Juliette Gordon Low, British and American Scout and Guide leaders found themselves in profound disagreement on the nature of the girls' movement. Certainly, British Guide and American Girl Scout leaders corresponded frequently during World War I and into the early 1920s, and a genuine spirit of cooperation and advice seemed to flourish. Often personnel from one movement would journey to the other country to attend events, offer criticism, or to raise funds. Even before the establishment of the international organization, leaders from the two countries relied on each other. The one issue that really divided leaders was the question of the naming of the girls' movement. British leaders continually pressed the Girl Scouts to adopt the name "Guides," arguing that only confusion could result.

After the battles in Britain to create a separate and appropriate girls movement of a different name, it seemed that the American Girl Scout movement could only cause uncomfortable questions about the nature of British Guiding. All the questions of respectability and femininity were raised again, only on a worldwide scale. The American girls' organization had always been known as Girl Scouts, and some other countries also instituted movements with this name. Despite repeated attempts by the Guide association in Britain to convince the Americans to change, Girl Scouting was well-established and beloved. Following a visit to Britain in 1920 Helen Storrow, Vice-President of the Girl Scouts of the U.S.A., wrote a report for her council on the trip and she sent a report to the Girl Guides. In her report to the British leaders, she made the American position on the question of naming clear. She explained and proposed her own solution:

> Our name, Girl Scouts, is very dear to us, and seems to us the logical name. The terms scout and scouting apply to girls and their activities as appropriately as to boys, and represent the same law and ideals. The idea that we are trying to make boys out of the girls is soon dissipated when the girls show their increased usefulness at home, and demonstrate womanly activities at their rallies. The suggestion to change the name met with determined opposition from both our girls and their officers, and we shall in all probability remain scouts. I wish most heartily we might share the same name. Would the Guides consider changing? I wish they would.[56]

After ten years of emphasizing that Girl Scouts did not exist in Britain, Guide leaders were as unlikely to change their name as the Americans were to embrace the Guide name and emblem. The relationship between the organizations remained cordial in the interwar period except for issues that addressed naming. Real problems arose in the 1920s as the World Association began to recognize official movements in new countries. Apparently, Girl Scout and Girl Guide organizations existed side by side in some places, and in other cases, Guide and Scout organizers squabbled over the naming of the new organization. The British and American leaders became quite territorial in the matter of new organizations, and correspondence between the two countries reflected a continuing tension over how to name the girls' movement.

Siam was one such country of contention when in 1921 girls began to organize a sister movement to Boy Scouting. Olave Baden-Powell wrote to the Girl Scout leaders in the United States, urging the Americans to allow her leaders to "guide" Siam in its development. She pointed out that strong Guide organizations existed in neighboring Malaya, Hong Kong, and Burma, but she also noted that a Guide organizer had already been dispatched to the area. After a delicate reference to the fact that Guide and

Scout work are the same "except in name," Baden-Powell launched into her real objections. Baden-Powell pointed to problems in Palestine and India with Girl Scouts wrecking local Guide movements and causing confusion about the "true" nature of Guiding. Above all, she worried that Girl Scouting was equated with masculine pursuits, especially in non-western countries:

> It is not the name IN AMERICA that matters, but the misinterpretation that is ALWAYS put upon it in other countries. It so obviously shows that it is to all intents and purposes the same thing for the girls as "scouting" is for boys, and good as we know that to be in a strange, and especially an Eastern, land, it goes against the movement . . .[57]

In short, she believed that Girl Scouting would be considered the same movement as Boy Scouting and that parents would envision coeducational activities, which she thought would be counterproductive. As she noted in her letter, "pushing Western ideas onto Eastern peoples needs care and tact," implying that the British had a better understanding of such process-es than the Americans:

> We have to reckon, in promoting this quite modern and Western idea, with Caste, Creeds of all kinds, Climate, Languages, Customs, Racial feelings and National feel-ings, as well as Politics and it really is most important that where it is being pushed it must be done by the right people in the right way![58]

Of course, underlying Baden-Powell's surface objections to the name was the desire for British headquarters to control new movements spring-ing up, but her comments also illustrate the continuing importance of the gendered nature of the movements in Britain and abroad. Perhaps this concern was best expressed by Boy Scout leaders, who felt compelled to comment on the question of girls. At the Boy Scout International Conference in Paris in 1922, a resolution was passed to request that Guides stop using the name "Scout" or "Eclaireuse," echoing the strong disapproval many boys' organizations felt over what they saw as girls aping boys. As Hubert Martin pointed out in a memo to Baden-Powell, "It is one of her [a woman's] jobs in life to guide—not to Scout, which is the man's job." He continued:

> But my personal anxiety about many Guide companies is the danger that they, through wrong leadership, will produce a race of tomboys, than which there is noth-ing more objectionable. . . . It seems to me that the use of the term "Girl Scout" is a big question of principle and that the persistence of its use is symptomatic of the tom-boy, aping the man, instead of concentrating on woman's most important sphere—the home . . .

Martin really touched on the heart of the issue: had girls become too mas-culine? Were they losing their femininity and their domestic skills? As he wrote in his report, "The tendency amongst the girls of today is to neglect their own sphere, the home, and try to ape the man—hence the collar and tie, the 'Eton crop' etc. etc."[59] As with many of the tensions confronting the

Scout and Guide movements in the interwar period, international expansion also brought to the fore old anxieties about teaching and reinforcing appropriate notions of femininity and masculinity.

⚜ CONCLUSION

Throughout the interwar period international peace was a stated priority, if not always a reality, in the two movements. The Scouts and Guides had concrete ideas about how to bring peace and to make the "brotherhood" and "sisterhood" a reality even if they continually ran into obstacles in the countries they entered. Members were encouraged to camp abroad whenever possible, and pen-pal schemes were created as well. World, national, and regional camps were held on a regular basis, with Scout World Jamborees every four years, and Guide World Camps every two years. Additionally, goodwill missions and expeditions were held, such as the "Argosy of Peace" cruise on the *Calgaric* in the summer of 1933. This joint Scout and Guide cruise had more than 600 adult members of the movements visiting northern Europe by ocean liner. It was followed by cruises to the Mediterranean in 1934 and to the Arctic Circle in 1938.[60]

In addition, the world movements each got a boost with the acquisition of international camping and training facilities in Switzerland. The Scout hostel, Kandersteg, was purchased in 1923 by donors, and surrounding land was acquired in 1929. It remains a training and camping center to this day. The Guide hostel, "Our Chalet," in Adelboden, Switzerland, was paid for by U.S. Girl Scout executive Helen Storrow. "Our Chalet" opened in July 1932 as a training and camping center like Kandersteg. Beyond these well-known Swiss centers, smaller training and camping facilities opened around the world in the 1920s and 1930s.

As the physical spaces of world Scouting and Guiding were developing, the movements worked to make the two organizations more accessible to a variety of youth. Translation of Scout and Guide literature had high priority in the interwar years. *Scouting for Boys* was translated into almost thirty languages by the early 1930s, including Indian vernaculars, Cantonese, Swahili, Russian, and Braille. *Girl Guiding* was available in Singhalese, Greek, Norwegian, Afrikaans, and more than a dozen other languages by 1933. The Scouts and Guides were ahead of some other organizations in this respect and could attribute some of their success internationally to the availability of their literature. For instance, in South Africa both *Scouting for Boys* and *Girl Guiding* were translated into Afrikaans by 1927; the Bible had only been translated into that language in 1925.[61]

The expansion of Guiding and Scouting internationally was a great boost for the movements in Britain and it won them acclaim from educators, government officials, social organizations, and even the League of Nations. However, the extension of the Scout and Guide program into other countries produced problems both abroad and at home, as contradictions appeared in the ideologies and activities of the organizations. The movements began to recognize the deep divisions with the "Anglo coalition" that they sought to create, as British and American visions of the movements' directions diverged. More importantly, however, Scouting and Guiding, while attempting to make their imagined worldwide white settler community a reality, faced increasing pressure from nonwhite groups drawn to the programs. Practically, this meant that the organizations had to accommodate different races, religions, languages, and nations in its new global brotherhood/sisterhood while in the process of defining the meaning of the international movements.[62] This became particularly problematic in countries with serious political divisions based on race or religion, and it was those countries where the Scout and Guide vision of the postwar world foundered. By the outbreak of World War II, it seemed that the two organizations would have to again redefine their mission in Britain and in the empire in order to survive.

ENDNOTES

[1] Address by Baden-Powell in USA, n.d; Baden-Powell Collection (946–986), Reel 8, Manuscripts 1930s; Boy Scouts of America, Murray, Kentucky.

[2] On the Victorian re-creation of the Anglo-Saxon myth, see Robert H. MacDonald, *The Language of Empire: Myths and Metaphors of Popular Imperialism, 1880–1918* (Manchester: Manchester University Press, 1994), 4, 53–54; and Kathryn Tidrick, *Empire and the English Character* (London: I. B. Taurus & Co., Ltd., 1990), 49–50. The best general introduction to British imperial thought is still: Bernard Semmel, *Imperialism and Social Reform: English Social Imperial Thought* (New York: George Allen & Unwin, Ltd., 1960).

[3] Ann L. Stoler, "Making Empire Respectable: The Politics of Race and Sexual Morality in 20th Century Colonial Cultures," *American Ethnologist* 16:4 (November 1989), 635.

[4] Vronwyn M. Thompson, *1910 . . . and Then? A Brief History of the Girl Guides Association* (London: Girl Guides Association, 1990), 33. *75 Years of Scouting: A History of the Scout Movement in Words and Pictures* (London: Scout Association, 1982), 55.

[5] See, in particular, Ann Stoler, *Race and the Education of Desire: Foucault's History of Sexuality and the Colonial Order of Things* (Durham and London: Duke University Press, 1995).

[6] Girl Guides Association, *Annual Report 1919*, 21; Mrs. Herbert Hoover, "The Girl Guide International Conference," TS, 14 May 1926, WAGGGS–International Council folder; *The WAGGGS* (London: WAGGGS, May 1938), 2; GSUSA–New York.

[7] Rose Kerr, *The Story of A Million Girls* (London: Girl Guides Association, 1936), 388–390.

[8] *The History and Organization of World Scouting* (London: Boy Scouts Association, n.d. [approx. 1938]), 2, TC/183, SA–London. R.T. Lund, "History of World Scout Bureau," TS,

1971, 1–3, TC/86, SA–London. John S. Wilson, *Scouting Round the World* (London: Blandford Press, 1959), 44–45.

[9] For a good treatment of the politics and realities of the Empire Settlement Act and interwar migration, see: Stephen Constantine, ed., *Emigrants and Empire: British Settlement in the Dominions Between the Wars* (Manchester: Manchester University Press, 1990). The classic study of interwar migration is G.F. Plant, *Oversea Settlement: Migration from the United Kingdom to the Dominions* (London: Oxford University Press, 1951). Especially useful is Plant's discussion of the drop in emigration to the U. S. on pages 91–92.

[10] Keith Williams, "A way out of our troubles? The Politics of Empire Settlement, 1900–1922," in *Emigrants and Empire British Settlement in the Dominions between the Wars*, ed. Stephen Constantine (Manchester: Manchester University Press, 1990), 22–26. For emigration figures, see introductory essay by Stephen Constantine, "Introduction: Empire migration and imperial harmony," in the same volume. A comprehensive look at interwar migration schemes in Britain is Kent Fedorowich, *Unfit for Heroes: Reconstruction and Soldier Settlement in the Empire between the Wars* (Manchester: Manchester University Press, 1995).

[11] Alex G. Scholes, *Education for Empire Settlement: A Study of Juvenile Migration* (London/New York: Longmans, Green & Co., 1932), 80.

[12] Gillian Wagner, *Children of the Empire* (London: Weidenfeld and Nicolson, 1982), xi–xiii, 220. See also Philip Bean and Joy Melville, *Lost Children of the Empire* (London: Unwin Hyman, 1989).

[13] Janice Gothard, "'The Healthy, Wholesome British Domestic Girl': Single Female Migration and the Empire Settlement Act, 1922–1930," 72–95, in Constantine, *Emigrants and Empire*, 1990. As Gothard points out, even with free or drastically reduced passages, fewer than 100,000 women were induced to emigrate as domestics under the provisions of the Empire Settlement Act. For a longterm history of female emigration and its problems, see A. James Hammerton, *Emigrant Gentlewomen: Genteel Poverty and Female Emigration, 1830–1914* (London: Croom Helm, 1979).

[14] Society for the Oversea Settlement of British Women, *Britain's Call from Overseas* (London, 1929), 2–4. Girl Guides Association, *Annual Report* (London: Girl Guides Association, 1930), 77. On the official history of the development of women's migration, see Una Monk, *New Horizons: A Hundred Years of Women's Migration* (London: HMSO, 1963).

[15] Scholes, *Education for Empire Settlement*, 79.

[16] Beltana Troop of Overseas B.P. Boy Scouts (At Sea) to Captain Wade, 21 June 1913; TC/215, SA–London.

[17] On adventure, see Martin Green, *The Adventurous Male: Chapters in the History of the Male Mind* (University Park: Pennsylvania State University Press, 1993). On adventure and the frontier ethos in Scouting, see Robert MacDonald, *Sons of the Empire: The Frontier and the Boy Scout Movement, 1890–1918* (Toronto: University of Toronto Press, 1993), 8–9, 119, 143–146.

[18] Boy Scouts Association (Migration Dept.), *The Call of Empire* (London: Boy Scouts Association, 1939), 1–2.

[19] On the Te Poi project, E. Fox to Robert Baden-Powell, Christmas 1930, TC/27, SA–London. On types of employment migrating Scouts took, see "Peopling the Vacant Spaces," *Annual Report* (London: Scout Association, 1931), 48. Information on T. H.

Whitehead and his scholarships can be found in Wilson, *Scouting Round the World*, 82. Memo on Migration figures from 1924 to 1932, TC/27, SA–London, shows that seventy-seven Whitehead scholarships were taken.

[20] Migration figures are drawn from annual reports and quarterly migration statistical reports; TC/215, SA–London.

[21] Scholes, *Education for Empire Settlement*, 83.

[22] Boy Scout Diaries of Doris Mason, 1925–1934, TC/296, SA–London; Scout Migration Eynsham Hall folder, TC/295, SA–London. The Eynsham Hall materials include letters to Doris Mason from the boys and the log books for the overseas troops.

[23] Report on Boy Scout Training Camps for Migration of Pit Lads, 1929, TC/215, SA–London.

[24] MacDonald, *Sons of the Empire*, 9, 40, 45. MacDonald is especially persuasive in his discussion of the connections between the frontiersman myth in American culture and the empire-builder myth in Britain.

[25] Tom Martin to Doris Mason, 1930; Isaac West to Doris Mason, 17 November 1930; TC/295, SA–London.

[26] Charlie Whiting to Doris Mason, 7 October 1929 and 31 May 1932; Isaac West to Doris Mason, 12 October 1929; T. Milburn to Doris Mason, nd.; S. R. Davidson to Doris Mason, 24 September 1933; TC/295, SA–London.

[27] Empire Migration and Settlement and the Ottawa Conference, Confidential Memo by Joint Committee of Parliamentary Migration Committee and the Migration Committee of the Royal Empire Society; Scout Migration Scheme Reports, TC/215, SA–London. Scouts members of the Royal Empire Society were Kenneth Lindsay and the head of the Scout Migration Department, C. J. Sutton.

[28] "Boy Scout Migration," *The Scouter*, 30:11 (November 1936), 407.

[29] World Association of Girl Guides and Girl Scouts, WAGGGS *Information* [pamphlet], (London: WAGGGS, 1 May 1938), 11. WAGGGS/General, GSUSA–New York.

[30] Miscellaneous jottings of Baden-Powell, Founder files, TC/95, SA–London.

[31] For the official religious policies of the two movements, see Boy Scout Association, *Policy, Organisation and Rules* (London: Boy Scout Association, 1911), 11–12; and Girl Guides Association, *Policy, Organisation and Rules* (London: Girl Guides Association, 1916), 5–6.

[32] Robert Baden-Powell, *Scouting for Boys* (London: C. Arthur Pearson, 1942), 248, 323.

[33] Eileen K. Wade, *The Piper of Pax: The Life Story of Sir Robert Baden-Powell* (London: C. Arthur Pearson, 1924), 11, 13.

[34] *Scouting and the Church*, TS, 30 July 1917, 8–9, 11; TC/25, SA–London.

[35] Knotted crucifixes hang in the chapel at Gilwell today. "The Catholic Share in the Girl Guide," *The Catholic Women's Outlook*, 2 (April 1925), 45, religious policy folder, GA–London. Marguerite de Beaumont, "Log of a Lilywhite Cadet," description of Commissioner's Conference, 4–11 October 1920, at Swanwick, GA–London.

[36] James Obelkevich, "Religion," in *The Cambridge Social History of Britain, 1750–1950*, ed. F. M. L. Thompson (Cambridge: Cambridge University Press, 1990), 346–348, 355–356; J. M.

Winter, "Spiritualism and the First World War," in *Religion and Irreligion in Victorian Society* ed. R. W. Davis and R. J. Helmstadter (London: Routledge, 1992), 185–200. For work on religion in the late nineteenth and early twentieth centuries, see Jeffrey Cox, *The English Churches in a Secular Society: Lambeth 1870–1930* (Oxford: Oxford University Press, 1982); Hugh McLeod, *Class and Religion in the Late Victorian City* (London: Croom Helm, 1974); Norman Vance, *The Sinews of the Spirit: The Ideal of Christian Manliness in Victorian Literature and Religious Thought* (Cambridge: Cambridge University Press, 1985).

[37] Marquerite de Beaumont, *The Wolf That Never Sleeps: A Story of Baden-Powell* (London: Girl Guides Association, 1944; reprinted 1984), 79.

[38] "Verbatim Report of East London Conference on the Churches and the Boy Scout Movement," held 22 November 1930 at People's Palace, Mile End Road, 19–21; TC/229, SA–London.

[39] Robert Baden-Powell to H.R. Harvey, 17 November 1921, TC/25, SA–London.

[40] H. F. Hutton, *It Happened This Way: The Story of A Scout Group 1908–1957* (Privately printed, 1957), 7, 25, SA–London. "H. Geoffrey Elwes," *Down East* (Roland House magazine), 28 (Christmas 1936), 5; TC/294, SA–London.

[41] H. Geoffrey Elwes to Robert Baden-Powell, 21 November 1921, TC/25, SA–London.

[42] Robert Baden-Powell to H. Geoffrey Elwes, 22 November 1921, TC/25, SA–London.

[43] "Scouting and Religion." TS Adult Training Notebook, 1920s, 203, 212–214; TC/124, SA–London.

[44] Mira Mladejovska, "The Guide and Religion," *Council Fire* 8:3 (July 1938), 38–39. Janice Brownfoot, "Sisters under the Skin Imperialism and the Emancipation of Women in Malaya, c. 1891–1941," 46–73, in J. A. Mangan, ed., *Making Imperial Mentalities: Socialisation and British Imperialism* (Manchester: Manchester University Press, 1990), 61–64.

[45] Olave Baden-Powell's notebook on Dominions and Colonies, November 1930, MALTA; GA–London.

[46] Gwendolyn Lake (Trinidad and Tobago) to D. Vinter (St. Lucia), 16 October 1925; Country History box–St. Lucia, GA–London.

[47] D. Vinter (St. Lucia) to Gwendolyn Lake (Trinidad and Tobago), 6 October 1925; Country History box–St. Lucia, GA–London.

[48] On the United States, see two articles by Elisabeth Israels Perry: "From Achievement to Happiness: Girl Scouting in Middle Tennessee, 1910s–1960s," *Journal of Women's History* 5:2 (Fall 1993), 75–94; "'The Very Best Influence': Josephine Holloway and Girl Scouting in Nashville's African-American Community," *Tennessee Historical Quarterly* 52:2 (Summer 1993), 73–85. I am indebted to Kari Frederickson for these references.

[49] Olave Baden-Powell's Notebook on Dominions and Colonies, November 1930, St. Helena; Memo to Olave Baden-Powell Re: St. Helena, 1936, Country History box–St. Helena, GA–London.

[50] See, for example: Jean Allman, "Making Mothers: Missionaries, Medical Officers and Women's Work in Colonial Asante, 1924–1945," *History Workshop Journal* 38 (1994), 23–47; and Andrew Ross, *John Philip, 1775–1851: Mission, Race and Politics in South Africa* (Aberdeen: Aberdeen University Press, 1986).

[51] Wilson, *Scouting Round the World*, 19–20; Brownfoot, "Sisters under the Skin," 64.

[52] Eton Scout—Watkin Williams, Diary of Dutch Jamboree, 14, 18, 23; TC/243, SA–London.

[53] Wilson, *Scouting Round the World*, 88.

[54] Katharine Furse, "Looking Forward," *Council Fire* 8:3 (July 1938), 35–37.

[55] Katharine Rathbone to Olave Baden-Powell, 4 May 1921; GSUSA–New York.

[56] Helen Storrow, "Girl Guiding from the Point of View of a Girl Scout,"(June 1920), Girl Guide Box, GSUSA–New York.

[57] Olave Baden-Powell to Miss Clendenin, 2 June 1921; WAGGGS, GSUSA–New York.

[58] Ibid., 2 June 1921; WAGGGS, GSUSA–New York.

[59] Memo to Robert Baden-Powell from Hubert S. Martin (International Director), 13 August 1926; forwarded to Miss Arnold (Girl Scouts of USA) 15 August 1926; WAGGGS, GSUSA-New York.

[60] Boy Scouts Association, *Year Book* 1927–28 (London: Boy Scouts Association, 1928), 7. Several in-house publications chart these trips, see Rose Kerr, *The Cruise of the Calgaric* (London: Girl Guides Association, 1933); *The Cruise of the Adriatic* (London: Girl Guides Association, 1934); *The Cruise of the Orduna* (London: Girl Guides Association, 1938); GA–London.

[61] Robert Brandon (Pearson's) to Miss Mcintyre (Girl Guides Assoc.) 24 May 1946; TS List of *Girl Guiding* Translations, 1951; Guiding Publications file, GA–London. Leonard Thompson, A *History of South Africa* (New Haven/London: Yale University Press, 1990), 160. Previously, the Bible had been read in either English or Dutch.

[62] Tammy Proctor, "'A Separate Path': Scouting and Guiding in Interwar South Africa," *Comparative Studies in Society and History*, 42:3 (July 2000), 605–631.

CONCLUSION
Gender-Free Scouting?

Just over eighty years after a mismatched group of girls demanded that they be recognized as Scouts, the organization "opened its tents to girls." In the spring of 1990, the Scout Association invited interested girls of all ages to join its ranks, allowing for the creation of Girl Scouts in Britain for the first time since those unofficial groups of early girls. Girls had been part of the senior "Venture Scout" scheme since the 1970s, but had never before been welcome in the younger sections.[1] By 1993, when the Scout Law was revised to reflect this so-called "Gender-free Scouting," a little under 20,000 girls were enrolled in the movement in Britain, bringing Scout membership to just more than 650,000.[2]

Boys' reactions to the 1990 ruling seem to have been mixed. One Scout leader wrote *The Times* to say that his Scouts had voted to admit girls, after being promised that their own sisters would not be included.[3] In another letter a few days later, ten-year old Scout Adam Smith expressed his concerns with the new scheme:

> I do not think it is right to let the girls join Scouts because sometimes boys like to be without the girls for they have the rest of the week to be with the girls. Over the last week I have asked my friends to sign a petition against girls joining Scouts. Forty per cent of the girls signed it and all of the boys . . .

Besides, as Smith reasoned: "If all the girls join Scouts there will be nothing left of the Guides."[4] Young Adam Smith had discovered the crux of the problem. Guiding had been created to fill a need for a Scout-like organization for the girls who wanted desperately to be Scouts. With the opening of

Scouting to girls, would girls still want to be Guides? The Guide Association, with more than 700,000 members in Britain in 1989–90, was now in the odd position of competing with the Scouts for the allegiance of British girls; these two organizations that had been created as complementary and cooperating were vying for the same population of children and youth.[5] In newspaper reports, the Scouts denied trying to steal the Guides' members, but the decision to accept girls did seem to be a betrayal of the founding vision of the movements. Scouts were not asking the female-led Guides to change into Girl Scouts, thereby amalgamating into one organization. Instead, they were simply admitting girls to their movement and ignoring the impact on Guiding. The boundaries of appropriate masculinity and femininity that had been so painstakingly constructed by the founders of Guiding and Scouting between 1909 and the 1930s had been crossed, creating fear and uncertainty about the future of both associations.

These fears echoed concerns both movements have been confronting since 1908. As I have argued, although products of Edwardian Britain, Scouting and Guiding experienced their greatest growth in the interwar period, eventually becoming the largest voluntary youth organizations in the world. Today, there are more than thirty-eight million Scouts and Guides in over 200 countries and territories around the world.[6] Estimates of those who have been involved in the movements at some point in their lives are difficult to calculate, but the organizations have maintained astounding membership figures both in Britain and abroad for almost one hundred years. In addition, Scouts and Guides function as popular cultural icons, appearing in films, books, political cartoons, and news media. In short, both have been hugely popular and extremely influential.

In the 1920s and 1930s the Scouts and Guides assuaged adult fears about generational conflict and gender transgression, while attracting millions of young people to their ranks. The shift in the movements' ideology and image that followed the Great War reflected a need in Britain to find in its youth symbolic assurance of an imagined past and an ideal future. With the advent of World War I, the gendering of the two movements took on new and important meaning when the promise to serve was redefined. Suddenly Scouts literally sacrificed their lives for God, nation, and humanity in record numbers, while Guides threw themselves wholeheartedly into work outside of the home. After the war the organizations became even more important to a nation scrambling to legitimate and memorialize the deaths of so many. Scouts and Guides functioned as a living memorial to the fallen and as a public reminder of the resilience of youth. Serving the nation came to signify the highly gendered roles of men as hero-martyrs and women as mothers in the Scout and Guide movements after the war. The war also catapulted the movements to an international prominence that became vital to the interwar vision. Beginning with the United States and the

Commonwealth countries in the 1910s, Guiding and Scouting spread to the rest of the empire and to most other parts of the world by the 1920s. The spread of Guiding and Scouting overseas made British members feel even more that they were involved in an important mission, as vital as that of the missionaries and explorers of a century earlier. The international nature of the organizations allowed youth of many countries to interact on a personal basis, breaking down some racial barriers, but not all.

Just as World War I transformed the organization, World War II brought new changes as well. The initial vigor and excitement of Scouting and Guiding in Britain seemed to disappear with the end of World War II. Leadership, which had waned from 1939–45 as men joined the armed forces and women also joined the war as workers, auxiliaries, and volunteers, did not immediately rebound. In fact, postwar membership figures in general declined in the late 1940s, and only rebounded after changes had been made in the organizations. Whereas World War I had provided impetus to the movements and helped them gain respectability, the Second World War showed both leaders and youth the world of options opening up for them. The death of Robert Baden-Powell on January 8, 1941, in Kenya, also had taken a toll on the organizations. Even though he had been increasingly inactive in his last few years, he had remained a spiritual force at the center of the movement. B-P's yearly Christmas cards, his newsreels, books, and articles had been a defining force in the two movements for more than thirty years. His death left a vacuum, but it also freed the leadership of the Scouts and Guides to make some significant changes. New handbooks were written, badges were altered, uniforms became more modern, and fresh leadership entered the organizations by the mid-1950s. However, as Tim Jeal points out, these changes did not create a sense of excitement in older boys and girls, they merely served to expand the younger sections of the movements: Brownies and Cubs. In fact, today the bulk of the movements' members are under 12.[7]

Perhaps Guiding and Scouting had lost their ability to picture their organizations as arenas of freedom from parental supervision by the 1950s. As eminently respectable and highly structured institutions, the two movements no longer had the spontaneity of their earlier years. By the 1950s, Scouting and Guiding had to combat images of their members as old-fashioned, stodgy, and traditional. National gatherings such as jamborees and Gilwell reunions saw a mixture of Old Scouts/Guides (aged 30–50) and very young members. For teens, other organizations and leisure activities seemed to provide more excitement, and a younger crowd. The vision that had made the groups popular had changed. Despite the temporary drop in membership in the 1940s, the organizations still exist as the largest voluntary youth movements in the world, and the Scouts are already planning for their centenary celebration in 2007. Festivities in Britain and around the world will mark one hundred years of Scouting and celebrate that first camp at Brownsea Island in 1907. The longevity and success of these youth organizations owes much to the creation of flexible movements in the first 30 years of Guiding and Scouting. Between 1908–1940, the Guides and Scouts had created a youth subculture that provided important outlets for members. They were part of an internationally respected organization, yet they could exercise some freedom from political authority. They felt a part of Britain's national and imperial destiny, yet they could pursue that destiny in a fun way. Members believed they belonged to something larger than themselves, as is evident from the uniforms and other signs of membership, yet they could retain an individual identity within their local groups.

By focusing on interwar Scouting and Guiding at home and in the empire, this book demonstrates how a reconstructed and gendered vision of youth served national and imperial requirements, while at the same time providing opportunities for millions of young people to shape their own identities. The Guides and Scouts became a unique space for youth that allowed boys and girls to stretch gender and generational boundaries, and the importance of the two organizations should not be underestimated in the 1920s and 1930s. Scouts and Guides represented a nostalgia for the nineteenth century with its imperial splendor, its veneer of respectability, and its moral code, while simultaneously embodying the modern: consumption, stimulation, and body culture. These two youth movements had created a reality that straddled two worlds for a generation seeking comfort from the war's shattering of illusions and from the bewildering speed of postwar society.

Baden-Powell quoted Benjamin Kidd in his conclusion to *Girl Guiding*, written just at the end of World War I. This passage encapsulates the mission and the vision, only partially fulfilled, that the Scout and Guide movements chased between the wars:

> Oh! You wise men who would reconstruct the world! Give us the young. Give us the young. Do what you will with the world, only give us the young. It is the dreams which we teach them: it is the Utopias which we conceive for them: it is the thoughts which we think for them, which will rebuild the world.[8]

ENDNOTES

[1] "Scouting Prepares for Girls," *The Times* (9 February 1990), 10.

[2] "Three Cheers Postponed," and "Gender Free Scouting," *Scouting* 87:11 (November 1993), 9–13.

[3] Trevor E. Parry to the Editor, *The Times* (15 February 1990), 15.

[4] Adam Smith to the Editor, *The Times* (19 February 1990), 15.

[5] "Eighty Years on, a Bastion Crumbles," *The Times* (9 February 1990), 1; and "Scouting

Prepares for Girls," *The Times* (9 February 1990), 10. In 1990, forty-one percent of all 8-year-olds in Britain were Guides.

[6] Figures are taken from fact sheets published by the Scout and Guide Associations on their web pages. For the Scouts, the Scout Information Centre's World Scouting report (based on 1999 figures) appears at *www.scout.org*. The Guide current membership information is listed on the World Association of Girl Guides and Girl Scouts page at *www.wagggsworld.org*.

[7] Tim Jeal, *The Boy-Man: The Life of Lord Baden-Powell* (New York: William Morrow, 1990), 574. The Guides and Scouts now have new sections for very young children. For boys, the new group is the Beavers, and for girls, it is the Rainbows.

[8] Robert Baden-Powell, *Girl Guiding* (London: C. Arthur Pearson, 1921), 200.

SELECT BIBLIOGRAPHY

I. ARCHIVES AND COLLECTIONS

Beinecke Rare Books and Manuscripts Collection–Yale University
Boy Scouts of America (BSA)–Murray, KY
Brunel University Library
Girl Scouts of the U.S.A. (GSUSA)–New York, NY
Guide Association Archives (GA)–London
Guide records in possession of Jane Frenneaux, Doncaster, Yorks.
Guide records in possession of Margaret Pearson, Grimsby, S. Humb.
Guide records in possession of Sheila Marks, Ilkley, Yorks.
Imperial War Museum–London
Kirklees Sound Archive, Huddersfield, Yorks.
New York Public Library
Reed Book Services Library, Rushden, Northants.
School of Oriental and African Studies–University of London
Scout and Guide archives, Sheffield, Yorks.
Scout Association Archives (SA)–London
Scout center (formerly Roland House) of East London
Scout records in possession of Gwen Pearson, Huddersfield, Yorks.
Southwark Local Studies Library
Uxbridge Local Studies Library

II. ORAL HISTORY INTERVIEWS

Madge Bamford
Anthony Bolton
Phyllis Bratt
J. Derek Breakey
Muriel Brown
B. Cobb (Cobbie)
Margery Collins
Wyn Everett
Dench Gibbons
Harold Green
Hazel Harrison
George Herridge
Freda Hollamby
Jeanne Holloway
Hilda Holmes
Phyllis Holmes
Leslie Horsfall

Joan Joscelyne
Peter Kimpton
Eileen Mace
Peggy McGill
Margaret McMillan
Malcolm Pearson
Betty Prance
Daisy Priest
Win Ritchie
Marjorie Robbins
Lady Marjorie Stopford
Dennis Trotter
Margaret White
Ralph Whiteley
Cath Wilson
Marjorie Yonwin

III. NEWSPAPERS, PERIODICALS, JOURNALS

Berrow's Worcester Journal
Birkenhead Advertiser
The Catholic Women's Outlook
Daily Express
Daily Mail
Daily Mirror
Daily Worker
Down East
Dundee People's Friend
Home Chat
Ikwezi le Afrika

Illustrated London News
Liverpool Daily Courier
Natal Mercury
Newbury Weekly News
Punch
Race Relations
S.P.G. Mission
The Spectator
Times
Yorkshire Post

IV. PUBLISHED PRIMARY SOURCES

A. SCOUT ASSOCIATION PUBLICATIONS

The Akela Leaders Handbook. 1924
Annual Competitions: Rules and Conditions.
    London, January 1913
Annual Report. 1909–
Boy Scouts and What They Do. London:
    Oldfields, 1914
Headquarters Gazette

The Pathfinder
Policy, Organisation, and Rules. London,
    1911–
The Scout
Scouter
Scouting

B. GUIDE ASSOCIATION PUBLICATIONS

Annual Report. 1912–
Council Fire
Girl Guides Gazette
The Guide

Guider
Home Notes
Policy, Organisation, and Rules. 1916–

C. OTHER PRIMARY SOURCES

Aldis, Janet. *A Girl Guide Captain in India*. Madras: Methodist Publishing House, 1922.

Booth, Charles. *Life and Labour of the People in London*. London/New York: Macmillan, 1902.

Census of England and Wales 1921. London: His Majesty's Stationery Office, 1924.

Census of England and Wales 1931. London: His Majesty's Stationery Office, 1934.

Smith, Hubert Llewellyn. *The New Survey of London Life and Labour* (vol. IX). London: P.S. King and Son Ltd., 1935.

Society for the Overseas Settlement of British Women. *Britain's Call from Overseas*. London: HMS Office, 1929.

Statistical Abstract for the United Kingdom: No. 72 (1913–1927). London, 1929.

Synge, Violet. *Royal Guides: A Story of the 1st Buckingham Palace Company*. London: Girl Guides Association, 1948.

V. HANDBOOKS AND OFFICIAL HISTORIES

Baden-Powell, Agnes. *The Handbook for Girl Guides, or How Girls Can Help Build the Empire*. London: Thomas Nelson and Sons, 1912.

Baden-Powell, Olave. *Training Girls as Guides*. London: C. Arthur Pearson, 1917.

Baden-Powell, Robert. *Girl Guiding*. London: C. Arthur Pearson, 1921.

_____. *The Great Trek of the Early Scouts of South Africa for Rovers, Patrol Leaders and King's Scouts*. London: Jackson & Co., 1936.

_____. *Pamphlet A: Girl Guides*. 1910.

_____. *Quick Training for War*. New York: Duffield and Company, 1914.

_____. *Rovering to Success: A Book of Life-Sport for Young Men*. London: Herbert Jenkins Ltd., 1922.

_____. *Scouting for Boys*. London: C. Arthur Pearson, 1942 (memorial edition).

_____. *The Wolf Cub Handbook*. London: C. Arthur Pearson, 1916.

Baden-Powell, Robert, and Olave Baden-Powell. *Report on the Boy Scouts and Girl Guides in South Africa*. London: Boy Scouts Association, 1927.

Barnes, Kitty. *Here Come the Girl Guides*. London: Girl Guides Association, 1956.

Boy Scouts Association (Migration Dept.), *The Call of Empire*. London: Boy Scouts Association, 1939.

Campbell, Marjorie, comp. *The Story of Guiding in Kent, 1910–1960*. Dartford: Perry Song & Lack, Ltd., n.d.

Collis, Henry, Fred Hurll and Rex Hazlewood. *B-P's Scouts: An Official History of the Boy Scouts Association*. London: Collins, 1961.

Girl Wayfarers Association. *Handbook of Rules and Organisation "Upward."* 1926.

Kerr, Rose. *The Story of a Million Girls*. London: Girl Guides Association, 1936.

_____. *The Story of the Girl Guides*. London: Girl Guides Association, 1954.

Liddell, Alix. *The Girl Guides, 1910–1970*. London: Frederick Muller, 1970.

Philipps, Roland. *The Patrol System and Letters to a Patrol Leader*. London: C. Arthur Pearson, 1917.

75 *Years of Scouting: A History of the Scout Movement in Words and Pictures*. London: Scout Association, 1982.

Thompson, Vronwyn M. *1910 . . . and Then? A Brief History of the Girl Guides Association*. London: Girl Guides Association, 1990.

The WAGGGS. London: WAGGGS, May 1938.

Wilson, J. S. *Scouting Round the World*. London: Blandford Press, 1959.

World Association of Girl Guides and Girl Scouts. WAGGGS *Information* [pamphlet]. London: WAGGGS, May 1938.

VI. AUTOBIOGRAPHIES, BIOGRAPHIES, AND MEMOIRS

Baden-Powell, Olave, as told to Mary Drewery. *Window on My Heart*. London: Hodder & Stoughton, 1973.

Bagnold, Enid. *Letters to Frank Harris and Other Friends*. London: William Heineman Ltd, 1980.

Baker, Michael. *Our Three Selves: The Life of Radclyffe Hall*. New York: Morrow, 1985.

Batchelder, W.J. and David Balfour. *The Scout's Life of Baden-Powell*. London: Collins Clear-Type Press, 1929.

Bermant, Chaim. *Coming Home*. London: George Allen & Unwin, 1976.

Brittain, Vera. *Testament of Youth*. USA: Wideview Books, 1980.

Brookes, Edgar H. R. J. Johannesburg: The South African Institute on Race Relations, 1953.

Cotton, William. *I Did It My Way: The Life Story of Billy Cotton*. London: Harrap, 1970.

Dark, Sidney. *The Life of Sir Arthur Pearson*. London: Hodder & Stoughton, 1922.

De Beaumont, Marguerite. *The Wolf That Never Sleeps: A Story of Baden-Powell*. London: Girl Guides Association, 1944; reprinted 1984.

Ezard, Edward. *Battersea Boy*. London: William Kimber, 1979.

Furse, Katharine. *Hearts and Pomegranates*. London: Peter Davies, 1940.

Hattersley, Roy. *A Yorkshire Boyhood*. London: Pan Books, 1990.

Holmes, G. V. *The Likes of Us*. London: Frederick Muller, Ltd., 1948.

Holt, William. *I Haven't Unpacked: An Autobiography*. London: George Harrap and Co., 1939.

Holtby, Winifred. *Women and a Changing Civilisation*. New York: Longman, Green, and Co., 1936.

Horwood, Wally. *A Walworth Boy: Looking Back on Growing Up 1922–1939*. Southwark Local Studies Library, 1977.

The Island: Life and Death of an East London Community, 1870–1970. London: Centerprise, 1979.

Izzard, Molly. *A Heroine in her Time: A Life of Dame Helen Gwynne-Vaughan, 1879–1967*. London: MacMillan, 1969.

Jeal, Tim. *The Boy-Man: The Life of Lord Baden-Powell*. New York: William Morrow, 1990.

Kiernan, R.H. *Baden-Powell*. London: George G. Harrap, 1939.

Linton, Alice. *Not Expecting Miracles*. London: Centerprise Trust Ltd., 1982.

Renshaw, Winifred. *An Ordinary Life: Memories of a Balby Childhood*. Doncaster: Doncaster Library Services, 1984.

Rodaway, Angela. *A London Childhood*. London: B. T. Batsford Ltd., 1960.

Scannell, Dorothy. *Mother Knew Best: Memoir of a London Girlhood*. USA: Pantheon, 1974.

Tucker, William. *Autobiography of an Astrologer*. Sidcup: Pythagorean, 1960.

Wade, Eileen K. *The Piper of Pax: The Life Story of Sir Robert Baden-Powell*. London: C. Arthur Pearson, 1924.

_____. *Twenty-Seven Years with Baden-Powell*. London: Blandford Press, 1957.

Weir, Molly. *Shoes Were for Sunday*. London: Hutchinson & Co, 1970.

Wilson, Harold. *Memoirs: The Making of a Prime Minister*. London: Weidenfield & Nicholson and Michael Joseph, 1986.

VII. SECONDARY WORKS

Adas, Michael. *Machines as the Measure of Men*. Ithaca/London: Cornell University Press, 1989.

Alberti, Johanna. *Beyond Suffrage: Feminists in War and Peace, 1914–1928*. London: MacMillan, 1989.

Alexander, Sally. "Becoming a Woman in London in the 1920s and 1930s." In *Metropolis London: Histories and Representations since 1800*, eds. David Feldman and Gareth Stedman Jones. London: Routledge, 1989.

Allman, Jean. "Making Mothers: Missionaries, Medical Officers and Women's Work in Colonial Asante, 1924–1945," *History Workshop Journal* 38 (1994), 23–47.

Anderson, Benedict. *Imagined Communities: Reflections on the Origins and Spread of Nationalism*, rev. ed. London/New York: Verson, 1991.

Anderson, Olive. "The Growth of Christian Militarism in Mid-Victorian Britain." *English Historical Review* 86 (January 1971), 46–72.

Ballhatchet, Kenneth. *Race, Sex and Class Under the Raj: Imperial Attitudes and Policies and their Critics, 1793–1905*. New York: St. Martin's Press, 1980.

Bean, Philip, and Joy Melville. *Lost Children of the Empire*. London: Unwin Hyman, 1989.

Beddoe, Deirdre. *Back to Home and Duty: Women between the Wars, 1918–1939*. London: Pandora, 1989.

Blanch, Michael. "Imperialism, Nationalism and Organized Youth." In *Working Class Culture: Studies in History and Theory*, eds. John Clarke, Charles Critcher, and Richard Johnson. Birmingham: Centre for Cultural Studies, 1979.

Bourke, Joanna. *Dismembering the Male: Men's Bodies, Britain and the Great War*. London: Reaktion Books, 1996.

Branson, Noreen. *Britain in the Nineteen Twenties*. London: Weidenfield and Nicholson, 1975.

Brantlinger, Patrick. *Rule of Darkness: British Literature and Imperialism, 1830–1914*. Ithaca/London: Cornell University Press, 1988.

Braybon, Gail. *Women Workers in the First World War*. London/New York: Routledge, 1989.

Brittain, Vera. *Lady into Woman*. New York: MacMillan, 1953.

Brod, Harry, ed. *The Making of Masculinities: The New Men's Studies*. Boston: Allen & Unwin, 1987.

Brogan, Hugh. *Mowgli's Sons: Kipling and Baden-Powell's Scouts*. London: Jonathan Cape, 1987.

Brook, Roy. *The Story of Huddersfield*. London: MacGibbon and Kee, 1968.

Brown, Kenneth D. "Modelling for War? Toy Soldiers in Late Victorian and Edwardian Britain. *Journal of Social History* 24:2 (1990): 237–254.

Brown, Victoria Bissell. "Golden Girls: Female Socialization among the Middle Class of Los Angeles, 1880–1910." In *Small Worlds: Children and Adolescents in America, 1850–1950*, eds. Elliott West and Paula Petrik. Lawrence: University of Kansas Press, 1992.

Brownfoot, Janice. "Sisters under the Skin: Imperialism and the Emancipation of Women in Malaya, c. 1891–1941." In *Making Imperial Mentalities: Socialisation and British Imperialism*, ed. J. A. Mangan. Manchester: Manchester University Press, 1990.

Bryder, Linda. "'Wonderlands of Buttercups, Clover and Daisies:' Tuberculosis and the Open Air School Movement in Britain, 1907–1939." In *In the Name of the Child: Health and Welfare, 1880–1940*, ed. Roger Cooter. London/New York: Routledge, 1992.

Budd, Michael Anton. "Heroic Bodies: Physical Culture, Commerce and the Promise of the Perfected Self, 1898–1918." PhD diss., Rutgers, October 1992.

Burke, Timothy. *Lifebuoy Men, Lux Women: Commodificaiton, Consumption, and Cleanliness in Modern Zimbabwe*. Durham: Duke University Press, 1996.

Burnett, John. *Destiny Obscure: Autobiographies of Childhood, Education and Family from the 1830s to the 1920s*. Harmondsworth: Penguin, 1984.

Calloway, Helen. *Gender, Culture, and the Empire*. Urbana: University of Illinois Press, 1987.

Cannadine, David. "The Context, Performance and Meaning of Ritual: The British Monarchy and the Invention of Tradition." In *The Invention of Tradition*, eds. Eric Hobsbawm and Terence Ranger. Cambridge: Cambridge University Press, 1983.

Cell, John. *The Highest Stage of White Supremacy: The Origins of Segregation in South Africa and the American South*. Cambridge: Cambridge University Press, 1982.

Chaudhuri, Nupur and Margaret Strobel, eds. *Western Women and Imperialism: Complicity and Resistance*. Bloomington: University of Indiana Press, 1992.

Childs, Michael. *Labour's Apprentices: Working-class Lads in Late Victorian and Edwardian England*. London: Hambledon Press, 1992.

Clarke, John, Charles Critcher and Richard Johnson, eds. *Working-Class Culture: Studies in History and Theory*. Birmingham: Centre for Cultural Studies, 1979.

Coates, A. J. *The Ethics of War*. Manchester: Manchester University Press, 1997.

Cohen, Lizabeth. "Encountering Mass Culture at the Grassroots: the Experience of Chicago Workers in the 1920s." *American Quarterly* (March 1989), 6–33.

Cohen, Phil. *Subcultural Conflict and Working-Class Community*. Birmingham: CCCS, 1972.

Constantine, Stephen. *Buy and Build: The Advertising Posters of the Empire Marketing Board*. London: HMSO, 1986.

_____. *Emigrants and Empire: British Settlement in the Dominions between the Wars*. Manchester: Manchester University Press, 1990.

Cooter, Roger, ed. *In the Name of the Child: Health and Welfare, 1880–1940*. London/New York: Routledge, 1992.

Cornell, Richard. "The Origins and Development of the Communist Youth International 1914–1924." PhD diss., Columbia University, 1965.

Cox, Jeffrey. *The English Churches in a Secular Society: Lambeth 1870–1930*. Oxford: Oxford University Press, 1982.

Davidoff, Leonore. "The Family in Britain." In *The Cambridge Social History of Britain,1750–1950*, ed. F. M. L. Thompson. Cambridge: Cambridge University Press, 1990.

Davies, Robert. "Mining Capital, the State, and Unskilled White Workers in South Africa, 1901–1913." *Journal of South African Studies* 3:1 (October 1976), 41–69.

Davin, Anna. *Growing Up Poor: Home, School and Street in London, 1870–1914*. London: Rivers Oram Press, 1996.

_____. "Imperialism and Motherhood." *History Workshop Journal* 5 (1978), 9–65.

Davis, Fred. *Fashion, Culture, and Identity*. Chicago/London: University of Chicago Press, 1992.

Davis, R. W., and R. J. Helmstadter, eds. *Religion and Irreligion in Victorian Society*. London: Routledge, 1992.

Dedman, Martin. "Baden-Powell, Militarism, and the 'Invisible Contributors' to the Boy Scout Scheme, 1904–1920." *Twentieth Century British History* 4:3 (1993), 201–223.

de Grazia, Victoria. *How Fascism Ruled Women*. Berkeley: University of California Press, 1992.

Dickson, Lovat. *Radclyffe Hall at the Well of Loneliness*. New York: Scribner's, 1975.

Doan, Laura. "Passing Fashions: Reading Female Masculinities in the 1920s." *Feminist Studies* 24:3 (Fall 1998): 663–700.

Dwork, Deborah. *War is Good for Babies and Other Young Children: A History of the Infant and Child Welfare Movement in England, 1898–1918*. London/New York: Tavistock, 1987.

Dyhouse, Carol. *Feminism and the Family in England, 1880–1939*. Oxford/New York: Basil Blackwell, 1989.

_____. *Girls Growing Up in Late Victorian and Edwardian England*. London: Routledge, 1981.

Eksteins, Modris. *Rites of Spring: The Great War and the Birth of the Modern Age*. New York: Doubleday, 1989.

Enloe, Cynthia. *Bananas, Beaches and Bases*. Berkeley: University of California Press, 1989.

Fedorowich, Kent. *Unfit for Heroes: Reconstruction and Soldier Settlement in the Empire between the Wars*. Manchester: Manchester University Press, 1995.

Feldman, David and Gareth Stedman Jones, eds. *Metropolis London: Histories and Representations since 1800*. London: Routledge and Kegan Paul, 1989.

Fletcher, Sheila. *Women First: The Female Tradition in English Physical Education, 1880–1980*. London/Dover, NH: Athlone Press, 1984.

Formes, Malia. "Beyond Complicity versus Resistance: A Review of Recent Work on Gender and European Imperialism." *Journal of Social History* 28:3 (March 1995), 629–641.

Fowler, David. *The First Teenagers: the Lifestyle of Young Wage-Earners in Interwar Britain*. London: Woburn Press, 1995.

Fussell, Paul. *The Great War and Modern Memory*. London: Oxford University Press, 1975.

Gaitskell, Deborah. "Female Mission Initiatives: Black and White Women in Three Witwatersrand Churches, 1903–1939." PhD. Diss. University of London, 1981.

Galbraith, Gretchen. *Reading Lives: Reconstructing Childhood, Books, and Schools in Britain, 1870–1920*. New York: St. Martin's Press, 1997.

Gardner, Brian. *Mafeking: A Victorian Legend*. London: Cassell, 1966.

Geyer, Michael. "The Militarization of Europe, 1914–1945." In *The Militarization of the Western World*, ed. John Gillis. New Brunswick: Rutgers University Press, 1989.

Gilbert, Sandra. "Soldier's Heart: Literary Men, Literary Women, and the Great War." In *Behind the Lines: Gender and the Two World Wars*, eds. Margaret Higonnet et al. New Haven: Yale University Press, 1987.

Gillis, John, ed. *Commemorations: The Politics of National Identity*. Princeton: Princeton University Press, 1994.

_____. ed. *The Militarization of the Western World*. New Brunswick: Rutgers University Press, 1989.

_____. *Youth and History: Tradition and Change in Early Age Relations, 1770–present*. New York: Academic Press, 1974.

Girouard, Mark. *The Return to Camelot: Chivalry and the English Gentleman*. New Haven/London: Yale University Press, 1981.

Gittins, Diana. *Fair Sex: Family Size and Structure, 1900–1939*. London: Hutchinson, 1982.

Gorham, Deborah. *The Victorian Girl and the Feminine Ideal*. Bloomington: Indiana University Press, 1982.

Gothard, Janice. "'The Healthy, Wholesome British Domestic Girl': Single Female Migration and the Empire Settlement Act, 1922–1930." In *Emigrants and Empire: British Settlement in the Dominions between the Wars*, ed. Stephen Constantine. Manchester: Manchester University Press, 1990.

Gould, Jenny. "Women's Military Services in First World War Britain." In *Behind the Lines: Gender and the Two World Wars*, eds. Margaret Higonnet et al. New Haven: Yale University Press, 1987.

Gould, Peter. *Early Green Politics: Back to Nature, Back to the Land, and Socialism in Britain, 1880–1900*. New York: St. Martin's Press, 1988.

Grayzel, Susan. "'The Outward and Visible Sign of Her Patriotism': Women, Uniforms, and National Service During the First World War," *Twentieth Century British History* 8:2 (1997): 145–164.

_____. *Women's Identities at War: Gender, Motherhood, and Politics in Britain and France during the First World War.* Chapel Hill and London: The University of North Carolina Press, 1999.

Green, Martin. *The Adventurous Male: Chapters in the History of the Male Mind.* University Park: Pennsylvania State University Press, 1993.

Gullace, Nicoletta. "White Feathers and Wounded Men: Female Patriotism and the Memory of the Great War," *Journal of British Studies* 36:2 (1997): 178–206.

Hall, Stuart, and Tony Jefferson, eds. *Resistance through Rituals.* London: Hutchinson, 1977.

Hammerton, A. James. *Emigrant Gentlewomen: Genteel Poverty and Female Emigration, 1830–1914.* London: Croom Helm, 1979.

Hantover, Jeffrey P. "The Boy Scouts and the Validation of Masculinity," *Journal of Social Issues* 34:1 (1978).

Hargreaves, Jennifer. *Sporting Females: Critical Issues in the History and Sociology of Women's Sports.* London/New York: Routledge, 1994.

Harrison, Brian. *Prudent Revolutionaries: Portraits of British Feminists between the Wars.* New York: Oxford University Press, 1987.

_____. *Separate Spheres: The Opposition to Women's Suffrage in Britain.* New York: Holmes and Meier Publishers Inc., 1978.

Hebdige, Dick. *Subculture: The Meaning of Style.* London: Methuen, 1979.

Hendrick, Harry. *Images of Youth: Age, Class and the Male Youth Problem, 1880–1920.* Oxford: Clarendon Press, 1990.

Hey, David. *Yorkshire from A.D. 1000.* London: Longman, 1986.

Higonnet, Margaret et al., eds. *Behind the Lines: Gender and the Two World Wars.* New Haven/London: Yale University Press, 1987.

Hirsch, Eric. "Voices from the Black Box: Folk Song, Boy Scouts and the Construction of Folk Nationalist Hegemony in Hungary, 1930–1944." *Antipode* 29:2 (1997): 197–215.

Hobsbawm, Eric and Terence Ranger, eds. *The Invention of Tradition.* Cambridge: Cambridge University Press, 1983.

Hobsbawm, Eric. *Nations and Nationalism since 1780: Programme, Myth, Reality.* Cambridge: Cambridge University Press, 1990.

Hoggart, Keith and David R. Green, eds. *London: A New Metropolitan Geography.* London: Edward Arnold, 1991.

Holtzman, Ellen. "The Pursuit of Married Love: Women's Attitudes towards Sexuality and Marriage in Britain, 1918–1939," *Journal of Social History* 16 (1982), 39–51.

Hunt, Felicity, ed. *Lessons for Life: The Schooling of Girls and Women.* Oxford: Basil Blackwell, 1987.

Hynes, Samuel. *The Edwardian Turn of Mind.* Princeton: Princeton University Press, 1968.

_____. *A War Imagined: The First World War and English Culture.* New York: Atenaeum, 1990.

Inglis, K. S. "The Homecoming: The War Memorial Movement in Cambridge, England." *Journal of Contemporary History* 27:4 (October 1992), 583–605.

Johnstone, F.A. *Class, Race and Gold: A Study of Class Relations and Racial Discrimination in South Africa.* London: Routledge, 1976.

Jones, Gareth Stedman. "Class Expression versus Social Control? A Critique of Recent Trends in the Social History of Leisure." In *Languages of Class: Studies in Working Class History, 1832–1982,* ed. Gareth Stedman Jones. Cambridge: Cambridge University Press, 1983.

Joseph, Nathan. *Uniforms and Nonuniforms: Communication through Clothing*. New York: Greenwood Press, 1986.

Kahane, Reuven. *The Origins of Postmodern Youth: Informal Youth Movements in a Comparative Perspective*. Berlin/New York: Walter de Gruyter, 1997.

Kalloway, Peter, ed. *Apartheid and Black Education: The Education of Black South Africans*. Johannesburg: Ravan Press, 1984.

Kennedy, Dane. "Imperial History and Post-Colonial Theory." *Journal of Imperial and Commonwealth History* 24:3 (1996): 345–363.

_____. "The Imperial Kaleidoscope." *Journal of British Studies* 37:4 (1998): 460–467.

Kent, Susan Kingsley. "Gender Reconstruction after the First World War." In *British Feminism in the Twentieth Century*, ed. Harold L. Smith. Amherst: University of Massachusetts Press, 1990.

_____. *Making Peace: The Reconstruction of Gender in Interwar Britain*. Princeton: Princeton University Press, 1993.

_____. "The Politics of Sexual Difference: World War I and the Demise of British Feminism." *Journal of British Studies* 21:3 (July 1988): 232–253.

_____. "Remembering the Great War." *Journal of British Studies* 37:1 (January 1998): 105–110.

_____. *Sex and Suffrage in Britain, 1860–1914*. Princeton: Princeton University Press, 1987.

Koven, Seth. "From Rough Lads to Hooligans: Boy Life, National Culture and Social Reform." In *Nationalisms and Sexualities*, eds. Andrew Parker, Mary Russo, Doris Somer and Patricia Yaeger. New York/London: Routledge, 1992.

Langhamer, Claire. *Women's Leisure in England, 1920–1960*. Manchester: Manchester University Press, 2000.

Laqueur, Thomas W. "Memory and Naming in the Great War." In *Commemorations: The Politics of National Identity*, ed. John R. Gillis. Princeton: Princeton University Press, 1994.

Laqueur, Walter. *Young Germany: A History of the German Youth Movement*. New York: Basic Books, 1962.

Leed, Eric. *No Man's Land: Combat and Identity in World War I*. Cambridge: Cambridge University Press, 1979.

Levine, Philippa. "'Walking the Streets in a way No Decent Woman Should': Women Police in World War I." *Journal of Modern History* 66 (March 1994), 1–45.

Liddington, Jill, and Jill Norris. *One Hand Tied Behind Us*. London: Virago, 1978.

Light, Alison. *Forever England: Femininity, Literature and Conservatism between the Wars*. London: Routledge, 1991.

MacDonald, Robert H. *The Language of Empire: Myths and Metaphors of Popular Imperialism, 1880–1918*. Manchester: Manchester University Press, 1994.

_____. "Reproducing the Middle-Class Boy: From Purity to Patriotism in the Boys' Magazines, 1892–1914." *Journal of Contemporary History* 24:3 (July 1989), 519–539.

_____. *Sons of the Empire: The Frontier and the Boy Scout Movement, 1890–1918*. Toronto: University of Toronto Press, 1993.

Mackenzie, John, ed. *Imperialism and Popular Culture*. Manchester: Manchester University Press, 1986.

Macleod, David I. *Building Character in the American Boy: The Boy Scouts, YMCA, and Their Forerunners, 1870–1920*. Madison: University of Wisconsin Press, 1983.

Maier, Charles. "Between Taylorism and Technocracy: European Ideologies and the Vision of Industrial Productivity in the 1920s." *Journal of Contemporary History* 5:2 (April 1970), 27–61.

Mangan, J. A. *Athleticism in the Victorian and Edwardian Public School*. Cambridge: Cambridge University Press, 1981.

_____, ed. *Making Imperial Mentalities: Socialisation and British Imperialism.* Manchester: Manchester University Press, 1990.

_____, ed. *Shaping the Superman: Fascist Body as Political Icon.* London/Portland: Frank Cass, 1999.

_____, ed. *Tribal Identities: Nationalism, Europe, Sport.* London/Portland: Frank Cass, 1996.

_____, and Roberta Park, eds. *From "Fair Sex" to Feminism: Sport and the Socialization of Women in the Industrial and Post-Industrial Eras.* London/Totowa, NJ: Frank Cass, 1987.

_____, and James Walvin, eds. *Manliness and Morality: Middle-class Masculinity in Britain and America, 1800–1940.* New York: St. Martin's Press, 1987.

Marks, Shula. "History, the Nation, and Empire: Sniping from the Periphery." *History Workshop Journal* 29 (1990), 111–119.

Matthews, Jill Julius. "They Had Such a Lot of Fun: The Women's League of Health and Beauty between the Wars." *History Workshop Journal* 30 (Autumn 1990), 22–54.

Mazumdar, Pauline. *Eugenics, Human Genetics, and Human Failings: The Eugenics Society, Its Sources and Its Critics in Britain.* London: Routledge, 1992.

McCracken, Grant. *Culture and Consumption: New Approaches to the Symbolic Character of Consumer Goods and Activities.* Bloomington: Indiana University Press, 1988.

McCrone, Kathleen. *Playing the Game: Sport and the Physical Emancipation of English Women, 1870–1914.* Lexington: University of Kentucky Press, 1988.

McLeod, Hugh. *Class and Religion in the Late Victorian City.* London: Croom Helm, 1974.

McRobbie, Angela, and Mica Nava, eds. *Gender and Generation.* London: MacMillan, 1984.

Melville, Joy. *Lost Children of the Empire.* London: Unwin Hyman, 1989.

Miller, Richard O. "The New Feudalism: The Origins of the Boy Scout Movement in Edwardian England." Ph.D. diss., University of Missouri–Columbia, December 1981.

Mitchell, Sally. *The New Girl: Girls' Culture in England, 1880–1915.* New York: Columbia University Press, 1995.

Monk, Una. *New Horizons: A Hundred Years of Women's Migration.* London: HMSO, 1963.

Morris, A. J. A. *The Scaremongers: The Advocacy of War and Rearmament 1896–1914.* London: Routledge and Kegan Paul, 1984.

Mosse, George. *Fallen Soldiers: Reshaping the Memory of the World Wars.* New York/Oxford: Oxford University Press, 1990.

_____. *Nationalism and Sexuality: Middle-Class Morality and Sexual Norms in Modern Europe.* Madison: University of Wisconsin Press, 1985.

Mowat, Charles. *Britain Between the Wars, 1918–1940.* Chicago: Chicago University Press, 1955.

Nava, Mica. "Youth Service Provision, Social Order, and the Question of Girls." In *Gender and Generation,* eds. Angela McRobbie and Mica Nava. London: MacMillan, 1984.

Nelson, Claudia, and Ann Sumner Holmes, eds. *Maternal Instincts: Visions of Motherhood and Sexuality in Britain, 1875–1925.* New York: St. Martin's Press, 1997.

Neubauer, John. *The Fin-de-Siecle Culture of Adolescence.* New Haven/London: Yale University Press, 1992.

Obelkevich, James. "Religion." In *The Cambridge Social History of Britain, 1750–1950,* ed. F. M. L. Thompson. Cambridge: Cambridge University Press, 1990.

Pakenham, Thomas. *The Boer War.* London: Weidenfeld and Nicolson, 1979.

Parker, Andrew, Mary Russo, Doris Somer, and Patricia Yaeger, eds. *Nationalisms and Sexualities.* New York/London: Routledge, 1992.

Pedersen, Susan. "The Failure of Feminism in the Making of the British Welfare State." *Radical History Review* 12 (1989), 86–110.

_____. *Family, Dependence, and the Origins of the Welfare State: Britain and France, 1914–1945.* Cambridge/New York: Cambridge University Press, 1993.

Peiss, Kathy. *Cheap Amusements: Working Women and Leisure in Turn-of-the-Century New York*. Philadelphia: Temple University Press, 1986.

Penn, Alan. *Targeting Schools: Drill, Militarism, and Imperialism*. London/Portland, OR: Woburn Press, 1999.

Perry, Elisabeth Israels. "From Achievement to Happiness: Girl Scouting in Middle Tennessee, 1910s–1960s." *Journal of Women's History* 5:2 (Fall 1993), 75–94.

_____. "'The Very Best Influence': Josephine Holloway and Girl Scouting in Nashville's African-American Community." *Tennessee Historical Quarterly* 52:2 (Summer 1993), 73–85.

Peukert, Detlev. *Inside Nazi Germany: Conformity, Opposition, and Racism in Everyday Life*. New Haven: Yale University Press, 1987.

Pill, David H. *Yorkshire: The West Riding*. London: B. T. Batsford, 1977.

Pimlott, J. A. R. *Toynbee Hall: Fifty Years of Social Progress, 1884–1934*. London: J. M. Dent and Sons, Ltd., 1935.

Plant, G. F. *Oversea Settlement: Migration from the United Kingdom to the Dominions*. London: Oxford University Press, 1951.

Posel, Deborah. "The Meaning of Apartheid before 1948: Conflicting Interests and Forces within the Afrikaner Nationalist Alliance." *Journal of Southern African Studies* 14:1 (October 1987), 123–139.

Proctor, Tammy M. "Gender, Generation, and the Politics of Scouting and Guiding in Interwar Britain." PhD diss., Rutgers University, October 1995.

_____. "'A Separate Path': Scouting and Guiding in Interwar South Africa." *Comparative Studies in Society and History* 42:3 (July 2000): 605–631.

_____. "Scouts, Guides and the Fashioning of Empire, 1919–1939." In *Fashioning the Body Politic: Gender, Dress, Citizenship*, ed. Wendy Parkins. London/New York: Berg Publishers [forthcoming].

_____. "(Uni)Forming Youth: Girl Guides and Boy Scouts in Interwar Britain, 1908–1939." *History Workshop Journal* 45 (Spring 1998), 103–134.

Pugh, Martin. *Women and the Women's Movement in Britain, 1914–1959*. Basingstoke: MacMillan, 1992.

Reader, W. J. *At Duty's Call: A Study in Obsolete Patriotism*. Manchester: Manchester University Press, 1992.

Reese, Dagmar. "Emancipation or Social Incorporation: Girls in the Bund Deutscher Mädel." In *Education and Fascism: Political Identity and Social Education in Nazi Germany*, eds. Heinz Sünker and Hans-Uwe Otto. London: The Falmer Press, 1997.

Rempel, Gerhard. *Hitler's Children: The Hitler Youth and the S.S.* Chapel Hill: University of North Carolina Press, 1989.

Reynolds, Sian. *France Between the Wars: Gender and Politics*. London/New York: Routledge, 1996.

Rich, P. J. *Elixir of Empire: The English Public Schools, Ritualism, Freemasonry, and Imperialism*. London: Regency, 1989.

Rich, Paul. *Race and Empire in British Politics*. Cambridge: Cambridge University Press, 1986.

Richards, Jeffrey, ed. *Imperialism and Juvenile Literature*. Manchester: Manchester University Press, 1989.

Roberts, Mary Louise. *Civilization without Sexes: Reconstructing Gender in Postwar France 1917–1927*. Chicago/London: University of Chicago Press, 1994.

Rochberg-Halton, Eugene. *Meaning and Modernity: Social Theory in the Pragmatic Attitude*. Chicago/London: University of Chicago Press, 1986.

Rose, Jacqueline. *The Case of Peter Pan, or, The Impossibility of Children's Fiction*. London: MacMillan, 1984.

Roseman, Mark, ed. *Generations in Conflict: Youth Revolt and Generation Formation in Germany, 1770–1968.* Cambridge/New York: Cambridge University Press, 1995.

Rosenthal, Michael. *The Character Factory: Baden-Powell and the Origins of the Boy Scout Movement.* New York: Pantheon Press, 1986.

Ross, Andrew. *John Philip, 1775–1851: Mission, Race and Politics in South Africa.* Aberdeen: Aberdeen University Press, 1986.

Ross, Ellen. *Love and Toil: Motherhood in Outcast London, 1870–1918.* New York/Oxford: Oxford University Press, 1993.

_____. "'Not the Sort that Would Sit on the Doorstep': Respectability in Pre-World War I London Neighborhoods." *International Labor and Working-Class History* 27 (Spring 1985), 39–59.

Rotundo, E. Anthony. *American Manhood: Transformations in Masculinity from the Revolution to the Modern Era.* New York: HarperCollins, 1993.

Samuel, Rafael, ed. *Patriotism: The Making and Unmaking of British National Identity.* London: Routledge, 1989.

Scholes, Alex G. *Education for Empire Settlement: A Study of Juvenile Migration.* London/New York: Longman, Green & Co., 1932.

Semmel, Bernard. *Imperialism and Social Reform: English Social Imperial Thought.* New York: George Allen & Unwin Ltd., 1960.

Shear, Keith. "'Not Welfare or Uplift Work': White Women, Masculinity and Policing in South Africa." *Gender and History* 8:3 (1996), 393–415.

Showalter, Elaine. *The Female Malady: Women, Madness, and English Culture.* New York: Pantheon, 1985.

Smith, Harold L., ed. *British Feminism in the Twentieth Century.* Amherst: University of Massachusetts Press, 1990.

Søland, Birgitte. *Becoming Modern: Young Women and the Reconstruction of Womanhood in the 1920s.* Princeton: Princeton University Press, 2000.

Soloway, Richard A. *Birth Control and the Population Question in England, 1877–1930.* Chapel Hill: University of North Carolina Press, 1982.

Springhall, John. *Coming of Age: Adolescence in Britain, 1860–1960.* Dublin: Gill & Macmillan Ltd., 1986.

_____. *Youth, Empire and Society: British Youth Movements, 1908–1930.* London: Croom Helm Ltd., 1977.

Stachura, Peter. *The German Youth Movement, 1900–1945: An Interpretive and Documentary History.* London: Macmillan, 1981.

_____. *Nazi Youth in the Weimar Republic.* Santa Barbara/Oxford: Clio, 1975.

Stewart, Susan. *On Longing: Narratives of the Miniature, the Gigantic, the Souvenir, the Collection.* Baltimore/London: Johns Hopkins University Press, 1984.

Stoler, Ann L. "Making Empire Respectable: The Politics of Race and Sexual Morality in 20th-century Colonial Cultures." *American Ethnologist* 16:4 (1989), 634–660.

_____. *Race and Education of Desire: Foucault's History of Sexuality and the Colonial Order of Things.* Durham and London: Duke University Press, 1995.

_____. "Rethinking Colonial Categories: European Communities and the Boundaries of Rule." *Comparative Studies in Society and History* 31:1 (January 1989), 134–161.

Strachey, Ray. *The Cause.* London: Virago, 1978.

Strobel, Margaret. *European Women and the Second British Empire.* Bloomington: Indiana University Press, 1991.

Summers, Anne. *Angels and Citizens: British Women as Military Nurses, 1854–1914.* London: Routledge and Kegan Paul, 1988.

_____. "Edwardian Militarism." *Patriotism: The Making and Unmaking of British National Identity* [volume I: History and Politics], ed. Raphael Samuel, 236–256. London: Routledge, 1989.

Tabili, Laura. "The Construction of Racial Difference in Twentieth-Century Britain: The Special Restriction (Coloured Alien Seamen) Order, 1925." *Journal of British Studies* 33 (January 1994), 54–98.

Taylor, A. J. P. *English History, 1914–1945.* New York: Oxford University Press, 1965.

Thompson, F. M. L., ed. *The Cambridge Social History of Britain, 1750–1950.* Cambridge/London: Cambridge University Press, 1990.

Thompson, Leonard. *A History of South Africa.* New Haven: Yale University Press, 1990.

Tickner, Lisa. *The Spectacle of Women: Imagery of the Suffrage Campaign, 1907–1914.* Chicago: University of Chicago Press, 1988.

Tidrick, Kathryn. *Empire and the English Character.* London: I. B. Taurus & Co., Ltd., 1990.

Titmuss, Richard. *The Gift Relationship: From Human Blood to Social Policy.* New York: Pantheon Books, 1971.

Vance, Norman. *The Sinews of the Spirit: The Ideal of Christian Manliness in Victorian Literature and Religious Thought.* New York/Cambridge: Cambridge University Press, 1985.

Vicinus, Martha. *Independent Women Work and Community for Single Women, 1850–1920.* Chicago: University of Chicago, 1985.

Voeltz, Richard. "'. . . A Good Jew and a Good Englishman': The Jewish Lads' Brigade, 1894–1922." *Journal of Contemporary History* 23:1 (January 1988), 119–127

_____. "The Antidote to 'Khaki Fever'? The Expansion of the British Girl Guides during the First World War." *Journal of Contemporary History* 27 (September 1992), 627–638.

Wagner, Gillian. *Children of the Empire.* London: Weidenfeld and Nicolson, 1982.

Walker, Pamela. *Pulling the Devil's Kingdom Down: The Salvation Army in Britain.* Berkeley: University of California Press, 2001.

Warren, Allen. "Citizens of the Empire: Baden-Powell, Scouts and Guides, and an Imperial Ideal." In *Imperialism and Popular Culture*, ed. John Mackenzie. Manchester: Manchester University Press, 1986.

_____. "Mothers for the Empire." In *Making Imperial Mentalities: Socialisation and British Imperialism*, ed. J. A. Mangan. Manchester: Manchester University Press, 1990.

_____. "Popular Manliness: Baden-Powell, Scouting and the Development of Manly Character." In *Manliness and Morality: Middle-class Masculinity in Britain and America, 1800–1940*, eds. J. A. Mangan and James Walvin. New York: St. Martin's Press, 1987.

_____. "Sir Robert Baden-Powell, the Scout Movement, and Citizen-Training in Britain, 1900–1920." *English Historical Review* 101 (1986), 376–398.

Warwick, Peter. *Black People and the South African War, 1899–1902.* Cambridge: Cambridge University Press, 1983.

Weaver, Kitty. *Bushels of Rubles: Soviet Youth in Transition.* Westport, CT/London: Praeger, 1992.

Weeks, Jeffrey. *Sex, Politics and Society.* London: Longmans, Green and Co., 1981.

West, Elliott, and Paula Petrik, eds. *Small Worlds: Children and Adolescents in America, 1850–1950.* Lawrence: University of Kansas Press, 1992.

Whitney, Susan. "The Politics of Youth: Communists and Catholics in Interwar France." PhD diss., Rutgers University, 1994.

Wilkinson, Paul. "English Youth Movements, 1908–1930." *Journal of Contemporary History* 4:2 (April 1969), 3–23.

Williams, Keith. "A way out of our troubles? The Politics of Empire Settlement, 1900–1922." In *Emigrants and Empire: British Settlement in the Dominions between the Wars*, ed. Stephen Constantine. Manchester: Manchester University Press, 1990.

Winter, J. M. *The Great War and the British People*. London: MacMillan, 1985.

_____. "Spiritualism and the First World War." In *Religion and Irreligion in Victorian Society* ed. R. W. Davis and R. J. Helmstadter. London: Routledge, 1992.

Winter, Jay. *Sites of Memory, Sites of Mourning: The Great War in European Cultural History*. Cambridge: Cambridge University Press, 1995.

Wohl, Robert. *The Generation of 1914*. Cambridge: Harvard University Press, 1979.

Woollacott, Angela. "'Khaki Fever' and Its Control: Gender, Class, Age and Sexual Morality on the British Homefront in the First World War." *Journal of Contemporary History* 29:2 (April 1994), 325–347.

_____. *On Her Their Lives Depend: Munitions Workers in the Great War*. Berkeley: University of California Press, 1994.

Yeo, Eileen, and Stephen Yeo, eds. *Popular Culture and Class Conflict 1590–1914: Explorations in the History of Labor and Leisure*. New Jersey: Humanities Press, 1981.

INDEX